Twentieth-century Mass Society in Britain and the Netherlands

Twentieth-century Mass Society in Britain and the Netherlands

Edited by
Bob Moore and Henk van Nierop

Oxford • New York

English edition
First published in 2006 by
Berg
Editorial offices:
First Floor, Angel Court, 81 St Clements Street, Oxford OX4 1AW, UK
175 Fifth Avenue, New York, NY 10010, USA

Berg is the imprint of Oxford International Publishers Ltd.

Library of Congress Cataloging-in-Publication Data
Twentieth-century mass society in Britain and the Netherlands /
edited by Bob Moore and Henk van Nierop.
    p. cm.
Includes bibliographical references and index.
ISBN-13: 978-1-84520-525-6 (cloth)
ISBN-10: 1-84520-525-1 (cloth)
  1. Mass society. 2. Popular culture—Great Britain—History—
20th century. 3. Popular culture—Netherlands—History—20th
century. I. Moore, Bob, 1954- II. Nierop, Henk F. K. van.

HM866.T93 2006
306.0941--dc22   2006021127

British Library Cataloguing-in-Publication Data
A catalogue record for this book is available from the British Library.

ISBN-13 978 1 84520 525 6
ISBN-10 1 84520 525 1

Typeset by Avocet Typeset, Chilton, Aylesbury, Bucks
Printed in the United Kingdom by Biddles Ltd, King's Lynn

www.bergpublishers.com

Contents

Contributors

Theo Beckers has held a chair in leisure studies in the Faculty of Social and Behavioural Sciences of Tilburg University since 1987. His research is focused on the allocation and use of time, technology and time-spatial dynamics, sustainable consumption and the global impact of tourism. He is the scientific director of *Telos*, an interdisciplinary research network on sustainable development in the province of Brabant. He is member of the Scientific Council of the European Centre for Nature Conservation. He is now member of the governmental Advisory Council on Rural Policy and acts as a consultant and advisor for various national and international organizations.

Clare Griffiths is Lecturer in Modern History at the University of Sheffield. She has written on various aspects of politics and culture in early and mid-twentieth century Britain. Her publications include *Labour and Countryside: The Politics of Rural Britain between the Wars* (2006), and she is currently working on a study of the Fabian Socialists G.D.H. and Margaret Cole.

Ido de Haan is Professor of Political History at the University of Utrecht. His work focuses on the political history of Western Europe in the nineteenth and twentieth century, the history of political thought, and on the history and memory of large-scale violence, especially the Holocaust. He is currently working on a comparative study of political and cultural reconstruction in France and the Netherlands around 1600, 1815 and 1945. His publications include *Na de ondergang. De herinnering aan de Jodenvervolging in Nederland 1945–1995* (The Hague, 1997) and *Het beginsel van leven en wasdom. De constitutie van de Nederlandse politiek in de negentiende eeuw* (Amsterdam, 2003).

Bob Moore is Reader in Modern History at the University of Sheffield. He is the author of *Refugees from Nazi Germany in the Netherlands 1933–1940* (Dordrecht, 1986) and *Victims and Survivors: The Nazi Persecution of the Jews in the Netherlands 1940–1945* (London, 1997). His most recent publication is *Prisoners of War, Prisoners of Peace* (Oxford, 2005) co-edited with Barbara Hately-Broad.

Henk van Nierop is Professor of Early Modern History at the University of Amsterdam and Academic Director of the Amsterdam Centre for the Study of the Golden Age. Among his publications is *The Nobility of Holland: From Knights to*

Regents, 1500–1650 (Cambridge, 1993) and *Het verraad van het Noorderkwartier. Oorlog, terreur en recht in de Nederlandse Opstand* (Amsterdam, 1999).

Bill Osgerby is Reader in Media, Culture and Communications at London Metropolitan University. His research focuses on twentieth-century British and American cultural history, and his books include *Youth in Britain since 1945* (Oxford, 1998), *Playboys in Paradise: Youth, Masculinity and Leisure-style in Modern America* (Oxford/New York, 2001) and *Youth Media* (London, 2004).

Douglas Reid is Senior Lecturer in Social History in the Department of History at the University of Hull. Best known for his work on 'Saint Monday', he has written on various aspects of the history of leisure (and religion) in Britain between the eighteenth and twentieth centuries, including 'Playing and Praying' in the *Cambridge Urban History of Britain*, volume 3.

Joop M. Roebroek studied political science and economics at the University of Nijmegen. From 1978 to 1985 he lectured in state theory and political economy at the Institute for Political Studies at the University of Nijmegen, and from 1986 until 1998 he worked in the Department of Labour and Social Security at the University of Tilburg. He completed his dissertation on a comparative study of the long-term evolution of welfare states in 1993 and now lectures part-time in the Department of Organization Studies at the University of Tilburg, and combines this with work as a film-maker, writer, consultant and initiator of social projects.

Piet de Rooy is Professor of Contemporary Dutch History at the University of Amsterdam. He has published on nineteenth and twentieth-century social and political history. Works currently in print include *Republiek van Rivaliteiten. Nederland sinds 1813* (Amsterdam, 2002).

Pat Thane is Leverhulme Professor of Contemporary British History and Director of the Centre for Contemporary British History at the Institute of Historical Research, University of London. Her publications include *Old Age in English History: Past Experiences, Present Issues* (Oxford, 2000); *Labour's First Century: The Labour Party 1900–2000* (Cambridge, 2000), co-edited with D. Tanner and N. Tiratsoo; *The Foundations of the Welfare State* (second edition, 1996); 'Women Graduates: Earning and Learning, 1920s–1950s', *Women's History Review* (2004); 'What Difference Did the Vote Make? Women and Politics in Britain since 1918', in Amanda Vickery (ed.), *Women, Privilege and Power* (Stanford/Cambridge, 2001). She also chairs the Social History Society of the United Kingdom.

Henk te Velde is Professor of Dutch History at Leiden University. Until 2005 he was Professor of Political Culture in the Modern Age at the University of Groningen. He has coordinated or directed several research projects in the field of the history of political culture and has also published on nationalism and bourgeois culture. In 2002 he published a comparative study of Dutch political leadership: *Stijlen van leider-schap. Persoon en politiek van Thorbecke tot Den Den Uyl* (Amsterdam 2002).

Frank van Vree is Professor of Journalism at the University of Amsterdam. He is the author of several books on the history of the media, modern history, historiography and memory.

Kevin Williams is Professor of Media and Communication Studies at the University of Swansea. His latest publication is *European Media Studies* (2005) and he is presently completing a history of the British newspaper.

Preface

Since the late 1950s there have been regular meetings of leading scholars from the historical profession in Britain and the Netherlands to compare ideas on major themes and debates. The results of these conferences have been published as an occasional 'Britain and the Netherlands' series, of which this is the fifteenth volume.

The choice of twentieth-century 'mass society' as the theme of the conference hosted by the University of Swansea in 2003 brought together specialists from many fields of contemporary history. The development of politics, welfare, leisure, media and youth culture were all discussed in depth and this book provides both a British and a Dutch perspective on all five of these themes. Some of the chapters derive from papers given at the conference, but the editors would like to extend special thanks to Dr Clare Griffiths (University of Sheffield), Dr Bill Osgerby (London Metropolitan University) and Professor Piet de Rooij (Universiteit van Amsterdam) for their specially commissioned contributions, and to Professor Ido de Haan (Rijksuniversiteit Utrecht) for his analytical and thought-provoking introduction to the collection as a whole. Thanks are also due to Dr Hugh Dunthorne, who so ably organized the conference at Swansea, and to the staff of the Dylan Thomas Centre in Swansea and the National Botanic Garden of Wales at Llanarthne, who were excellent hosts for particular sessions.

Financial assistance is an essential element in the organization of international conferences, and the organizers are pleased to acknowledge the support received from both sides of the North Sea. From Britain, there was a generous subvention from the British Academy and further contributions from the University of Hull, the University of Wales Swansea and the Association for Low Countries Studies in Great Britain and Ireland. From the Netherlands, the Instituut voor Nederlandse Geschiedenis, the University of Amsterdam and the University of Utrecht all made valuable contributions.

On a more personal note, the editors would like to thank Ben Schofield from the Centre for Dutch Studies at the University of Sheffield for his translation work, and colleagues in the History Departments at the universities of Sheffield and Amsterdam for their invaluable help and advice. Finally, we would also like to acknowledge the role played by Kathryn Earle, Kathleen May and their colleagues at Berg Publishers in bringing this project to fruition.

Bob Moore and Henk van Nierop
Sheffield/Amsterdam

Between Stupidity and Creativity
Mass Society in Britain and the Netherlands in the Twentieth Century

Ido de Haan

From the beginning of the nineteenth century, many people in Western Europe noted the emergence of a mass society. They observed grand social processes, like urbanization, industrialization and democratization, which obliterated the distinctions that had previously divided society into clearly separated ranks and communities. In this new environment, individuals were thrown together in an undifferentiated mass, which had to be addressed in a new, non-rational way and seemed to behave according to, as yet unknown, social laws. The description of the masses was never neutral. As Asa Briggs has argued in his seminal article on the language of mass and masses in nineteenth-century England, the masses were considered to be easy to manipulate and a threat to creative individuality, yet at the same time as a force which might be used to obliterate undesirable social distinctions and, as Gladstone had said, to mobilize 'the masses against the classes'.[1] However, in the twentieth century the language of the masses served mainly as a diagnosis of a social pathology, the occurrence of which appeared to be inevitable the more it was described as an objective phenomenon.

Mass society may thus be analysed from two, or perhaps even three, perspectives. On the one hand, it can be understood as the product of objective processes and as an object of empirical and historical description and explanation. On the other hand, mass society can be analysed as a central concept in the discourse about modern society as it emerged at the end of the nineteenth century. These are not necessarily mutually exclusive approaches to mass society: discourses about modern society reflect, and reflect upon, the changes in the nature of societies. At the same time, the nature of mass society is influenced by the discourse that is woven around it. Moreover, from a third perspective, one of the distinctive traits of mass societies may very well be the emergence of a certain type of discursive practice, dominated by mass media appealing to popular sentiments, replacing the bourgeois public sphere of reasonable gentlemen.[2]

In all of these perspectives, specific national characteristics come into play. Even though mass societies transcend traditional boundaries of community and kin, both as social processes and as discourses and discursive practices, they are constrained by institutional and cultural boundaries. In the context of this volume of comparative studies of Britain and the Netherlands, it is assumed that there are not only similar trends but also distinctively British and Dutch conditions in the rise of a mass society and of the development of a discourse on the role of the masses. As a result, the grand social processes that lead to the formation of the masses might differ in nature, pace and effect in both countries. Also, British and Dutch traditions of intellectual debate and cultural criticism, as well as the organization of the public debate and the development of mass media, are likely to exhibit just as many differences as similarities.

Historiographical Traditions

In order to develop a framework for a historical comparison of the rise and development of mass society in both countries, this introduction aims to identify a number of comparative questions that seem relevant to the practice and discourse of mass society. The chapters that follow address most of these issues. Yet at the same time they reveal a difference in British and Dutch historical scholarship that serves to complicate a comparative approach still further. It appears that social history is much stronger on the British side of the North Sea, while the Dutch historical profession has developed a stronger interest in cultural history and in the history of political culture. As a result, Dutch scholars tend to focus more on the development of the discourse of mass society, while their British counterparts have more of an eye for the structural social characteristics and determinants of the role of the masses.

For instance, Pat Thane discusses, among other topics, the structural characteristics and the mechanisms of social exclusion of the British welfare state, Kevin Williams focuses on the organization of the media, and Douglas Reid investigates the relationship between labour and leisure time as one of the determinants of the development of a mass culture. However, none of the British contributors addresses what is, from a social (and that used to be in many cases a Marxist) historian's point of view, the most basic issue of all: the relations of production itself and, more specifically, the emergence of a system of mass production.

In general, the Dutch contributors focus more on the discourse of the masses. Thus Henk te Velde discusses fears of a volatile crowd and of a new barbarism in the early decades of the twentieth century, and Frank van Vree stresses the negative approach to popular culture in the development of mass media in the Netherlands. Time and again, the masses are accused of passivity and stupidity, as is demonstrated by Beckers' discussion of leisure and, contrary to the apparent academic division of labour, also by Bill Osgerby's discussion of novels like Hoggart's *The Uses of Literacy*, which framed the development of British youth culture in a history of degeneration.

Notwithstanding these differences in approach, in one way or another all contributors are confronted with the question of how to understand the relationship between the structural transformations of British and Dutch society after the end of the nineteenth century and the discourse of mass society that developed in tandem. Are we dealing here with the moral panic of a conservative elite, or does it involve a set of more or less rational responses to genuine, and genuinely problematic, changes in the social structure?

Moreover, this question needs to be addressed from a comparative perspective. Evidently, there are important differences between the Netherlands and the United Kingdom that must have had an influence on the emergence and development of a mass society. For instance, there is a clear difference in the timing and scope of the Industrial Revolution in the United Kingdom and the Netherlands. The nature and process of urbanization in both countries differed also. The role of religion and changing religious relations also made a difference. The different electoral systems definitely had an influence on the development of mass politics. But the difficult question is how to assess the weight and influence of all these differences.

There are also similarities and differences in the intellectual and public debate in both countries. What is the role and stance of public moralists, as Stefan Collini has called the British public intellectuals?[3] What is their relation to the churches? And are they connected to the universities? Do the social sciences play a role, and what kind of social science? In this respect, the influence of foreign intellectual traditions also plays an important role. For instance, how was the work of Gustave Le Bon and Gabriel Tarde received?[4] Did people read José Ortega y Gasset's *La rebelión de las masas*,[5] or the work of Theodor Adorno[6] or Elias Canetti?[7] What was the reaction to the critics of mass society of the 1950s, like David Riesman or William Kornhauser?[8] Is there a specific Dutch or British reception of Marcuse?[9]

These reactions might also be influenced by historical antecedents. The fear of the mob is nothing new, and since the eighteenth century a discourse on the problems of popular culture and the danger of popular sovereignty has circulated.[10] Yet it was not only the eighteenth century that was different in Britain and the Netherlands. The impact of the French Revolution and the Napoleonic regime, as well as the different development of constitutional monarchy and parliamentary democracy in the nineteenth century inevitably made a difference to the reaction to the emergence of the masses and of a mass society.

Creation and Organization of the Masses

To address these wide-ranging issues in a more systematic way, it seems appropriate to start with a basic approach to the concept of the masses: the dictionary. As the Dutch *Woordenboek der Nederlandse Taal* notes, '*massa*' is used to denote '*klomp van een of andere stof*' (amount of a certain substance), '*toebereide stof, zonder gedachte aan een bepaalde hoeveelheid of gedaante*' (substance prepared without intending a specific amount or shape) and 'chaos'. In later uses, the notion of the mass and the masses indicates a large and undifferentiated group of people, conceptually related to notions like *multitudo* and *vulgus*. The *Concise Oxford Dictionary of Etymology* suggests the word has a Greek root in *mâza*, meaning barley-cake, which is perhaps related to the verb '*mássein*', meaning 'to knead'. This etymological digression makes it clear that 'mass' and 'masses' always involve two aspects. Like dough, it first needs to be prepared by putting together different ingredients, and, second, it needs to be moulded and shaped into a certain form.

These two aspects can be understood as the basis for a first and very crude periodization. The second half of the nineteenth century may be viewed as the time of the creation of the masses. In the common understanding of the modernization of society, closely knit communities are replaced by loosely tied networks of individuals. Modern city life is often associated with atomism, creating an image of an undifferentiated mass of individuals chaotically swirling around one another. This image of a society adrift is reinforced by the idea that secularization destroys the authority of moral commands and the religious leaders who proclaim them.

This period is generally conceptualized in rather negative terms, as a period of transition from *Gemeinschaft* to *Gesellschaft*. Individuals in the mass are prone to various forms of loss: loss of social bonds, the blurring of social distinctions and the loss of autonomy, as atomized individuals become very susceptible to mass manipulation of a political or commercial nature. In general, the emergence of mass society is associated with alienation. In that sense, the problem of mass society is qualitatively different from the ancient fear of the mob. The latter was always a clearly distinct social category, which by its specific unruly nature posed a threat to a civil society. The emergence of the masses, however, involved the complete loss of distinction, even among the higher ranks of society. In a mass society, man did not necessarily become uncivil, but more importantly a *Mann ohne Eigenschaften*, an insignificant particle in an undifferentiated mass.

After this period of dissolution, the next phase in the emergence of a mass society may then be perceived as that of shaping the masses by way of organization: the emergence of new types of social and political associations and of political mobilization; the creation of new forms of political and social interaction, like mass manifestation and mass parties; the development of a mass culture dominated by the mass marketing of mass goods, produced in new processes of mass production; creating along the way new types of individuals, identified as consumers, listeners and viewers in a mass audience. Assuming the organizational forms of the masses are not just constraining the growth of the masses but actually enabling their emergence, in the same way as there is no dough without kneading the components, it makes perhaps more sense to perceive the creation and organization of the masses as two sides of the same coin, i.e. the constitution of a mass society.

The nature of this constitution is addressed in this volume from an Anglo-Dutch comparative perspective. From a Dutch point of view, the first half of the twentieth century still figures as the heyday of pillarization (*verzuiling*): the development of a web of associations, covering all aspects of life, divided by denominational and cultural characteristics and crowned by political parties representing the interests of the respective pillars at municipal, provincial and state level. Despite a certain weariness of the constant appeal, both by foreign and Dutch scholars, to the exceptionalism of the Dutch consociational model of democracy, the image of an extraordinarily strong civil society in the Netherlands remains very powerful.

However, in comparison to Britain, the consociational exceptionalism of Dutch history might not hold. To begin with, there is some discussion of whether associational life in Britain actually withered away after 1914. For instance, there is a strong tradition of associationalism, represented by guild socialists like the Webbs and pluralist like Cole and Laski.[11] There is perhaps also a conservative strand of thought stressing the importance of self-help and charity as the basis of citizenship. Moreover, Geoffrey Finlayson has argued that voluntary associations played an important role in the development of the British welfare state, even into the second half of the twentieth century.[12] Moreover, in both countries the role of the state has expanded and, consequently, the relevance of national parties able to represent the interests of their constituency at state level. This centralization of the state and the strength of associational life are not necessarily a zero-sum game: the expansion of the state might very well have contributed to the strength of associations, even when the latter become more connected to, and dependent on, the state.

This at least seems to be true for Dutch pillarization: instead of the development of an independent civil society, next to and even opposed to the state, it is more likely that Dutch civil associational life flourished to a large extent only because it was supported financially and legally facilitated by the state. It gave the tops of these pillars, i.e. the political elites organized in national political parties, a strategic position both as brokers of the denominational interests and as watchdogs of the social order, organized within civil associations but backed up by the power of the state. Schools, poor relief, social work, health institutions and leisure organizations were all embodiments of pillarized power as well as guardians of the public moral order.[13]

In this respect, what worried pillarized elites most of all was the fact that only part of the population were members of any of these organizations. Contrary to the view of a thoroughly organized civil society, a large proportion of youngsters, of the lower classes and of the urban population did not actually belong to the pillars of Dutch society. Therefore, the discourse of mass society in the Netherlands should be viewed not as a general critique of modern society but, as Henk te Velde argues, as a diagnosis of the problem that some groups remained outside the pillarized organizations and were therefore part of the masses or, as it was increasingly called, the '*massa-jeugd*', mass youth.

The chapters that follow all address the emergence of a mass society from a double perspective, emphasizing both the dissolution of social bonds and the fears of alienation and anomy it generates, and of mass society as a specific type of social organization, which moulds, or even manipulates, modern individuals in a certain societal form. Since the beginning of the twentieth century, there appear to have been at least four specific contexts in which mass societies took shape. To begin with, the political mobilization of the masses was necessitated by the enfranchisement of ever-wider groups of citizens. Second, both in reaction to the loss of communal care and in reaction to the supposedly alienating nature of market capitalism, the welfare state offered a stable framework for the life and well-being of the citizens. Third, as a result of technological innovations, it became possible to address ever widening audiences and in this way to mould the masses into a public for broadsheets, broadcast and widescreen cinema. Connected to the media revolution was the development of mass markets, in which consumers of mass-produced goods are invited by marketing to buy ever more goods.

All of these developments were generally perceived as signs of a time to come, which would be brought home all too soon by a new generation of youngsters. Especially after 1945, the new baby-boom generation was conceived as what Bill Osgerby in his chapter on youth culture calls 'an ideological vehicle' of the mass society. Yet mass society itself was generally associated with youthful, not to say puerile or infantile, characteristics – unreflective, lustful and undisciplined.

Mass Politics

One of the main concerns in the literature on mass society is the political role of the masses and the nature of mass politics. Around this theme, the discourse on mass society is at its most pessimistic. On the one hand, mass politics is perceived as the result of the 'nationalization of the masses', the emergence of a new type of politics in which leaders directly address the population, and in which the population, in turn, is massively involved in politics.[14] As such, this kind of 'politics in a new key', as Carl Schorske has called it, is a product of the democratization around the turn of the century.[15] However, mass politics is said to undermine the parliamentary form that democracy acquired in the nineteenth century, replacing political representation by plebiscitary acclamation. As William Kornhauser argued:

> Mass politics occurs when large numbers of people engage in political activity outside of the procedures and rules instituted by a society to govern political action. Mass politics in democratic society therefore is anti-democratic, since it contravenes the constitutional order. The extreme case of mass politics is the totalitarian movement, notably communism and fascism.

According to Kornhauser, 'modern democratic systems possess a distinct vulnerability to mass politics because they invite the whole population, most of which has historically been politically quiescent, to engage in politics'.[16]

From this perspective, one of the central tasks of political theory is to identify the conditions under which democratic participation is possible without degenerating into mass politics. The crucial tenet of the democratic theorist, frightened by the prospect of mass society, is that democracy can only thrive when there is a healthy balance between the population and a plurality of elites. A positive conception of democratic elitism is therefore implicit in most theories of mass politics. For instance, José Ortega y Gasset argues that

> in a right ordering of public affairs, the mass is that part which does not act of itself. Such is its mission. It has come into the world in order to be directed, influenced, represented, organized – even in order to cease being mass, or at least to aspire to this. But it has not come into the world to do all this by itself. It needs to submit its life to a higher court, formed of the superior minorities.[17]

From a comparative perspective, these considerations could lead to the question of to what extent this kind of cultural criticism can be retraced in the Dutch and British context, but, at the same time, they might also function as an introduction to the question as to how mass and elites are actually organized in both countries. In this respect, one of the remarkable, and moreover similar, characteristics of British and Dutch political history of the twentieth century is the lack of strong communist and fascist movements. Starting from the assumption that the growth of a mass society is an important precondition for the growth of these movements, one might conclude either that a mass society had only partly developed in these countries or that there were stronger counter-forces which channelled mass politics into less disruptive forms.

As Clare Griffiths argues in her chapter on the British case, the emergence of mass politics was viewed with much suspicion not only by the Conservatives, who bemoaned the hurried pace of modernization, but more importantly by Labour politicians, who clung to a nineteenth-century concept of enlightened citizenship. Paradoxically, the champions of the people were less well prepared to meet the challenge of mass society than the defenders of the establishment. It was the Conservative Party that started to experiment with new methods of mobilization and campaigning, enabling its leadership to gain an electoral advantage that lasted until Tony Blair discovered the power of political spin.

Another aspect Griffiths addresses is the pessimism about the power of reason in politics implied in the dominant visions of mass politics. While Griffiths stresses the productive aspect of this suspicion, as it formed the basis of contemporary electoral research, Henk te Velde in his chapter on the Netherlands stresses the negative aspects of this pessimism. He depicts Dutch politics between 1900 and 1960 as a form of brokerage between moral communities, legitimated by a Whiggish ideology of an age-old tradition of prudent accommodation by the elite to the demands of the population. In this context, non-aligned citizens, especially youngsters, were perceived by all major parties as susceptible to manipulative and potentially revolutionary rhetoric.

However, elements of mass politics were not entirely absent in the Netherlands. Many of the inter-war political organizations organized mass rallies, demonstrations and petitions, complete with sweeping oratory, flag waving, marching and chanting. One of the most remarkable examples of these mass manifestations in the Netherlands, given the problems of the German occupation, was the spectacular rise of the Nederlandsche Unie, which in the autumn of 1940 was able to attract a following of up to 800,000 people within a few months. This also occurred in later periods, for example in the 1980s when the peace movement twice brought around half a million people on to the streets to protest against the deployment of nuclear cruise missiles on Dutch soil. Characteristic of both examples, and perhaps for all these manifestations of mass action, is that they broke away from the parameters of party politics, bringing together people from different political backgrounds. From a comparative perspective, the emergence of the masses in politics is therefore perhaps most importantly a question about the connection between the party system and various interest groups, social movements and civil associations.

Mass Media

This leads to a further issue in the discussion of mass society: the mass media. As Kevin Williams demonstrates in his chapter, there was an enormous expansion of the British media after the First World War. The number of newspapers, movies and movie theatres increased tremendously, and the introduction of radio and television greatly expanded the reach of the media. The circulation of newspapers, movie attendance and radio and television audiences increased explosively. Frank van Vree highlights the same quantitative development in the Netherlands.

Yet there are striking, and even paradoxical, differences between the two countries. The expansion of the British press is to some extent due to the increase, both in number and in circulation, of the local press. Yet Williams argues that the British press and media in general have always stressed national unity and 'middlebrow' social values, perhaps as a way to veil very serious and possibly disruptive social cleavages. On the other hand, the growth of the Dutch press and of other media in the Netherlands was a phenomenon at the national level, yet it led to a substantial reinforcement of group identities instead of national unity. Newspapers especially were the mouthpieces of the pillars within Dutch society, often led by chief editors who were at the same time the leaders of national political parties. This all changed after 1960, confirming the impression that the cultural revolution of the 1960s was the moment of the nationalization of the masses in the Netherlands.

Perhaps one of the explanations for this paradox is the difference in scale, a factor that undoubtedly plays its role in all aspects of the discussion of mass society. In this case, the expansion of the British local press might be quantitatively equivalent to the development of a national press in the Netherlands, simply because Britain is five times larger than the Netherlands in size and population. But there are also other interpretations that might be instructive. One of the possibilities is that the media are, in organizational terms, locally or group based but substantially all doing very much the same thing. For instance, despite the fact that the Dutch pillarized media (and for that matter all pillarized organizations) are catering for their various constituencies, to a large extent they all stress the same set of moral values of work, family and civic responsibility. And, as Frank van Vree argues, they all manifested the same suspicion of popular culture, which was viewed as commercial empty-headedness or as a potentially disruptive glorification of folk ways. On the other hand, Kevin Williams presents examples of mediation of national unity which instrumentalize popular or lower-class culture: even though many British movie-actors were heard speaking with a local accent, the message they conveyed was distinctly national.

Another possibility is that the mass media did in fact manufacture both national and local or group identities, but that these identifications did not fit neatly into the patterns in which the masses were organized by other institutions. The mass media were to an important extent a commercial enterprise and as such very keen on keeping and expanding their market share. As a result, they might have been, and still are, reinforcing cultural tendencies that can undermine the structures in which the masses are organized. This is what seems to have happened to the public broadcast system in the Netherlands after the 1960s, and it might also explain some of the debates around the problematic national hegemony of the BBC.

In the end, these are not so much solutions to a riddle as indications of the issues that seem relevant to address from a comparative point of view. Were the media differently organized in Britain and the Netherlands? To what effect? Did the Dutch media strengthen group identity, or did they organize the nation in a way that is comparable with what the British media seem to have done? How is the identification the media offer related to the other modes of organizing a mass society? Did they always suppress more popular or populist interests, or did they perhaps utilize them for commercial or political reasons?

Mass Culture

The debate about the mass media is closely related to that about mass culture, in the sense that many of the products of mass culture are advertised, distributed and evaluated through the media. What would stardom be without the movies? Is the development of popular music thinkable without the radio and television? How would we survive a holiday in Benidorm (if at all) without the BBC World Service or the *Wereldomroep*? However, the debate about mass culture is not exhausted by a discussion of media consumption. As the chapters of Theo Beckers and Douglas Reid demonstrate, the development of a mass culture is to be located in both the sphere of consumption and that of production. In fact, a necessary precondition for the emergence of mass culture is not only the standardized production of consumer goods but also the creation of the wealth and income to buy them, and the organization of the free time to enjoy them. In all these respects, there are crucial comparative questions to address concerning the organization of labour, the introduction of new technology, the levels of national wealth and the distribution of incomes.

Also, mass culture, as a sphere of consumption, cannot be separated from its economic structure. Again, from a comparative perspective, the organization, functioning and transformation of the market for consumer goods are seminal issues to address. To what extent have national or international markets replaced local markets? How quickly are new consumer goods like cars, caravans, record players, radios, television sets, video recorders and home computers introduced, and how widespread is their ownership? To what extent did supermarkets replace local entrepreneurs, and how diversified are the goods on offer? How are these goods advertised? And what is the position of consumers, legally, politically and organizationally? What is to be made of the fact that the Dutch ANWB and the Consumentenbond (the equivalents of the Automobile Association and the Consumers' Association in Britain) have one of the highest levels of membership of all civil associations?

As both Reid and Beckers insist, one of the most crucial aspects from a cultural point of view is the division between work and 'free time'. The latter term needs to be put in quotes, since it is still deduced from the dominant term 'work', while the gist of the argument presented in these chapters is that leisure has become the more important domain of life. The rise of mass culture is also the rise of a sphere of leisure, which has replaced that of work as the sphere of personal development and identity formation. Free time has gradually been changing into quality time. Again, the comparative question would be how the organization of free time is arranged, both in terms of working hours and as a function of the organization of free time in holiday periods, time investment in play, sports and recreation, or the planning of recreational space (theatres, movies, sports facilities, holiday resorts or the market for travel and tourism). Moreover, as Reid argues, the enjoyment of leisure depends on the availability of the money to pay for it.

Now these are all matters of cultural hardware, so to speak. There are even more thorny questions, once we move to the cultural or discursive aspects of mass culture. As Patrick Brantlinger has argued, mass culture is very often conceived as the contemporary version of 'bread and circuses'.[18] In the technologically upgraded version of an age-old critique of luxury and popular taste, the spread of mass culture is perceived as the pathway to a totalitarian society in which citizens are turned into happy slaves, 'amusing themselves to death', as Neil Postman, one of the Cassandras of mass culture, has written.[19] The masses enjoying mass culture are accused of passivity, lack of taste and judgement, of being at the same time easy to manipulate and insensitive to reasoned argument.

However, as Becker stresses in his chapter, the development of mass consumption is also perceived as the precondition for the spread of modern individualism. The opportunity to create one's own personality, the power of self-development, which at the beginning of the twentieth century was only available to Veblen's leisure class and the bohemians of the cultural underground, has been democratized since the 1960s. We collectively aim at an ever more distinctive individualism. It appears that the emergence of this 'mass individualism' was nowhere more abrupt than in the Netherlands, which in a very short interval changed from one of the most traditional societies in Europe to a beacon of libertarianism. It seems that more than anyone else Dutch individuals strive to develop a unique personality, yet they do this in massive numbers and in often remarkably uniform ways.[20]

The Welfare State

The possibilities of mass individualism are conditioned by the mass production of consumer goods and the development of mass markets, but most of all they are facilitated and constrained by the development of the welfare state. The state in the twentieth century performs a crucial role in the development of mass societies in a number of ways. To begin with, it offers citizens the means to live their lives without being burdened by the necessities of existence. The limitation of the working day, reasonable payment, disability insurance and pensions, but also housing, health care, child support and homes for the elderly, all contribute to the possibility to buy and enjoy the goods of mass culture and society.

In this area of welfare provisions, the British and Dutch states perhaps constrain the development of a mass society in different ways. As Roebroek argues, the development of the Dutch welfare state is the result of an intricate relationship between state and society. The organizations within Dutch civil society are often closely connected with the state and can in many ways be considered as an extension of the state: hospitals, poor relief and housing corporations have often been part of the denominational or cultural network of Dutch society, yet financially, and also in terms of training and expertise, they have been dependent upon the state. Even though in Britain the number and spread of associations might be considerable, as is the connection with the welfare state, Pat Thane's chapter suggests that the development of the British welfare state is much more the result of the pressure of the labouring classes on the state, initially mediated by progressive politicians in the Liberal Party, to develop forms of social security and care on a national basis. However, in the post-war era, the British and Dutch welfare states seem to have followed more or less the same trajectory of a measured increase in scope during the 1950s, when social democrats put a higher priority on full employment than on extensive social security, a boom in social legislation at the end of the 1960s as a result of the culture shift of that era, and the rolling back of the state after the first oil crisis of 1973, leading to the neo-liberal austerity of Thatcher and Lubbers in the 1980s.

The welfare state had a profound influence on social relations. As Pat Thane stresses, it uprooted class distinctions and undermined the prestige of the British upper class. However, the Dutch case demonstrates that the welfare state could also reinforce social difference through the differential treatment of men and women in the area of health, education and care, but most importantly by sanctioning systems of payment and taxation that deeply influence the status of individuals within the family and that of families within society. Again, from a comparative perspective, one could ask whether the Dutch system, based on a family income earned by the male head of the household, is very different from the British gendering of the welfare state. How are the boundaries between public and private defined? Under what conditions do the products of mass culture enter the homes of families? Moreover, welfare state provisions, especially after the 'rights revolution' of the 1960s which contributed to the proliferation of entitlements, offer a broad spectrum of identifications and enable individuals to develop their personalities in a great many different ways. Yet again, differences in the nature of this revolution in Britain and the Netherlands can be of crucial importance for the development of citizenship in both countries.

Youth

One of the most important aspects of state intervention after 1945 is the massive investment in education. Both the British Education Act of 1944 and the much later Dutch *Mammoetwet* of 1965 gave a major boost to the participation in education, both socially and in terms of the amount of time spent at school. As Piet de Rooy argues, this led to a substantial shift in the social environment in which young people grew up, leading to a move from the family and the street to the peer group within the school as the most important formative context of the child's soul.

The expansion of education is one of the major determinants in the development of a youth culture. The development of a mass society cannot be separated from the changing place of young people in Western societies. Very often the emergence of mass society was perceived as an infantilization of culture, and as such a retreat in the history of civilization. As William Wordsworth put it in his poem 'Illustrated Books and Newspapers': 'A backward movement surely we have here, / From manhood – back to childhood; for the age – / Back towards caverned life's first rude career'.[21] The mirror-image to this pessimistic vision was the expectation, promoted by the idealistic youth movement of the 1920s and 1930s, that youth had the ability to overcome the short-sightedness and irresponsibility of the old regime, which had sent its youth to be slaughtered in massive numbers in the trenches of Verdun and Passchendaele.

The accusation of childishness and the fear of the unruliness of mass youth predominated from 1945 until the end of the 1950s, but as Piet de Rooy argues for the Dutch case, following the work of Hans Righart and others, this negative evaluation of youth culture gradually disappeared at the end of the 1950s, making room for an uneasy recognition that youth again had the future.[22] Everywhere in the Western world, youth culture has become dominant, as is demonstrated by clothing, recreation and musical taste. From a comparative Anglo-Dutch perspective, it could be argued that this tendency is particularly strong in the Netherlands, which has experienced a more radical 'culture shift' in the 1960s than any other Western country, and where giving in to the demands of a younger generation seems to have been culturally programmed by a long tradition of elite accommodation.[23] According to De Rooy, the emergence of a new youth culture even resulted, after 1970, in a general longing for youthfulness among adults.

However, two caveats seem to be warranted. To begin with, the emergence of a youth culture did not erase older social markers altogether. Class distinctions between working-class 'rockers' and *nozems*, and middle-class 'mods' and *Pleiners* and later on also the Dutch 'Provos', were still very much in place. This even seems to hold for the present day, when differences between youth subcultures have become much more refined; yet the class distinctions between '*altos*' and '*Anitas*', to give just one Dutch example of social demarcations of some years ago, is still plainly visible. A second remark stems from the chapter of Bill Osgerby, who stresses the more gloomy side of youth culture after 1979. The rise of Margaret Thatcher was accompanied by the sounds of the Sex Pistols and New Order, replacing the 'love is all you need'-spirit of 1968 by the doom of the 1980s. Yet even then youth remained the messenger of a new era of society, defined by a mixture of hyper-individualism and mass culture.

Conclusion

The chapters in this volume address most of the issues raised above and offer new and important insights into the development of mass societies. On the one hand, they underline the fruitfulness of the notion of mass society as an approach to the history of the twentieth century from a comparative point of view. The authors shed light on the ambiguous nature of the concept and the practice of mass society, combining individualism and collectivism, stupidity and creativity, passivity and unruliness – all crucial aspects of contemporary history. Moreover, the comparison between Britain and the Netherlands makes clear to what extent the development of mass societies is conditioned by the nature of the political system, the organization of the public sphere, the material and cultural preconditions of mass consumption, and the development of the welfare state. Finally, it becomes clear that the evaluation of mass societies is strongly dependent on the status awarded to the younger generation, both as the messenger of times to come and as the prime example of infantilization of the masses.

Yet, as all inspiring historical scholarship is supposed to do, these chapters also raise new questions. To what extent are the developments described in this volume specific to Britain and the Netherlands? Is there a specific northwest European path towards mass societies, or is there no substantial difference from, for example, Russia, the US or the Mediterranean countries? Or, from a more localized perspective, how is the development of mass society influenced by regional identities? What is the impact of the almost proverbial British working-class identity on the development of mass culture, as compared to the Dutch identification with societal pillars? What is the role of distinctions between city and countryside, old and new ethnic boundaries, styles, trends and brands? To what extent is it possible to speak of a mass culture, given the multifarious social and cultural distinctions that define it?

This is not the place to answer all these issues, and perhaps it will be impossible to arrive at definitive answers. The multifaceted nature of mass society leads to the paradoxical insight that its emergence has created a mass individualism. But even when we all try to be different in similar ways, there may still be differences between the Netherlands and Britain that really distinguish one mass society from another.

Notes

1. Asa Briggs, 'The Language of "Mass" and "Masses" in Nineteenth-century England', in David E. Martin and David Rubinstein (eds), *Ideology and the Labour Movement: Essays Presented to John Saville* (London/Totowa, 1979), pp. 62–83.

2. Jürgen Habermas, *Strukturwandel der Öffentlichkeit: Untersuchungen zu einer Kategorie der bürgerlichen Gesellschaft* (Darmstadt, 1962).

3. Stefan Collini, *Public Moralists: Political Thought and Intellectual Life in Britain 1850–1930* (Oxford, 1991).

4. Susanna Barrows, *Distorting Mirrors: Visions of the Crowd in Late Nineteenth-century France* (New Haven, 1981); Jaap van Ginneken, *Crowds, Psychology, and Politics, 1871–1899* (Cambridge, 1989).

5. José Ortega y Gasset, *La rebelión de las masas* (Madrid, 1929), English translation: *The Revolt of the Masses* (London, 1932), Dutch translation: *De opstand der horden* ('s-Gravenhage, 1933).

6. Theodor Adorno, *Minima Moralia: Reflexionen aus dem beschädigten Leben* (Berlin, 1951).

7. Elias Canetti, *Masse und Macht* (Hamburg, 1960).

8. David Riesman (with Nathan Glazer and Reuel Denney), *The Lonely Crowd: A Study of the Changing American Character* (New Haven, 1950); William Kornhauser, *The Politics of Mass Society* (London, 1960).

9. Herbert Marcuse, *One-dimensional Man: Studies in the Ideology of Advanced Industrial Societies* (Boston, 1964).

10. Sandor Halebsky, *Mass Society and Political Conflict: Toward a Reconstruction of Theory* (Cambridge, 1976), pp. 10–35.

11. David Runciman, *Pluralism and the Personality of the State* (Cambridge, 1997); Cécile Laborde, *Pluralist Thought and the State in Britain and France, 1900–25* (Basingstoke/New York, 2000).

12. Geoffrey Finlayson, *Citizen, State, and Social Welfare in Britain, 1830–1990* (Oxford, 1994).

13. Ido de Haan, *Het beginsel van leven en wasdom. De constitutie van de Nederlandse politiek in de negentiende eeuw* (Amsterdam, 2003).

14. George L. Mosse, *The Nationalization of the Masses: Political Symbolism and Mass Movements in Germany from the Napoleonic Wars through the Third Reich* (New York, 1975).

15. Carl E. Schorske, *Fin-de-siècle Vienna: Politics and Culture* (New York, 1979).

16. Kornhauser, *The Politics of Mass Society*, p. 227.

17. Ortega y Gasset, *The Revolt of the Masses*, chapter 13.

18. Patrick Brantlinger, *Bread and Circuses: Theories of Mass Culture as Social Decay* (Ithaca/London, 1983).

19. Neil Postman, *Amusing Ourselves to Death: Public Discourse in the Age of Show Business* (New York, 1985).

20. Jan Willem Duyvendak and Menno Hurenkamp (eds), *Kiezen voor de kudde. Lichte gemeenschappen en de nieuwe meerderheid* (Amsterdam, 2004).

21. William Wordsworth, *Complete Poems* (Oxford, 1965), p. 383, quoted in Brantlinger, *Bread and Circuses*, p. 278.

22. Hans Righart, *De eindeloze jaren zestig. Geschiedenis van een generatieconflict* (Amsterdam, 1995); Ger Tillekens (ed.), *Nuchterheid en nozems. De opkomst van de jeugdcultuur in de jaren vijftig* (Muiderberg, 1990); Paul Luykx and Pim Slot (ed.), *Een stille revolutie? Cultuur en mentaliteit in de lange jaren vijftig* (Hilversum, 1997); Hans Righart and Paul Luykx (ed.), *Generatiemix. Leeftijdsgroepen en cultuur* (Amsterdam, 1998).

23. See James Kennedy, *Nieuw Babylon in aanbouw. Nederland in de jaren zestig* (Amsterdam/Meppel, 1995).

Part I
Politics

–2–

Politics and the People
Perceptions of the Masses in Dutch Politics
Henk te Velde

For the twentieth century the compound term 'mass politics' seems almost pleonastic. Most politics simply were mass politics. Curiously enough, however, in the Netherlands many contemporaries refused to accept the equation of politics with mass politics. They did not like the 'masses'. As this chapter sets out to demonstrate, this dislike presents a clue to understanding important aspects of Dutch politics and Dutch attitudes towards politics in the twentieth century.

Like many popular words in Dutch and other languages, the word 'masses' has had many different meanings. In 1940 the Dutch author of a theoretical dissertation about 'mass action and mass mentality' distinguished at least six meanings of the word 'masses' in the social sciences.[1] In practice, however, in the Netherlands the word was mainly used in two different, though intertwining, meanings. First, there was the *psychological* meaning of a volatile, excited crowd, mob or mass meeting, in which people behaved without thinking, irrationally and irresponsibly. Second, *cultural criticism* used the word in the sense of the 'average man', superficial, materialistic, uprooted, broken away from tradition, spineless, suggestible and depersonalized. For most of the twentieth century, Dutch politicians did not like the masses in either of these meanings. In order to give an overview of the attitude of Dutch politicians towards mass society, I will demonstrate this dislike and also investigate its meaning, beginning with the masses as defined in the psychological sense.

The Masses in Dutch Politics

Wim Kok, the Dutch prime minister from 1994 to 2002, once said that he hardly ever felt comfortable when receiving a standing ovation in a mass meeting. In fact, he generally did not like mass meetings and feared the capacity of crowds to work themselves up into a state of excitement. His experiences with mass activities had taught him to be careful, and to take to heart the lessons of history in this respect.[2] His predecessor Ruud Lubbers (1982–94) held similar views and, just like Kok, preferred sober administration to populist politics.[3] Kok, the trade union man, the social-democratic son of a carpenter, and Lubbers, the rich Catholic entrepreneur, came from different social backgrounds and belonged to different political parties, but they shared a dislike of mass ovations. This is no coincidence. For most of the twentieth century most Dutch politicians did not like crowds. Since the Second World War they did not normally like to be at the centre of a mass meeting. Even if they liked to remain in close contact with the members of their own party and also with the common workers, as Joop den Uyl – Kok's predecessor as leader of the Dutch Social Democratic Party and prime minister in the 1970s (1973–7) – did, they were incapable of the sort of populist theatricality that the occasion of a mass meeting sometimes called for. Dutch politics had to wait until the beginning of the next century and the advent of Pim Fortuyn before an influential political leader emerged who really liked to put on a performance. Especially during the first decades after the war, and then again in the 1980s and 1990s, Dutch prime ministers adopted a distant, restrained and administrative attitude. In the case of Willem Drees, the Attlee-like and by now legendary social democratic prime minister of the post-war period of austerity (1948–58), this was partly a reaction against pompous and antidemocratic leadership in the period before the war, and partly a result of the Dutch traditions of coalition governments that called for colourless managers. But it was also a new form of an older Dutch tradition of rule by distant and rather inconspicuous notables.[4]

In order to understand the attitude towards mass politics in the twentieth century, one has to go back to the society of the nineteenth century. There were remarkable parallels between the political development of Britain and that of the Netherlands. In the second half of the nineteenth century, liberalism with its agenda of constitutional reform and the rule of law dominated politics. Modern, organized parties appeared from the 1870s and 1880s onwards, although the Socialist Party only became a powerful force after the First World War, and suffrage was gradually broadened to reach male (and in the Dutch case also female) universal suffrage by the end of the First World War in both countries. Thus, the gradual development of parliamentary democracy and liberal traditions showed many similarities in the two countries. However, the atmosphere of politics differed widely. There were not many countries that mirrored the political development of Britain more closely than the Netherlands, but there were not many countries that differed so much from the British example in relation to both the culture and liveliness of political and public life. Until 1956 the small Dutch parliament only contained 100 members, and before the revision of the constitution in 1887 there had been even fewer. After the constitutional changes in 1956, the second chamber was enlarged to 150 members. The Dutch parliament was not nearly as popular as the British parliament and, compared to Britain, Dutch electoral campaigns were generally rather quiet. A distant, legal atmosphere permeated parliamentary politics. The notion of popular sovereignty did not enter the Dutch constitution in the nineteenth century, nor has it entered it since, and politicians have tended to stress the distance between the electors and the elected.

In the nineteenth century the representative system was valued just because it was *not* 'democratic'. At first most British liberals did not like 'democracy' either, but this common rejection of democracy as a theory masked major differences in terms of rhetoric and agitation. A passionate popular leader such as Gladstone was unthinkable in Dutch liberalism. There were charismatic leaders like him in the Netherlands, but they started as either orthodox Protestant or socialist outsiders. From the 1880s until the beginning of the twentieth century, there was a brief period of populist politics in the Netherlands. For the first time huge political mass meetings were organized, and Abraham Kuyper, founder and leader of the orthodox Protestant Antirevolutionaire Partij, not only enjoyed speaking to them, but also wrote a theoretical defence of the beneficial effects of mass meetings. According to him, they furthered the solidarity and spiritual strength of the people present: together they could move mountains.[5] His socialist counterpart Pieter Jelles Troelstra, leader of the Social Democratic Workers' Party (SDAP) founded in 1894, cherished his experiences in mass meetings even more. The new socialist and denominational parties realized that mass politics demanded new methods of appealing to the people, and the new politicians sometimes used populist methods. At the elections of 1905, for instance, so-called Catholic 'democrats' and socialist politicians alike campaigned under the slogan of fewer lawyers and more 'practical' men and workers in parliament.[6] This was clearly directed against the old liberals, who were often lawyers and whose leading politicians and intellectuals had often been professors of constitutional law. In 1918 Henriette Roland Holst, the left-wing socialist and Dutch Rosa Luxemburg, published a book about the important contributions of spontaneous revolutionary mass action to the progress of humanity.[7]

By then, however, the tide had turned. Roland Holst belonged to a breakaway socialist party that was turned into the Dutch Communist Party after the Russian Revolution. Mainstream social democrats now preferred organization to spontaneous action, and older social democrats began to warn against the dangers of the fickle crowd.[8] In 1934 the influential social-democratic criminologist and political scientist W.A. Bonger published a famous book about the 'problems of democracy'. Bonger wrote his book as a defence of parliamentary democracy and he committed suicide when the Germans invaded the Netherlands in May 1940. Bonger was interested in the necessary selective or even aristocratic aspects of representative systems and advocated strong leadership. He was very explicit: if there were no capable leaders, the masses would fall into the hands of demagogues or fanatics. The mass of average men were not capable of solving difficult problems, in particular when they were together and thus easily emotionalized.[9] On the subject of leaders and masses Bonger was more outspoken than most of his fellow socialists, but his remarks were in keeping with the growing concerns of his time, and so was his careful reading of the classics of mass psychology such as the work of Gustave Le Bon. Many Dutch intellectuals had read Le Bon and even more had heard of his ideas. Most of them concurred with the tendency of Le Bon's pessimistic conclusions about crowd behaviour. Few, however, were as pessimistic as G.J.P.J. Bolland, the right-wing philosopher, who thought that parliamentary democracy entailed mob rule and serving the vulgar herd hand and foot.[10] One is left wondering in what country Bolland was living, because after the introduction of universal suffrage the Netherlands had become a rather quiet country again. The period of populist politics was largely over, at least for the time being, and party and other mass organizations had disciplined what masses existed. A disciplined bourgeois culture dominated public life. When Virginia Woolf briefly visited the Netherlands in May 1935, she wrote in her diary:

> We are back in 1913. ... The people are dressed in perfect respectability. ... People immensely respectable. No sign of crisis or war. ... Not a beggar, not a slum. ... A feeling that Holland is a perfectly self respecting rather hard featured but individual middle aged woman. Conventions of 1913. No women smoking or driving cars. Only one man smokes a pipe in the streets.[11]

This is just the brief impression of a travelling tourist, and historians would add not only that the crisis certainly did make a deep impression on the Netherlands, but also that the country no longer lived in 1913 any more and was modernizing. Still, compared to countries such as Britain, Belgium or Germany, which had lived through the horrors of war and also possessed a larger share of mass industry and a much more clear-cut and separate working-class culture, the Netherlands must have seemed a quiet, bourgeois country. Thus, the apocalyptic visions of mass psychology were not very realistic in the Netherlands, not least because there were no cities the size of Paris. On the contrary, the aristocratic element that Bonger advocated very conspicuously dominated Dutch politics, not in the sense of a real nobility, but in the form of the untranslatable bourgeois *deftigheid* or stateliness, a restrained, aloof, very respectable and stiff attitude of dignitaries, administrators and politicians.

Linthorst Homan, a Conservative Liberal and provincial governor, was one of the leaders of the 'Nederlandse Unie', an organization that attempted to restructure Dutch political life during the German occupation in a way that was certainly not National Socialist and was perceived by many as an act of national resistance, but was not clearly directed against the Germans. Instead the Union was arguably first and foremost a criticism of Dutch pre-war political and social life. Linthorst Homan uttered fashionable complaints about the stalemate created by the hopelessly divided nature of Dutch parliamentary politics and also internal party politics, but interestingly he also complained about the 'distance' that separated administrators from the people and the parade of top hats that dominated public ceremonies and events. Even though one could object to his politics, his complaint sounds more convincing than the warning a few years later that the Netherlands had experienced the crumbling of 'authority' and 'decorum', even though this warning appeared in a respectable postwar book by the engineer S.H. Stoffel, prefaced by Willem Schermerhorn, the then Social Democratic prime minister.[12] When Johan Huizinga, the historian, wrote in his last and posthumously published book that democracy needed 'an element of aristocracy' because it would otherwise founder on the coarseness of 'the masses', he worried about the Netherlands, but there was no real need for this.[13] In Dutch the adjective *representatief* can mean, among other things, representative as in representative instead of direct democracy, but also presentable and respectable. Thus, Dutch democracy was very *representatief* in both meanings of the word, and the respectable side added to its very clear representative qualities.

Looking back from the beginning of the twenty-first century, the political situation seems very stable. Only a small percentage of floating voters existed. The mobilizing politics of the end of the nineteenth century had resulted in a new political configuration, with Catholic, Social Democratic and Protestant parties each having a stable share of the vote: Catholics about one third, Protestants about one quarter, and Social

Democrats almost the same percentage. At the same time, the Liberal vote dwindled away to around 10 per cent. The newly introduced system of proportional representation translated the percentages of the vote into exactly the same share of parliamentary seats. Political scientists and historians have said that Dutch elections during this period resembled a census. Just as in a census, voting did not imply choice but rather registration; it was in fact the expression of a permanent identification with a certain religious or political group.[14] Often this situation has been discussed as a kind of Dutch *Sonderweg*, and much has been made of the Dutch consociational democratic system of so-called 'pillarization' or *verzuiling*, which consisted of closed political communities that catered for their adherents from the cradle to the grave in separate political parties and societies, denominational schools, separate trade unions, newspapers, broadcasting corporations, etc.[15] One could argue, though, that this was instead a particular form, and also a very clear case, of 'party democracy', which the political scientist Bernard Manin discusses in his book on the principles of representative government. He concentrates on socialist parties and says: 'For most socialist or social democratic voters, the vote they cast was not a matter of choice, but of social identity and destiny.' A 'feeling of belonging and a sense of identification' dominated politics.[16] In the Dutch case this was perhaps even more true than in most other countries, and it was true in particular in the case of the religious groups.

It is easy to understand that many liberals were not happy with the new situation. In the early 1920s Dresselhuys, the political leader of the Conservative Liberals, still mourned the time when politics had been parliamentary politics dominated by individual notables, and culture had meant elite bourgeois culture. He thought that the introduction of universal suffrage entailed a politics of 'sentiments' and cheap propaganda instead of rational persuasion. Politicians now had to address huge masses and, according to him, mass psychologists had shown that masses were insensible to reason.[17] Dresselhuys' comments must perhaps be seen against the background of the first phase of universal suffrage. The 1917 changes in the constitution had not only introduced universal male suffrage (followed by universal female suffrage in 1919) but also proportional representation, enabling all kinds of small parties to enter the political scene that did not have any substantial ideology but sometimes practised modern methods of publicity.[18] However, they attracted almost exclusively potential Liberal voters. Dresselhuys' distinction between rational persuasion and mass propaganda may have been true in the Liberal case, when Liberal notables refused to do something about the distance that separated them from the common people, but in the cases of the denominational and socialist parties an ideology which appealed to reason and mass propaganda went hand in hand. The whole point of these parties was to lead, activate and mobilize the masses, but in each case this was mobilization of a specific group. Catholic politicians tried to mobilize the Catholic masses, Social Democrats wanted to activate the working classes. They sometimes used aggressive means of propaganda, but they seldom had the intention of temporarily rousing a crowd. In the nineteenth century, socialists and orthodox Protestants had started with the ambition to convert the whole nation, but by now they had resigned themselves to just mobilizing their share of the population, and their primary efforts were directed towards the retention and mobilization of their electoral heartland. Although there were fierce electoral campaigns, in the eyes of the politicians permanent organizations were much more important.

So the Dutch political scene was dominated by the masses, but these were organized, disciplined masses. For some international analysts of mass society, this made no difference at all, because the organizations were a part of the problem. A mass psychologist such as Le Bon had argued that even parliaments acted irrationally because they constituted a crowd. Most Dutch analysts, though, tended to differentiate, for instance, between crowds and masses. Depending on the author, a crowd would mean an unorganized and irrational group but a mass would mean a disciplined crowd or it could be the other way round (a crowd being an organized mass), but at least a difference was being made.[19] In most critical analyses of mass politics and mass society the negative connotations of mob behaviour could still be heard, but mostly a different meaning prevailed. When writing about 'masses', Dutch authors generally did not have in mind the psychological meaning with which I started this contribution, but rather cultural criticism.[20]

Cultural Criticism of the Masses

From the 1920s to the 1960s, a pile of books, articles and reports was written about the problems of mass society. The remainder of this contribution will be devoted to the political use of the word masses in this type of cultural criticism and the relevance of this criticism for Dutch politics. More often than not authors refrained from clearly defining their subject, but in 1946 the essay by the engineer Stoffel about 'the man in the crowd and his future' was an exception. The author did not want to use the word in the mass-psychological sense of crowd or mob as it was used by Le Bon, but meant the 'growing number of people broken away from traditional thinking and feeling'.[21] As so often in this type of literature, the masses were defined negatively by explaining what they lacked. Ortega y Gasset, in a book about the revolt of the masses that was immensely popular in the Netherlands, expressed it as follows: in the masses 'there is no culture; there is, in the strictest sense of the word, barbarism. Barbarism is the absence of standards.'[22] The masses were formed by people who had lost their traditional values and now led an empty, hedonistic, superficial life.

The opposite of masses was community. A community offered the individual everything the masses lacked: a sense of purpose, a haven in a heartless world, traditions to hold on to. The most important thing, though, was that people could be educated in order to stop being part of the masses and to join a community instead. So, according to Stoffel, the essential duty was education, and in this respect he was typical. Everybody agreed that education was the most important thing, and also that the modern world suffered from a lack of traditions and community. This included many writers from the religious and socialist groups alike. They did not consider their own group as a mass; the masses were the others, the ones who lacked culture or civilization. According to Koos Vorrink, the prominent socialist and leader of a famous socialist youth organization, modern man was lonely and uprooted; he devoted a chapter of his book on education and the new socialist community to 'the destruction of tradition'.[23] After the Second World War Willem Banning, the prominent, religiously inspired socialist, also wrote many articles and books about the hedonistic, 'uprooted' masses that had lost all sense of direction.[24] In the case of socialism in particular, this was a rather paradoxical message. Socialism had made a living out of the mobilization of the masses, the destruction of tradition and its replacement by a new socialist movement. On the other hand, however, social democracy was dominated by respectable workers (as well as intellectuals and teachers) and it was at the same time becoming a world of its own, with organizations, habits, celebrations, heroes and traditions. It is perhaps no coincidence that the socialist Eric Hobsbawm coined the term 'invention of tradition', because late nineteenth and twentieth-century socialism offers very nice examples of the idea.[25] Vorrink, for instance, introduced elements from the German socialist youth movement into his own organization, and he advocated folk dancing. In the movement as a whole the sense of tradition and history was strong.

Perhaps it could be argued that politics *needed* the concept of 'the masses' as a negative counter-image to true politics as long as politics, or at least political parties and movements, were based on tradition. It is at least intriguing that the concept was most popular in the years between 1920 and 1960, which was precisely the period in which the tradition-based political movements ruled supreme. As mentioned above, the masses were mostly defined negatively by pointing out that they lacked culture, traditions and the like. In analyses of 'the masses', they hardly constituted a concrete social group. Although many authors apparently had in mind jobless and uneducated members of the working classes when writing about the masses, there were many others who made a point of explaining that rich idlers or students could be men in the crowd (*massamensen*) too.[26] One of the characteristics of men in the crowd was precisely that they did *not* constitute a group in the proper sense of the word; they were uprooted, lonely individuals. Paradoxically, individuals, in the sense of loose atoms, and masses belonged together. In the eyes of politicians and intellectuals alike, they both belonged to a modern world without direction, an atomized world. Politics could offer a solution if it could provide for a community.

Because the question had so much to do with education, there was inevitably special attention paid to young people. A few years after the Second World War, the minister of education commissioned an investigation into the question of the degeneration and lawlessness of young people, the so-called *massa-jeugd*. In the Netherlands this was then the largest sociological survey research ever undertaken. Although the tone of the resulting report was worried,[27] it was clear to most sober observers that nothing much was the matter. Young people behaved as could be expected of them, and most of them looked more like pocket-sized responsible adults than degenerate idlers. When introduced into government policy, the concepts of the masses and man in the crowd thus proved powerless. Gerardus van der Leeuw, the minister who had launched the idea of the survey, had been a theologian and university professor, without any political experience to speak of, and was only minister for a couple of months before returning to his former employment, which, besides his work as a theologian, partly consisted in writing critical essays about the condition of mass society.[28] This makes one wonder what the relationship actually was between politics, on the one hand, and intellectual cultural criticism of the masses on the other. Did all the books and articles about the masses actually have a political significance? I think they did, but different levels of politics must be distinguished.

Dutch Conceptions of Mass Politics

As I argued above, there was a large distance between politicians and the people. This means not only that the authorities were seen as people from another world, but also that many people did not have much interest in or knowledge of politics in the strict sense of the word. A visit to parliament in The Hague was never a popular outing, such as a visit to Westminster in Britain; parliamentary politics were never part of cultural life in the Netherlands. Before the 1960s there was a strong bond of trust binding political leaders and their followers in the same religious or socialist group, but this implied that the followers trusted that their leaders would act in their best interest, even when not being supervised. Most leaders, on the other hand, regarded politics mainly as administration, in particular when they were part of the government, such as Prime Minister Drees. Normally they lived in a sober world in which worried observations about mass society only played a small part. There was a huge distance separating politics in The Hague from politics in one's own community.

Yet outside The Hague there was another level of politics. When political scientists such as Hans Daalder and Arend Lijphart began to write in the 1960s about the lack of interest that the Dutch people had almost always shown in politics,[29] they forgot that, to the adherents of the different political communities, politics not only meant administration but also, and sometimes even primarily, ideology and being part of a moral community. Concrete results were crucial of course, such as the equal financial treatment of denominational and state schools after 1917 or the introduction of state old age pensions by Drees after the war, but the activities of the ordinary followers concentrated on the organizations and meetings of their community. Political scientists wrote about the alleged political passivity of the Dutch population, but in these organizations and meetings the population was not passive at all. In the period before 1939 in particular there were all kinds of huge mass meetings of Catholics, Protestants and socialists, and election meetings also drew large numbers of people. Most people also belonged to at least a few of the cultural societies and other organizations that constituted the separate subcultures. Even today it is said that the Dutch are mainly interested in the moral side of politics; if this is true, one of the reasons for this may be this tradition of separation of the administration in The Hague and grass-roots moral communities.

At the level of politics in the moral communities, the concept of the masses was very useful. It served to demonstrate the superiority of the community over the lonely outsiders. According to Willem Banning, the lonely, alienated, spoiled men in the crowd could hardly be called human beings at all.[30] They needed a community to become mature persons. The community also protected the individual against mere enslavement to his animal passions. The connotation of the masses was of course exactly the opposite: they did not protect against, but aroused, the passions. The well-known sexual connotations of crowd behaviour were strongest in Le Bon-like analyses, but they were never entirely absent from the use of the concept of the masses in cultural criticism, which always fulminated against hedonism and egotism. Sober self-discipline in the service of the community, that was the attitude of the ideal citizen; the community was more important than the individual.[31] There were of course outstanding individuals who could be selected as the leaders of the communities, but even they were part of the community, because they had more often than not been born or at least raised in the community itself.

Of course, cultural criticism was not simply an instrument in the hands of political leaders which they could use to strengthen their electoral basis. It was more complicated than that. Cultural criticism often criticized political practices as well. Sometimes modern political parties were even considered as threats to democracy.[32] Thus the criticism the Liberal leader Dresselhuys had levelled against the crude propaganda used by modern politics was echoed by many later cultural critics. Political propaganda used sensation, suggestion and slogans instead of rational arguments.[33] Just as Dresselhuys seemed a bit nostalgic for nineteenth-century politics, many cultural critics did not really seem to accept twentieth-century politics. Their idea of politics was often elitist, intellectual and resembled the nineteenth-century idea of a rational debate between mature citizens. Joop den Uyl, the Socialist leader of the 1970s and 1980s, said that Banning, one of the most prominent cultural critics, still lived in the world of the nineteenth century.[34] Like nineteenth-century liberals, cultural critics tended to confuse democratization or even politics in general with education. Citizens should be well educated before they began to take part in politics at all. Politicians who devoted part of their time to the writing of cultural criticism, such as Banning, Vorrink and others, were first and foremost educators or teachers; more often than not their approach to politics was rather unbusinesslike.[35]

Conclusion

After the Second World War some cultural critics thought for a moment that their version of politics as moral education would replace the old and fossilized party system. This turned out to be a short-lived illusion. The old parties returned, albeit with new names and adapted to the new circumstances. The most significant change was the replacement of the old Social Democratic Party (SDAP) by the new 'Labour' Party (PvdA). This was meant as a breakthrough in the Dutch political system, which had until then to a large extent been based on religious divisions but would now turn into a British-like system of conservatives and progressives. Only a small minority of voters accepted the change, and in a matter of a few years it became clear that the PvdA was in fact mainly a continuation of the pre-war SDAP. The situation was even clearer in the case of the new 'Catholic People's Party' (KVP), which was no more than the old Catholic RKSP in new clothing, and the 'people's party for freedom and democracy' (VVD), which turned out to be a continuation of the pre-war Conservative Liberal Party.

The political system did not change fundamentally after the war, nor did the cultural critics. The worried observations about mass society continued to be very popular, as was demonstrated by the best-selling *Revolution of the Lonely* by the sociologist P.J. Bouman, a consideration of the existential fate of the 'lonely' men in modern society and a description of Europe in the first half of the twentieth century that continued the tradition of pre-war cultural criticism.[36] This book was published in the early 1950s and reprinted time and again. Had it been published fifteen years later, it would probably not have been very successful, as by the late 1950s ideas about uprooted and lonely crowds had begun to sound old fashioned. Almost overnight this vocabulary completely fell out of fashion in the 1960s. Strangely enough, the observations about men in the crowd (*massamensen*) began to disappear at exactly the time most people would argue that something that could be called mass society was developing very quickly. From the 1960s political parties had to deal with floating voters and partly changed into 'catch-all parties', the mass medium of television made its appearence, and mass consumption grew at an unprecedented pace. 'The Dutch have stopped being dull', a British journalist commented in 1967,[37] and the country was indeed changing rapidly.

The loss in popularity of cultural criticism could be partly explained by a new perception of the meaning of the masses. For example, in the early 1970s the left-wing sociologist W.F. Wertheim published a book about 'elites and masses' in which almost for the first time since Roland Holst in 1918 the emancipating power of the masses was emphasized, and their revolutionary potential was praised.[38] Much more important, however, was a different perception of the individual. Traditional communities were now considered to be oppressive rather than stimulating, let alone emancipating. Individuals should liberate themselves from the dead weight of traditions, and the hypocrisy of elites who propagated nostalgia for village communities after having left themselves should be exposed. Voting should cease to be a census and start to really be about choices.

We are all familiar with the problems this emancipation in turn brought in its wake. Some of the cultural critics certainly would have said, 'I told you so'. Nevertheless, it is clear that the old paternalism had ceased to be a viable political strategy decades ago. Nowadays, politicians have to deal with the realities of (post)modern society, and one of these is the disappearance of permanent loyalty to organizations and political parties. Le Bon and his like would certainly have considered the recent explosion in Dutch politics caused by Pim Fortuyn as a confirmation of their views about crowd behaviour: a charismatic leader, a volatile group, a sudden explosion of populism and even some disturbances. In the 1950s something like this would not have happened. Even if the Fortuyn movement addressed some real problems, it was the disappearance of mass parties that could bind their adherents for a lifetime that opened up the political theatre for newcomers in this way. On the whole, however, it could be argued that the Dutch political system has survived this severe challenge rather well. Perhaps it is fair to say that the normal state of a system of representative democracy is an at least latent tension between what could be called its elitist or aristocratic aspects and its populist or democratic aspects.[39] This is not to say that one should stop worrying, rather the reverse. Mass parties used to ease this tension, but in their old form they have largely disappeared, and the new situation is still rather unclear. Democracy will always be controversial and the topical question is how to combine the Dutch tradition of quiet, sober administration with the desire that politics should also address moral, ideological and cultural questions.

Notes

1. Julius Woltning, *Massa-actie en Massa-mentaliteit* (Assen 1940).

2. Peter Klein and Redmar Kooistra, *Wim Kok. Het taaie gevecht van een polderjongen* (Amsterdam, 1998), p. 55.

3. See, for example, some remarks in Jan Tromp and Erik van Venetië, 'Ik ben niet geschikt om te schrijden als De Gaulle', *de Volkskrant*, 2 November 1991, and Bert Steimetz, *Ruud Lubbers. Peetvader van het poldermodel* (Amsterdam, 2000), p. 169.

.4. See Henk te Velde, *Stijlen van leiderschap. Persoon en politiek van Thorbecke tot Den Uyl* (Amsterdam, 2002).

5. A. Kuyper, *Ons instinctieve leven* (Amsterdam, *c.* 1908).

6. J.H. Schaper, *Een halve eeuw strijd. Herinneringen*, 2 vols (Groningen etc., 1933–5) II, p. 210; Jos van Wel, cited by Hans Verhage, *Katholieken, kerk en wereld. Roermond en Helmond in de lange negentiende eeuw* (Hilversum, 2003), p. 173.

7. Henriette Roland Holst, *Revolutionaire massa-aktie. Een studie* (Rotterdam, 1918).

8. E.g. Schaper, *Halve eeuw*, I, pp. 162 and 168–9.

9. W.A. Bonger, *Problemen der demokratie. Een sociologische en psychologische studie* (1934; Amsterdam *c.* 1977), pp. 48 and 67.

10. G.J.P.J. Bolland, *De teekenen des tijds* (Leiden, 1921), p. 8.

11. Anne Olivier Bell and Andrew McNeillie (eds), *The Diary of Virginia Woolf*, IV (1982; London, 1983), pp. 309–10. I'd like to thank Prof. Coen Tamse who drew my attention to this text.

12. J. Linthorst Homan, *Aanpakken! Een hartekreet van een jongen Nederlander* (Haarlem, 1940), p. 13; S.H. Stoffel, *De massa-mensch en zijn toekomst. Proeve van een analyse onzer samenleving. Met een voorwoord van Prof. Ir. W. Schermerhorn* (Amsterdam, 1946), pp. 235–7.

13. J. Huizinga, *Geschonden wereld. Een beschouwing over de kansen op herstel van onze beschaving* (Haarlem, 1945), p. 110.

14. Joseph J. Houska, *Influencing Mass Political Behavior: Elites and Political Subcultures in the Netherlands and Austria* (Berkeley, CA, 1985), pp. 57–8, who is quoting Hans Daalder. More recently, Piet de Rooy has also used the metaphor of the census.

15. The oldest classic in English is Arend Lijphart, *The Politics of Accommodation: Pluralism and Democracy in the Netherlands* (Berkeley, CA, 1968).

16. Bernard Manin, *The Principles of Representative Government* (Cambridge, 1997), pp. 209 and 211.

17. H.C. Dresselhuys, *Om de democratie* (1924) p. 3; ibid., *Openingsrede uitge-*

sproken ter gelegenheid van de partij-vergadering en het congres van den Vrijheidsbond (1925), pp. 6–7.

18. Koen Vossen, *Vrij vissen in het Vondelpark. Kleine politieke partijen in Nederland 1918–1940* (Amsterdam, 2003).

19. H.T. de Graaf, *Om het hoogste goed* (Amsterdam, 1918), pp. 37–8 (*menigte* or crowd is an accidental mass gathering; *massa* is a group, bound by history, tradition and common beliefs); J.A. Sellenraad, *Massapsychologie en karaktervorming (Bibliotheek voor Bijbelsche opvoedkunde)*, 15 (1931) p. 5: in a *menigte* (crowd) each participant will keep his 'individuality', in a *massa* he will lose it.

20. A case in point is the sociologist P.J. Bouman, who used the two definitions of the masses indiscriminately but in fact limited himself to cultural criticism: Tity de Vries, *Complexe consensus. Amerikaanse en Nederlandse intellectuelen in debat over politiek en cultuur 1945–1960* (Hilversum, 1996), pp. 178–9.

21. Stoffel, *Massa-mensch*, p. 8.

22. José Ortega y Gasset, *The Revolt of the Masses* (New York, 1950), p. 52; ibid., *De opstand der horden* (The Hague, 1934), p. 69.

23. Koos Vorrink, *Om de vrije mens der nieuwe gemeenschap. Opvoeding tot het demokratiese socialisme* (Amsterdam, 1933).

24. For example, Willem Bouwman, '*Tijd en Taak*, blad voor Bannings idealen', in G. Harinck and D.Th. Kuiper (eds), *Anderhalve eeuw protestantse periodieke pers* (Zoetermeer, 1999), p. 129.

25. Eric Hobsbawm and Terence Ranger (eds), *The Invention of Tradition* (Cambridge, 1983). Hobsbawm is, for example, citing the socialist holiday of the First of May as a prominent example of the 'invention of tradition'.

26. For example, *Maatschappelijke verwildering*, pp. 20–1; J.H. van der Hoop, *Geestelijke vrijheid. I Massa, democratie, staat* (Arnhem, 1948), p. 142, footnote: this type of person may be found in every walk of life.

27. 'Maatschappelijke verwildering der jeugd. Rapport betreffende het onderzoek naar de geestesgesteldheid van de massajeugd in opdracht van de Minister van Onderwijs, Kunsten en Wetenschappen samengesteld' (The Hague, 1952). Cf. among other things Piet de Rooy, 'Vetkuifje waarheen? Jongeren in Nederland in de jaren vijftig en zestig', *Bijdragen en Mededelingen Betreffende de Geschiedenis der Nederlanden*, 101 (1986), pp. 76–94.

28. For example, G. van der Leeuw, *Balans van Nederland* (Amsterdam, 1945).

29. For example, Lijphart, *Politics of Accommodation.*

30. Bouwman, 'Bannings idealen', pp. 129–30.

31. Henk te Velde, 'Zedelijkheid als ethiek en seksueel fatsoen. De geschiedenis van een Nederlands begrip', in Remieg Aerts en Klaas van Berkel (ed.), *De pijn van Prometheus. Essays over cultuurkritiek en cultuurpessimisme* (Groningen, 1996), pp. 198–218.

32. Van der Hoop, *Geestelijke vrijheid*, pp. 156–7.

33. Stoffel, *Massa-mensch*, pp. 146–7.

34. H. van Wirdum-Banning, *Willem Banning 1888–1971. Leven en werken van een religieus socialist* (Amersfoort/Leuven, 1988), p. 187.

35. Piet de Rooy, in Remieg Aerts, Herman de Liagre Böhl, Piet de Rooy, Henk te

Velde, *Land van kleine gebaren. Een politieke geschiedenis van Nederland 1780–1990* (Nijmegen, 1999), p. 240.

36. P.J. Bouman, *Revolutie der eenzamen. Spiegel van een tijdperk* (Assen, 1953); ibid., *Revolution of the Lonely: Mirror of an Epoch* (London, 1954). Cf. E.H. Kossmann, *De Lage Landen 1780–1980. Twee eeuwen Nederland en België* II (Amsterdam/Brussels, 1986), p. 275.

37. Quoted by Henry Faas, *God, Nederland en de franje* (Utrecht/Antwerp, 1967), p. 135.

38. W.F. Wertheim, *Elite en massa. Een bijdrage tot ontmaskering van de elite-waan* (Amsterdam, 1974), pp. 36, 85 and *passim*.

39. Cf. Manin, *Principles of Representative Government*.

–3–

Dubious Democrats

Party Politics and the Mass Electorate
in Twentieth-century Britain

Clare Griffiths

On hearing about the landslide victory which brought in Britain's first Labour majority government in the summer of 1945, one woman registered her outrage in a remark which has become notorious: 'The country will never stand for that!', she insisted.[1] Her notion of what 'the country' was, and what right-thinking opinion might be, was clearly at variance with the verdict passed by the mass electorate. The implication in her comment was not that an argument had been lost, but that the general public had got it wrong and had come to a decision which could not be tolerated. The trouble with democracy is that it does not always deliver the answer you expect or want.

Attitudes towards mass democracy were often contradictory. Democracy was presented as a characteristic of modern Britain, and part of its civilizing mission in the rest of the world. The expansion of political participation became a key narrative in positivist Whig histories; the dates of the major steps towards achieving a more socially representative politics were canonized as milestones in the creation of the modern nation: 1832, 1867, 1884, 1918. Yet many commentators and politicians felt more uneasy about what had been achieved than such triumphalism might suggest. Alongside the periodic verdicts of the people through the ballot box, the notion of a more elitist political wisdom persisted. Those who solicited the electorate for their votes often held reservations about the intellectual capacity of voters to make the right choices. Moreover, as levels of general education, leisure time and access to a variety of media and communications rose, there was not a notable increase in standards of public engagement with the issues of the day. Arguably, Britain had enjoyed a more active culture of political discussion during the nineteenth century, in an era of extensive parliamentary coverage in the press, mass petitions and lengthy political oratory at public meetings. Mass enfranchisement, by contrast, was accompanied by a more popular, less serious-minded journalism, a focus on domestic and private life rather than the public sphere, and increasing degrees of political apathy. For most of the twentieth century, voter turn-out remained at a respectable level, at least for parliamentary elections, but any greater commitment, for example through party membership, was more unusual.

Developments in party politics against this background represent an interesting chapter within the history of British experience of the mass society. In the attitudes of politicians and political analysts during the twentieth century there were many overlaps with the anxieties about the 'masses' which arose in cultural criticism, sociology and psychology. These often dispiriting conclusions about the limited discernment of the mass audience had particular implications for political parties in determining their strategies and programmes. Politicians with any ambitions for electoral success have always targeted their campaigns on the basis of calculations about what will go down well with voters. However, this began to become more systematic from the 1920s onwards, with attempts to offer scientific approaches to describing and shaping public opinion, rather than depending on more anecdotal canvassing and expectations about certain interest groups within the electorate. Moreover, it was clearly the case that the political behaviour of voters came to be strongly influenced by features of mass society such as the growth of the modern media and the impact of advertising. The apparent susceptibility of the mass electorate to psychological rather than rational persuasion, and the power of presentation over policy, were assumptions behind much party strategy and electoral analysis throughout the twentieth century.

In the course of the twentieth century the British electorate changed in three major respects: the franchise was expanded to become universal (in 1918); it was redefined to acknowledge female participation (with equality established in 1928); and it was broadened to include younger voters (lowering the age of qualification from 21 to 18 in 1969). The effect of these measures, alongside rises in the domestic population, was a massive expansion in the electorate from around 6.7 million registered voters at the beginning of the century to over 44 million in 1997. The most dramatic leap came with the new registrations following the 1918 Representation of the People Act, when the size of the electorate was virtually tripled. This, as much as the disputed social make-up of the newly enfranchised, seemed to usher in a new politics.[2] 1918 was the first general election for which the whole country polled its votes on a single day. The practicalities of managing a constituency were complicated by the increased numbers of those registered to vote, yet at the same time both contemporaries and historians seem to have been particularly struck by the challenges of appealing to an electorate whose political education was assumed to be deficient. In the view of some later commentators, the character of the new electorate was so distinctive that it rewarded particular political approaches, notably to the disadvantage of the progressive liberalism which had enjoyed such electoral success before the First World War. McKibbin, Matthew and Kay argue that the new electorate was most appropriately targeted through slogan politics and organization, rather than rational appeals; the Liberals, by contrast, 'expected in democracy just those qualities most conspicuously absent from it – knowledge and a well-developed political intelligence'.[3]

Politicians in the nineteenth century were often very frank in their views on democracy, an idea which took a long time to attract respectability. Extensions of the franchise from 1867 onwards were hedged around with much discussion about responsibility, and the continued argument that voters must demonstrate that they 'deserved' the vote. Property and the payment of rates established the male electorate's standing within the community, while the receipt of assistance through the Poor Law was a disqualification from citizenship. The complexities of voter registration also acted as significant restraints. Despite the fact that many adult men were excluded from voting, whether by structural biases working against the interests of particular social groups or simply through flaws in the operation of the system, what is striking about the position before 1918 is how few people seem to have been concerned about any deficiencies in Britain's democracy. 'There is no need to fight the battle of the franchise,' commented the socialist Keir Hardie in the 1890s, 'our fathers did that.'[4] With the exception of the inescapable agitations of the women's suffrage campaigns, there appears to have been no great awareness of other major exclusions from the electorate. Even the enfranchisement of women became, in the later stages of the debate, largely an issue of party political calculation. The problem for politicians with all changes to the franchise was that the electoral consequences were difficult to predict. On the ready assumption that people voted out of self-interest rather than on consideration of intellectual questions, the obvious conclusion was that the admission of distinctive new categories into the electorate could alter the political balance – yet legislation had to be brought in under a government whose future interests might be damaged as a result.

The apparent difficulties in predicting the political consequences of expanding the electorate were further compounded by a pessimism about the suitability of many people to take on the responsibility of the vote. Politicians often had little faith in the good judgement of the mass electorate. As R.B. McCallum and Alison Readman wryly observed in 1947, any impartial commentary on an election had to negotiate between 'the tributes of the victors to the sound and fundamental sense of the politically stable and educated electorate and the scorn of the defeated for the gullible, ignorant, narrow-minded, and embittered dupes who were so easily impressed by unscrupulous demagogues'.[5] The latter attitude can be contrasted with some of the rhetoric surrounding the verdicts of 'the people' during the later nineteenth century, which suggested that the general public could deliver sound verdicts on the big questions of the day, whilst the political elite might be compromised by their private interests. In this ideal scenario, ordinary people were supposedly better able to see beyond narrow, selfish interests, which was especially valuable where policy might benefit from a moral perspective. It was in this spirit that W.E. Gladstone took up the rhetoric of appealing to the people as the force of moral authority on important questions, particularly foreign affairs.[6] His campaigning for the Midlothian seat (1878–80) became a marker for the setting of a new test of rectitude in public policy: that a popular vote might be less corrupt than a vote of the propertied classes and notables, and that one could seek legitimation of policy by bypassing the established political classes and going direct to the people. Midlothian has also been remembered for the development of new campaigning methods, responding to the needs of a new audience. Colin Matthew saw Gladstone's approach as a way of embracing the broader electorate which had resulted from the Second Reform Act, establishing new definitions of citizenship through a mixture of the rational and the 'charismatic'. Yet even in appealing to the people, Gladstone was clearly pleased to be able to exclude certain categories of the population altogether: he noted that no one suggested giving votes to the men who slept rough under Waterloo Bridge. Even a broad franchise contained implicit restrictions over who possessed the right qualities for political participation.[7]

While Midlothian appeared to illustrate an acknowledgement of the political faculties of the masses, Gladstone's campaigns actually rested on certain assumptions which were becoming less and less tenable. For all the innovations in addressing an audience, the heart of Midlothian was still about persuading the public of the rightness of a course of action through rational argument. What was changing by the early twentieth century was this basic faith in how that audience actually reached its decisions. The idea of the 'mass' was accompanied by scientific and pseudo-scientific studies of group psychology. John Carey comments that 'the difference between the nineteenth-century mob and the twentieth-century mass is literacy', but arguably the definition of the mass was about irrationality rather than the democratic liberations of education.[8] There seemed to be less scope than in Gladstone's world for assuming that the crowd was reachable through rational persuasion. Two features in this new vision of the masses were of particular importance for the political responses which developed. The mass was envisaged as having an agency of its own, an updated version of older notions of the mob. It seemed that people behaved differently in large numbers, whether united by physical proximity or by participation in a common, homogenized culture. The second element to this mass society was that it was believed to destroy natural connections between people, promoting an atomization and failure of community. Mass society was about the individual being lost in the crowd.

Anxieties about the political fitness of the newly enfranchised masses were by no means the sole prerogative of the political right. Those who claimed to be socially progressive also had concerns. The Labour Party leader, Ramsay MacDonald, commented that the enormous increase in the electorate in 1918 was 'like a flood of waters for which no preparation had been made', coming at a time when civic and political life had been severely disrupted. As a result, he observed, 'elections since the war have hardly shown political judgment'.[9] For MacDonald, the ability of the mass electorate to show proper judgement was in any circumstances severely limited. 'The mass of people are indifferent or are merely agitated,' he complained. 'They are responsive to suggestion, and primitive in their impulses.'[10]

MacDonald's reservations about the character of the electorate existed at two levels. In the first place, he was critical of its intellectual capabilities. The 'minds of the masses' he regarded as inherently restricted, since most people read very little, knew little history and were magnetically attracted to the lowest forms of journalism: 'It may seem, therefore, sheer folly and perversity to allow this mass to pass important judgments upon the highest and most complicated matters of State'.[11] But the problem in the quality of voters extended beyond individuals' deficiencies: MacDonald was also concerned about the way in which they functioned within a mass society, within that crowd in which the individual was apt to feel lost. He criticized the redistribution of seats in 1918 for defining constituencies on mathematical rather than geographical principles, turning the electorate into nothing more than a 'disorganized crowd', when 'national responsibility' could only flow through 'a sense of local community'.[12] The absence of pluralist associations seemed to limit the extent to which an 'unwieldy' mass democracy could function as a proper democracy at all. '[W]hen the body of electors became a great unorganized mass of individuals, grouped into constituencies that were purely artificial, and living no corporate life,' he reported, 'elections ceased to be of much value as indications of public need or opinion.'[13]

The Labour Party's response was to keep faith with its models of popular membership as a means of giving people power to change things, and as an education in democratic participation. The trade unions, socialist and cooperative societies, to which so many of its supporters were affiliated, offered models of institutions which might help to construct the pluralism which was the common prescription for overcoming the dislocations and atomization of mass society. The Labour party did not believe that it was enough to win people's votes; it had to secure their membership. After MacDonald had been disowned by his old party, Labour's electoral fortunes seemed to be going into reverse, but, in attempts to rebuild, the 1930s saw optimistic efforts to raise political engagement to new levels, expanding party organization to truly embrace the mass electorate. In 1937 the party launched its 'great campaign' to recruit 'New Socialist Millions'. Calculation and the practicality of party finance provided good reasons for this focus on the recruitment of paid-up members, rather than resting content with the transient loyalties of voters, won for one election but perhaps reverting to old loyalties at the next. But the campaigns for a mass membership also involved idealism about the potential, and necessity, for political education:

> There is a fashion for sneering at democracy and parliament. But it is a great error to despise men and women. All men and women have a philosophy however crude ... Labour respects the mind of the people and consequently has to accept the obligation to educate it and transmute it to a social attitude.[14]

Labour's membership 'crusade' was a big idea, reflecting the sense of having to respond to unprecedented challenges. The intention was to convert a million people a year to socialism, until Labour had the support of two-thirds of the nation and could 'save Europe for Peace and a New Civilization'. The stakes were high, requiring the message of socialism to be 'projected in a mass way'. Because Labour's campaigning was about educating people, it could be safely distanced from more suspect contemporary movements: 'The projection in a mass way of a free idea like the Socialist idea involves no disturbing doubts as to its morality. It is not the drilling of millions of minds with a prejudiced or narrow conception. It is not a numbing and enslaving of the intelligence.'[15]

The Socialist Millions campaign was not a great success. Like other political parties, Labour discovered that party membership was only ever a minority enthusiasm in British society. Labour's wish to believe in the better instincts of the mass electorate also continued to suffer against the realities of the ballot. In practice it was more often the political left rather than the right which had cause to regret the verdicts of the British electorate during the twentieth century. Those who had been the most enthusiastic supporters of the principle of political participation across the whole of British society frequently missed out on the rewards from achieving a mass electorate. David Marquand has called this the 'paradox of British democracy': that the establishment of manhood suffrage from 1918 ushered in a period dominated by Conservative governments.[16] Labour's frustration was that the majority of the modern population could be regarded as working class, by occupation or economic fortunes, yet the party seemed unable to take advantage of this. The Conservative Party looked at the problem from the other end, assuming after 1918 that, as the natural party of the majority of the population, the future must be Labour's. David Jarvis talks about the Conservatives' 'fear, trepidation and suspicion' in approaching the newly expanded electorate, despite its electoral success in the 1920s and 1930s, while Ewen Green has described the Conservatives as 'strangely unconfident', even after three electoral victories in a row during the 1950s.[17] Whereas Labour's disappointments rarely translated into creative approaches to win the electorate round, the Conservatives' anxieties resulted in innovations in publicity and electioneering.

To the historian, the dominant fact about the Conservative Party after the First World War is that it experienced tremendous electoral success. A significant factor in this was the deliberate attempt within the party to reshape itself, or at least its image, to address the interests of the modern electorate. On the basis of the depressing analysis that the electoral odds were now stacked against it, the Conservative Party forced through modernizations of its rhetoric and, perhaps most importantly, of the ways in which it communicated with the general public. It established a trend which distinguished Conservative electioneering into the 1990s, and which was only really overshadowed by the creation of a media-savvy, spin-doctored 'New Labour' in the run-up to the 1997 general election. Up until that point, the Conservatives almost always had the advantage of the more innovative publicity techniques and the more advanced approaches to canvassing.[18]

This trend began in the period of Stanley Baldwin's leadership, credited by many as the start of a new era in political communication. Baldwin's philosophy, as it was promoted, appeared almost anti-political: 'if I were not the leader of the Conservative party,' he mused in 1935, 'I should like to be the leader of the people who do not belong to any Party'.[19] His approach proved remarkably attractive to the electorate of the inter-war years. His successor as leader of the party, Neville Chamberlain, commented on Baldwin's 'singular and instinctive knowledge of how the plain man's mind works'.[20] Knowledge was not necessarily approval. Baldwin had anxieties about the arrival of a mass democracy before the country was ready for it. As he explained in a letter in 1935, 'my job is to try and educate a new democracy in a new world and to try and make them realize their responsibilities in their possession of power, and to keep the eternal verities before them'.[21]

Against the political left's use of rhetoric about class, Baldwin's Conservative Party identified with the more inclusive idea of a 'national' interest and continued to present itself as a counterpoise to sectionalism throughout most of the twentieth century, thereby promoting the notion that it was the 'natural' party of the country as a whole.[22] Crucially, it also proved highly successful in appealing to the new female electorate.[23] Such shrewd repositioning of the Conservative Party within the new electoral context of the inter-war years was only one part of the story. Baldwin's Conservatives also worked hard to get their message across, making use of the modern means of communication at their disposal. They took advantage of film as a form of propaganda, investing in a fleet of cinema vans to take cartoons and recorded addresses around the country.[24] Their attitude to the new medium of radio was also far more sophisticated than that of their political opponents. When Baldwin made his first broadcast in 1924, he demonstrated an easy grasp of the adaptations which it required. While other politicians treated it as a method for reaching a larger audience with their usual repertoire of public-meeting oratory, Baldwin realized the intimate, domestic quality of radio. He broadcast a specially scripted talk from a studio, while his wife sat knitting in front of him, as an embodiment of the invisible audience, many of whom Baldwin imagined would be doing likewise.[25] Like Franklin Roosevelt with his fireside chats, Baldwin's radio manner became an important element in constructing his image for the general public.

Through a variety of innovations, the Conservative Party brokered modern techniques in electioneering during the 1920s and 1930s, which were often more advanced than methods in common use during the period following the Second World War.[26] Baldwin was unusual for his day in relying on speech writers rather than scripting his own oratory.[27] The Conservatives also employed an advertising agency for the three general elections before the war – an approach which was still controversial a quarter of a century later. In 1960 the chair of the Labour Party's publicity committee was scathing about Conservative attempts to produce 'a so-called image of the Tory Party' by employing an advertising agency: 'I believe that in doing this it introduces something into our political life which is alien to our British democracy.'[28]

The importation of advertising techniques into political campaigning transformed the focus and tone of elections across the twentieth century. In 1922 a guide to practical electioneering advised campaigners that: 'Winning elections is really a question of salesmanship, little different from marketing any branded article.'[29] The power of commercial advertising and its ability to manipulate mass psychology was a subject of fascination, and suspicion, by the 1920s. Alongside an awed acceptance of the fact that advertising worked, it tended to be regarded as morally dubious and potentially disreputable. Fine distinctions between 'publicity' and the propaganda of advertising deterred many organizations from rushing to embrace new modes of communication and the use of modern design in putting their message across.[30]

As the comments from Labour's publicity committee in 1960 suggest, the Labour Party continued for a long time to be suspicious of the appropriateness of advertising in British politics. The Conservative Party was less fastidious. Its use of the Colman, Prentis and Varley agency from 1948, and of Saatchi and Saatchi in the Thatcher years, set new standards for political advertising. The party's campaign from June 1957 to the 1959 general election is cited as the beginning of a new type of political advertising, dominated by arresting images and powerful slogans. The medium quickly threatened to become the message, and in 1963 the *Sunday Times* was able to play the game of producing a composite political advert drawn from the main parties' campaigns, to create something which could readily apply to either.[31] Since the role of the agencies was to identify the most fruitful way to engage public interest, it is perhaps not surprising that rival camps often tended to emphasize the same sorts of things.

The use of advertising agencies was very expensive. One of the crucial shifts which they encouraged was towards a more national focus to election campaigning. While there were legal restrictions on election spending within each constituency, there were no limits placed on what a party could spend nationally. It seemed that high-impact advertising on a national level was also far more effective in winning votes than the traditional methods of door-step canvassing and leaflet distribution. Social and cultural changes reinforced the shift to elections in which the national campaign meant more to many voters than the contest in their local area. Already in the 1920s the proportion of electors experiencing the campaign through the wireless in the privacy of their own homes was greater than that attending public meetings.[32] The growth of television further encouraged this tendency for disembodied electioneering, in which contact with politicians in the flesh became far less significant than their projections through the media. The election of 1959 has been identified as the first 'TV election'.[33] In 1987 the Labour MP Austin Mitchell commented that local campaigning was becoming 'an arcane irrelevance', while the real election was acted out on television: there was no one at home to be canvassed during the day and in the evenings party workers risked interrupting the people's television viewing.[34] Even nostalgic returns to an older political culture were rarely what they seemed. When John Major took to his soap box during the 1992 general election, it was spun as a revival of traditional methods of electioneering, but whatever his good intentions may have been, even this seemingly honest approach became a staging for the media.[35] House-to-house campaigning took on the character of farce when Boris Johnson went knocking on doors as the Conservative parliamentary candidate for Henley in 2001. There were no voters around to canvass as he toured the commuter villages of the constituency while everyone was out at work, but of course he was accompanied by a fellow journalist to record this symbolic and shambolic gesture at campaigning in a safe seat where victory was almost a foregone conclusion.[36]

One of the early anxieties about the mass electorate was that it would be somehow unknowable: subject to irrational rather than rational influences, and therefore behaving in ways which could not be foreseen. During the second half of the twentieth century there were more concerted efforts to understand how elections actually worked, and why they provided the outcomes they did. In this endeavour, the British General Election series, often referred to as the 'Nuffield studies', have occupied a central place. The first of these dissected the general election campaign of 1945, in a study by R.B. McCallum and Alison Readman, published in 1947. This was the first attempt to document what actually went on during an election across the country as a whole, surveying election addresses and the progress of the party campaigns, and analysing what lay behind the final declaration.

McCallum and Readman's volume began a tradition which has continued unbroken, although the scope and analysis of the studies have evolved with passing general elections. The person most indissolubly linked with the Nuffield studies, and with the whole field of psephology in Britain, is David Butler, author of the volume on the 1951 general election and to varying degrees responsible for every one since.[37] Butler's intention in his analysis of the 1951 election was to broaden the parameters of electoral study, notably by bringing in more sociological perspectives. The focus began to move away from a relatively straightforward record of what happened during a campaign to the discussion of what lay behind the parties' disparate fortunes.[38] Indeed one of Butler's depressing observations was that the activities of the campaign itself mattered remarkably little. By the time an election was called, he argued, there was little that the candidates or their organizations could do to change the verdict which would be delivered in due course.[39] But it is the comments that accompany this observation which demonstrate Butler's limited expectations of the electoral process under his scrutiny. He dismissed what he characterized as a prevalent 'nineteenth-century rationalist myth', which continued, inappropriately, in his view, to influence people's assumptions about the experience of elections:

> An election is regarded as a practical plebiscite on men and measures, in which candidates in each constituency come forward and argue the issues of the day, before an enlightened public which, after listening intelligently to all the points that are raised, weighs them up and comes to a judicial verdict. Graham Wallas suggested that such a picture was largely false, but his work was not followed up. Recent research, however, has done much to demonstrate how right he was.[40]

Here, in the middle of the twentieth century, there were echoes of earlier notions about political behaviour in a mass society. The work which Butler was citing takes us right back to the Edwardian period, when Wallas, one of the first generation of Fabians, an educationalist and enthusiast for the relatively new discipline of psychology, published his *Human Nature in Politics*. Wallas' starting point was the observation that: 'Whoever sets himself to base his political thinking on a re-examination of the working of human nature, must begin by trying to overcome his own tendency to exaggerate the intellectuality of mankind.'[41] His interest in psychological studies encouraged him to focus instead on the influence of 'instinct' and 'impulse' in shaping people's political affiliations and support. He argued that it was impossible to talk about politics without articulating one's views on the nature of man. Political thinkers of the past had developed philosophies about political engagement which were inseparable from their ideas about human nature, yet modern discussions seemed to feel no need to engage with the latest ideas about psychology and individual and social behaviour. Wallas' book became a classic, marrying psychology and politics and, in the process, providing plenty of evidence to deepen suspicions that modern democracy was not necessarily a way to reach sound decisions on public policy.

Human Nature in Politics first appeared in 1908, going through second and third editions in 1910 and 1920. In the preface to the 1920 edition, Wallas was able to update his comments on the inherent irrationality of most human behaviour with reference to the experience of the First World War. In 1948, sixteen years after Wallas' death, the book was reissued, with a preface by historian and one-time Labour candidate A.L. Rowse, who commented that events of recent times had only provided further support for Wallas' rejection of the 'Rationalist fallacy': 'We in our time, alas, know what fatuous nonsense this is … Yet this assumption underlies most liberal and democratic thinking on the subject of politics.' As Rowse saw it, political approaches which assumed too much intelligence on the part of the electorate were doomed to failure: 'No wonder Liberalism has been so ineffectual: it consigns itself to futility by clinging to what is so patently untrue of human behaviour in the mass.'[42] His identification with Wallas was over what he characterized as 'the leadership of the irrational by the rational'.[43] Rowse, the scholarship boy who made his new home in the common room luxuries of All Souls in Oxford, was a natural elitist, dismissive of the 'idiot people' on whom he had 'wasted' his time in Labour politics.[44]

Wallas himself was not so pessimistic about the intellectual potential of the ordinary voter: just because it was a mistake to assume that people act on rational motives, that did not mean that they could not consciously rise above their impulses to act with more determined calculation. At the same time, he talked about the processes of democratic politics in ways which made them seem not just open to active manipulation, but even organized with that as an inherent rationale within the system. Representative democracy he defended not as a way of giving people a voice, so much as a mechanism for forming opinion. And in influencing people to throw their vote behind a political position, Wallas regarded the political parties as doing nothing more than commercial businesses were engaged in when they targeted consumers with advertising. He made explicit comparisons between party propaganda and advertisements for tea, in which the party label represented the brand which people were able to recognize, and he suggested that the lessons from psychology offered politicians little choice other than to court the public's 'affection'.[45] Democracy, in Wallas' eyes, had turned out very differently from the high expectations of its advocates: 'the democratic movement which produced the constitutions under which most civilized nations now live, was inspired by a purely intellectual conception of human nature which is becoming every year more unreal to us'.[46]

Wallas' ideas about the shortcomings of modern democracy and the realities of political culture find echoes in two important areas, which reveal that such observations became more than simply detached commentaries on the nature of the mass electorate. First, these interpretations of the crowd's susceptibility and inherent irrationality began to influence the practical strategies adopted by political parties. Second, as Butler's reference to Wallas implies, they also found their way into analyses of politics, and particularly of electoral politics. In these ways, views which were articulated as part of particular psychological and cultural discussions of mass society in the early years of the twentieth century gained an enduring and influential presence within electoral campaigning and the modes of analysing it, with a legacy long after the rhetorics themselves had become much less common. In other words, although the specific anxieties about 'the masses' connected to cultural elitism were voiced less frequently after the Second World War, the ramifications of their impact on understandings of political behaviour had become integral to the system. It grew difficult to separate out the question of how the mass electorate *actually* behaved from *assumptions* about how it would behave. Such assumptions came to be built into the organization of party activity and expectations of electoral behaviour, in ways which turned anxiety about the mass electorate into a self-fulfilling prophecy.

Within both the electoral studies and party strategies, the position of the individual voter was problematic. In their study *Political Change in Britain*, first published in 1969, Butler and Stokes argued that electoral analysis must look for explanations of individual decision-making within 'a wider political or social milieu', involving 'both the reduction or disaggregation of mass phenomena to individual terms and also the aggregation of individual phenomena to explore effects in the full electorate'.[47] One of the most influential aggregations of individual choices was through the model of electoral 'swing', a cornerstone of post-war electoral commentating. Whatever was happening in individual constituencies became swallowed up in generalizations about how political opinion was moving across the country as a whole. As a mode of understanding electoral behaviour, it was founded on interpretations about how mass politics worked, whilst also feeding back into political parties' approaches to their campaigning, confirming the trend towards a focus on political contests on a national level.

By the 1980s, in response to trends in party political communication, and the immediate electoral history which demonstrated overwhelming national swings of political opinion, electoral analysis became predominantly concerned with explaining 'mass changes in alignments'. Just as parties themselves had lost confidence in traditions of electoral support and the significance of sociological determinants, so analysts also looked at politics in ways which tended to aggregate public opinion. Analysis was sometimes explicit in dismissing the agency of the individual elector: in the mid-1980s Patrick Dunleavy and Christopher Husbands defended their use of models which moved away from a concern with individual choice, on the grounds that studies of voting behaviour should deal with 'aggregate social phenomena, focusing on shifts of party support in a mass electorate', and that these phenomena had their own 'collective properties and identity'.[48] In other words, the mass electorate behaved in a way which was more than simply the sum of many individual, rational decisions.

There had long been attempts to understand this behaviour by quantifying it. The woman who believed that 'the country' would never stand for the popular verdict at the 1945 general election was expressing shock at an apparently unthinkable outcome – but it was a result which opinion polls had in fact predicted with considerable accuracy.[49] Opinion polling was then still in its infancy, having been first used to survey voter intentions from 1938 onwards, but 1945 seemed to prove its value, and it gradually established a key role in offering insights into political opinion which became indispensable for political punditry and also shaped party strategies.[50] This was a further example of politics becoming more national and less constituency-based. Whereas parties had once assembled their picture of the electorate on the basis of local canvass returns, from the 1950s they commissioned research on public opinion using methods borrowed from market research. While political scientists talked about 'consumer models' for political choice,[51] political parties increasingly targeted their audience on the basis of an understanding of what the public wanted, and what kinds of presentation would have the greatest appeal.

In the final years of the twentieth century, political commentators concentrated much of their attention on parties' skill at this kind of political calculation, at the way in which they used the media, and their success in promoting their own brand of 'designer politics'.[52] This was proclaimed the age of 'spin' and presentation. The soundbites and photo opportunities of electoral campaigning in the 1990s seemed the ultimate consequence of essentially pessimistic expectations about the abilities of the mass electorate to engage in meaningful political debate. In the promotion of 'New Labour' a new model seemed to be emerging, which has been labelled a 'post-modern' form of campaigning. In this tactical approach to identifying winnable political territory, and despite an often extreme form of centralized control of the party, there were signs that the mass was once more being disaggregated. By the end of the century, politicians seemed more interested in eliciting the qualitative views of electors through the invention of the 'focus group', rather than tracking aggregated opinion through the quantitative evidence of polling.

Democracy and the mass electorate did not always sit easily together. In analyses of how political opinion was formed within mass society, it was very tempting for politicians to adopt a cynical approach to their campaigning, taking lessons from commercial advertising in how to exploit mass psychology. But after the examples of regimes in the 1930s, the power of mass suggestion carried damning political associations. When the Labour MP Robin Cook murmured his doubts about whether the party's ill-fated Sheffield rally in 1992 would 'work', his colleague John Prescott quipped: 'It did in Nazi Germany.'[53] In fact political communication was far more concerned with identifying a party with what the masses appeared to want, than with attempting to manipulate public opinion: in Wallas' phraseology, courting the public's 'affection'. From the 1920s onwards, party politics in Britain underwent a series of changes which can interpreted as a process of adapting to a mass electorate. Parties, with varying degrees of enthusiasm, adopted new means of communication, found new mechanisms for monitoring political opinion, and shifted the focus of their organization towards running campaigns at a national rather than a predominantly local level. The electorate itself was redefined and expanded, and its experience of politics was increasingly mediated through individuals' engagement with a virtual national community, shaped by broadcasting and the press. Alongside these cultural shifts in the communication between politicians and the public, it is difficult to tell how far mass politics had led to the qualitative decline in political activity which many had predicted. As parties became ever more concerned to gauge popular opinion, to target policies and to focus their organizations to reflect voters' concerns, it is probably true to say that the electorate ended up with political parties shaped in its own image. However dubious many commentators had been about the political wisdom of the masses, the great ambition of politicians in the twentieth century was to find themselves thinking along the same lines.

Notes

1. Quoted in Peter Hennessy, *Never Again: Britain 1945–1951* (London, 1993), p. 56. The comment is supposed to have been overheard in the dining room at the Savoy Hotel in London.

2. A key contribution to the historiography about the significance of the 1918 Act was H.C.G. Matthew, R.I. McKibbin and J.A. Kay, 'The Franchise Factor in the Rise of the Labour Party', *English Historical Review*, 91 (October 1976) (reprinted in Ross McKibbin, *The Ideologies of Class: Social Relations in Britain 1880–1950* (Oxford, 1991), pp. 66–100). Aspects of the heated debate which followed are summarized in Duncan Tanner, 'The Parliamentary Electoral System, the "Fourth" Reform Act and the Rise of Labour in England and Wales', *Bulletin of the Institute of Historical Research* (1983), pp. 205–19.

3. McKibbin, *Ideologies of Class*, p. 97.

4. McKibbin, *Ideologies of Class*, p. 68.

5. R.B. McCallum and Alison Readman, *The British General Election of 1945* (London, 1947), p. xi.

6. David Marquand, *Decline of the Public* (Oxford, 2004), p. 58.

7. H.C.G. Matthew, *Gladstone 1875–1898* (Oxford, 1995), pp. 41–60.

8. John Carey, *The Intellectuals and the Masses* (London, 1992), p. 5.

9. Ramsay MacDonald, *Socialism: Critical and Constructive* (London, 1921), p. 228.

10. MacDonald, *Socialism*, p. 2.

11. MacDonald, *Socialism*, p. 234.

12. MacDonald, *Socialism*, pp. 253–4.

13. MacDonald, *Socialism*, p. 228.

14. Harold Croft, *New Socialist Millions* (Labour Party leaflet, 1937), p. 3.

15. Croft, *New Socialist Millions*, p. 4.

16. David Marquand, *The Progressive Dilemma* (London, 1991), pp. 8–9, *et passim*.

17. David Jarvis, 'The Shaping of the Conservative Electoral Hegemony, 1918–1939', in Jon Lawrence and Miles Taylor (eds), *Party, State and Society: Electoral Behaviour in Britain since 1820* (Aldershot, 1997), pp. 131–52, and E.H.H. Green, 'The Conservative Party, the State and the Electorate, 1945–1964', ibid., pp. 176–200.

18. Richard Cockett, 'The Party, Publicity, and the Media', in Anthony Seldon and Stuart Ball (eds), *Conservative Century: The Conservative Party since 1900* (Oxford, 1994), pp. 547–77.

19. Radio broadcast, 5 February 1935.

20. Cited in J.A. Ramsden, 'Baldwin and Film', in Nicholas Pronay and D.W. Spring (eds), *Propaganda, Politics and Film, 1918–1945* (London, 1982), p. 139.

21. Letter to his niece, 22 December 1935, quoted in Philip Williamson, *Stanley Baldwin: Conservative Leadership and National Values* (Cambridge, 1999), p. 143.

22. See discussions in Robert Waller, 'Conservative Electoral Support and Social Class', in Seldon and Ball, *Conservative Century*, pp. 579–610; Ross McKibbin,

'Class and Conventional Wisdom: the Conservative Party and the "Public" in Inter-war Britain', in *Ideologies of Class*, pp. 259–93; Philip Williamson, 'The Doctrinal Politics of Stanley Baldwin', in Michael Bentley (ed.), *Public and Private Doctrine* (Cambridge, 1993), pp. 181–208.

23. David Jarvis, 'Mrs Maggs and Betty: the Conservative Appeal to Women Voters in the 1920s', *Twentieth Century British History*, 5(2) (1994), pp. 129–52.

24. T.J. Hollins, 'The Conservative Party and Film Propaganda between the Wars', *English Historical Review*, XCVI(379) (1981), pp. 359–69.

25. J.A. Ramsden, 'Baldwin and Film', in Pronay and Spring, *Propaganda, Politics and Film*, pp. 139–43; Martin Rosenbaum, *From Soapbox to Soundbite: Party Political Campaigning in Britain since 1945* (Basingstoke, 1997), p. 43.

26. Rosenbaum, *From Soapbox to Soundbite*, p. 1.

27. Williamson, *Stanley Baldwin*, p. 161.

28. Quoted in Mark Abrams, 'Opinion Polls and Party Propaganda', *Public Opinion Quarterly*, 28(1) (1964), p. 13.

29. Henry James Houston and Lionel Valdar, *Modern Electioneering Practice* (London, 1922).

30. See Mariel Grant, *Propaganda and the Role of the State in Inter-war Britain* (Oxford, 1992).

31. Rosenbaum, *From Soapbox to Soundbite*, p. 10.

32. On the changing role of public meetings, see Jon Lawrence, 'The Transformation of British Public Politics after the First World War', *Past and Present*, 190 (2006), pp. 185–216.

33. John Bartle and Dylan Griffiths, *Political Communications Transformed: From Morrison to Mandelson* (Basingstoke, 2001), p. 3

34. *New Statesman*, June 1987.

35. Rosenbaum, *From Soapbox to Soundbite*, p. 272.

36. *Sunday Times*, 27 May 2001.

37. See David Butler, 'British Psephology 1945–2001: Reflections on the Nuffield Election Histories', in Wm Roger Louis (ed.), *Still More Adventures with Britannia* (London and New York, 2003), pp. 249–63.

38. Jon Lawrence and Miles Taylor discuss the influence of electoral sociology and its place in the Nuffield studies in the introduction to their edited volume *Party, State and Society*, pp. 4–5.

39. David Butler, *The British General Election of 1951* (London, 1952), p. 4.

40. Butler, *The British General Election of 1951*, p. 3.

41. Graham Wallas, *Human Nature in Politics* (London, 1948, reissue of third edition from 1920), p. 45.

42. A.L. Rowse, introduction to Wallas, *Human Nature in Politics*, p. 2.

43. Wallas, *Human Nature in Politics*, p. 3.

44. A.L. Rowse, *A Cornish Childhood: Autobiography of a Cornishman* (London, 1942), p. 224.

45. Wallas, *Human Nature in Politics*, pp. 53–5, 110. It was as late as the 1980s that British political parties took their 'branding' seriously, adopting unified corporate identities and party symbols within a few years of each other.

46. Wallas, *Human Nature in Politics*, p. 215.

47. David Butler and Donald Stokes, *Political Change in Britain: The Evolution of Electoral Choice* (second edn, London, 1974), pp. 6–7, 19, 20.

48. Patrick Dunleavy and Christopher T. Husbands, *British Democracy at the Crossroads: Voting and Party Competition in the 1980s* (London, 1985), p. 18.

49. The Gallup poll for the *News Chronicle* predicted the share of the vote to within 1 per cent (McCallum and Readman, *The British General Election of 1945*, p. 242).

50. On early attitudes towards opinion polling, see Laura Dumond Beers, 'Whose Opinion? Changing Attitudes Towards Opinion Polling in British Politics, 1937–1964', *Twentieth Century British History*, 17 (2) (2006), pp. 177–205.

51. See, for example, Hilde T. Himmelweit, Patrick Humphreys and Marianne Jaeger, *How Voters Decide* (London, 1981).

52. Margaret Scammell, *Designer Politics: How Elections Are Won* (Basingstoke, 1995).

53. Rosenbaum, *From Soapbox to Soundbite*, p. 137.

Part II
Welfare

The Arrival of the Welfare State
in Twentieth-century Mass Society
The Dutch Case

Joop M. Roebroek

At the end of the twentieth century European welfare states had become mature and comprehensive structures. Whereas at the beginning of the century only a small and largely elitist minority of the population was covered by the first insurance schemes, by the end of the century almost all citizens were covered within the system against all possible forms of risk. The Dutch welfare state was no exception to this. In the early years of the century, unemployment meant dependency on poor relief institutions that provided barely enough to sustain life. By the 1990s each unemployed person was given extensive help to re-enter the labour market as soon as possible. Nor was state support confined to social security arrangements or labour market programmes but covered a broad range of provisions and services that enhanced the welfare provision for its people; from educational opportunities, housing facilities, health care provisions and social work activities to relatively new programmes in the field of emancipation and the multicultural society. This chapter studies the relationship between the coming of the mass society in the Netherlands and the evolution of the welfare state. The central hypothesis can be formulated as follows: the welfare states constitutes an essential instrument in the organization of mass society, that is to say a society in which individuals became citizens with political and social rights, a society in which individual citizens became freed from the bare necessities of existence and obtained the possibility of participating in the adventures of modern society.

In order to study this relationship between mass society and the welfare state it is essential to use a series of more specific perspectives. First, there is the historical approach. The origins of both mass society and the welfare state can be found in the transition from the eighteenth to the nineteenth century. Second, as it is impossible to survey the whole range of welfare state programmes and arrangements, the main focus will be on social security and labour market policies as these constitute the major branches of the welfare state in terms of the number of beneficiaries and the proportion of the welfare expenditure they consume. Other spheres of the welfare state will be considered insofar as this is necessary to give a complete picture. Third, although the welfare state, its programmes, institutions and structures are the main focus, the analysis is nevertheless broadened to include the wider perspective of 'social politics'. That is to say that the social and political activities of classes, social groups and individuals can be regarded as the basis of welfare state evolution.

The relationship between the evolution of the Dutch welfare state and the arrival of mass society can be seen in four distinct periods. In contrast to more conventional studies of the history of the welfare state,[1] the intention here is to examine the relationship between welfare state (social politics) and mass society across a longer time perspective. Where conventional analyses start around the 1880s, this analysis will begin in the late eighteenth century.

The Historical Roots of the Welfare State and Mass Society

Although the starting point of the 'modern' welfare state can be located at the end of the eighteenth century, its historical roots go back to the medieval experiences of local poor relief. First provisions were usually almost unconditional, but ruling elites soon used social politics to control and discipline large parts of the population in order to integrate them into the prevailing economic and social relations. From the sixteenth century onwards, social politics became more and more embedded in the transition process from feudal relations to pre-capitalist and then later to the first manufacturing-capitalist economic and social relations. This orientation on the labour market became the central element. Based on the principle of the 'duty to work', social politics were structured along specific lines: a prohibition of begging, the introduction of forced labour (the *Grande Renfermement*), a centralization of local relief funds, the provision of minimal benefits limited to strict levels of subsistence and the individualization of relief according to explicitly formulated criteria. These general characteristics dominated social politics up until the middle of the eighteenth century.

Such social politics actually created a rather incoherent pattern of provisions, including many irrationalities and contradictions. However, it was precisely this pattern that formed the core of a learning process through which ruling elites, both in the Netherlands and elsewhere, developed their interventionist strategies, capacities and institutions, and similarly the lower classes and their allies strengthened their counteracting forces. From the Middle Ages until the Industrial Revolution that began in the Netherlands at the end of the eighteenth century, social elites, groups and classes prepared the ground for the evolution of modern social politics, and their accompanying political and organizational institutions.

In the long period from the Middle Ages until the eighteenth century, social politics slowly advanced from the periphery of society to the centre of social and political life. This was not a linear and continuous process, but rather an evolution full of wayward patterns. Long periods of relative immobility were followed by phases in which social politics underwent rapid change. Initially, social politics remained embedded in the feudal mode of production and absolutist political relations. Later on they moved from home industry and the first forms of industrial production in towns and villages to the larger productive areas of major cities, and from a clientele consisting of mainly pilgrims, vagabonds and beggars, along with the handicapped, poor, elderly, sick, widows and orphans, through to the industrial working classes of the modernizing nation state.

Against this background, and driven by the arrival of national industrial and labour relations and the first attempts to establish a stable political order, a broad social debate on social politics emerged from 1780 onwards. The Dutch economy became increasingly intertwined in the international economy, while larger parts of the population became directly dependent on the fluctuations of the economy. Rising levels of unemployment and the increased use of child labour, with all its social consequences, as well as aggravating social destitution, also touched the day-to-day lives of large parts of the population. This produced the first demands for a national social policy. A movement for economic and social reform emerged from urban bourgeois circles via organizations such as the Maatschappij tot Nut van 't Algemeen (Society for Public Welfare) in 1784 and some time later the Maatschappij van Weldadigheid (Benevolent Society) in 1818. These organizations formulated ideas and proposals for the extension and improvement of the economic, social and cultural condition of the (working) population. More pragmatically, they proposed public intervention in the provision of work, popular education, vocational training and moral regeneration.[2] These proposals were taken up by the *Patriotten* (Patriots), a radical-liberal movement that, supported by a French invasion army, seized power in the winter of 1794/5 and proclaimed the Batavian Republic in 1796. Mirroring the French *Déclarations des droits de l'homme et du citoyen*, the Patriots declared in their constitution, the *Staatsregeling* of 1798, poor relief as a public (national) responsibility and developed plans for the provision of public work. However, these plans never came to fruition, since the Republic lacked any executive national framework to convert the ideas into concrete social policy initiatives.

During the 1830s and 1840s the call for public poor relief re-emerged. Ecclesiastical and private charity clearly failed to address existing problems. The Liberal statesman Thorbecke, who introduced the Constitution for a democratic parliamentary system in 1848, submitted a draft Poor Law in 1851, which aimed at complete public (state) responsibility for poor relief. The Thorbecke draft led to fierce and fundamental debates both inside and outside parliament. The lines of argument were clearly drawn. The Liberal group, supported by some Catholic members of parliament, characterized the draft as excellent and responsive to the needs of the time. Their opponents, Conservatives, right-wing Liberals, Protestant-Christians and a majority of the Catholic members of parliament, directed their attacks at the *charité légale*, as it was called, as a system of '*étatist* omnipotence, which will destroy private and ecclesiastical charity'.[3] The draft never reached the statute book as the Thorbecke government fell in the course of 1853. The new government presented a new Poor Law Draft in December 1853. The leading principle of this proposal was clearly formulated: 'No public poor relief institution is allowed to support the poor, except in case it is evident that these poor cannot obtain support from ecclesiastic or private institutions, and then only in cases where it is completely unavoidable.'[4] In other words, the state was only allowed to interfere in social relations if no other ecclesiastic or private institution took responsibility. This version of the Poor Law was given parliamentary approval in 1854, and it was this principle that dominated Dutch social politics for the decades to come.

Besides the debate on poor relief, a second theme played an important role in the debate on state intervention. This was the question of child labour. The first debates began in the 1830s with the intervention of some academics. In the course of the nineteenth century a whole series of actions, inquiries, petitions, statements and demonstrations took place. Some came from regional and local governments, others from social organizations, employers' organizations, teachers, scientists, entrepreneurs, doctors and representatives of the churches. In the midst of these deliberations the government established a Royal Commission in 1863 in order to study the situation of factory children and to suggest possible legal measures. It was more than four years before the Commission published its report. The outcome was highly unsatisfactory. A large majority of the Commission argued that only the introduction of compulsory attendance at school could help to reduce child labour. Only the chairman of the Commission, De Vries Robbé, made the case for the legal restriction of child labour, linked with the introduction of compulsory education.[5] Partly because the Commission had not been unanimous and partly because of its strong aversion to social intervention, the government consistently argued that the time was not ripe for legislative action. However, the general public and a whole range of social and political organizations refused to accept this non-interventionist stance, and this was reflected in a further outpouring of articles, requests and scientific reports. The broad societal debate was now linked with social and political action. On 30 October 1870 the Comité ter bespreking van de Sociale Quaestie (Committee to discuss the Social Question) was founded. Between 1870 and 1873 this Committee organized a whole series of meetings in which legislation, and more precisely the formulation of a concrete draft law, formed a major theme. A prominent member of the Committee, the Liberal entrepreneur Samuel van Houten, proposed his private member's bill on child labour on 27 February 1873. The first Dutch labour union, the Algemeen Nederlandsch Werkliedenverbond (General Dutch Workman's Association), organized the first working-class demonstration in the Netherlands in favour of the Van Houten Draft on 19 April 1874.

The Draft was debated for five days in parliament, beginning on 29 April 1874. It is interesting to note that, in strong contrast to earlier debates, hardly any arguments against the measure were based on the principle of 'state abstinence'. This included even the Anti-Revolutionary Party and the majority of Catholic members of parliament, who had traditionally opposed any role of the state in social politics save in cases where it was 'completely unavoidable'. The *Kinderwet* (Child Labour Law) was promulgated on 19 September 1874, when it was published in the *Staatsblad* (Statute Book) under the eloquent title *Wet van den 19den September 1874, houdende maatregelen tot het tegengaan van overmatigen arbeid en verwaarlozing van kinderen*[6] (Law of 19 September 1874, concerning measures to prevent excessive labour and abandonment of children). This first labour law was followed in the 1880s by a series of parliamentary inquiry committees and new laws in the field of labour legislation and even the first aspects of social security, such as pensions and disability insurance, as incorporated into the *Arbeidswet* (Labour Law) of 5 May 1889.

The social policy experiences of the nineteenth century, or more precisely from the 1780s to the 1880s, not only meant a further step in the emergence of interventionist strategies, agencies and institutions, but also witnessed the arrival of more comprehensive conceptions of the role of the state in social politics. In the years before and during the Batavian Republic potentially 'radical' ideas were heard on the role of the state as 'representative of the nation'. Public (national) responsibility for poor relief and combating chronic unemployment, as well as public education, were loudly advocated in some quarters. In the decades that followed, this rather *étatist* option largely disappeared from the scene, although the introduction of the *Armenwet* (Poor Law) of 1854, the *Kinderwet* of 1874 and the *Arbeidswet* of 1889 represented the transition from earlier social policy practices, mainly based on local private and public initiatives and aimed at more marginal groups in society, to the first broader legislative actions by central government. Government operated under the new democratic parliamentary rules established by the Constitution of 1848 and was concerned with much broader sections of the population, and especially elements of the working population. The question of the *staatstusschenkomst* (state intervention) thus arrived on the social and political agenda. Was the state authorized to intervene under the banner of 'national interest' in domains that had been for so long the exclusive territory of parents, private institutions and entrepreneurs? It was a fundamental debate in which the foundations were laid for a new relationship between state and society and for a new kind of public intervention. Broader sections of the population, foreshadowing the twentieth-century 'mass society', asked for public intervention. The protection of factory children refers not only to child labour as such, or the physical protection of children *per se*, but also to aspects of upbringing, education and health. Furthermore, following on from child protection, the surveillance of women's labour and finally the labour of adult men became a public concern. And here, from the protection of adult men, the door was opened towards a new form of social intervention, beginning with social insurance initiatives on industrial injuries, insurance and pensions.

In the end, it was not a political initiative that provoked stronger interference by the state, or a greater level of public responsibility for social life. Politics was, until that time, mainly an affair of individual members of parliament without strong party ties. In was only after the late 1880s that political parties – the first being the Anti-Revolutionaire Partij (Anti-Revolutionary Party) founded in 1879 – started to act as parliamentary parties. The major actors, generating pressure for state action in respect of factory children and later on working conditions, comprised a broad spectrum of social organizations, associations and individual citizens. To a certain extent, therefore, the first expressions of a mass society at the end of the nineteenth century preceded ordinary parliamentary politics. Where central government representatives hesitated or even recoiled from taking action, social agitation and action led first to social measures and then public action in the field of labour legislation.

The Beginning of National Social Politics (1880–1918)

The socio-economic environment in the Netherlands changed drastically at the end of the nineteenth century. As industrial production developed rapidly, the Dutch economy became more and more integrated within the undulations of the international economic tide. From the early 1870s until the mid-1890s the economy was caught in the worldwide economic depression, but from that time onwards the Dutch economy was influenced by the positive upturn of the world economy. The population, and especially the working class centred in the larger cities, found traditional family structures weakened in favour of the nuclear family, and the vulnerable phases of the life cycle, youth and old age, became more strongly felt since child mortality diminished and the life expectancy of the population grew.

Social policy practice at the start of the new century showed new dimensions as the rather slow pace of development was accelerated after the turn of the century. This applied especially to the process of policy-making and the resultant decision-making in parliament. However, the implementation of the legislation that passed through parliament during the first two decades of the twentieth century suffered severe retardation. This contradiction between a relatively high tempo of decision-making and the slow process of implementation was the result of the fact that although there was general agreement on the necessity to introduce social insurance legislation for industrial injuries, sickness and old age, that these schemes needed to be compulsory (under state supervision) and that further expansion of state activities in housing, education and health care were also necessary, there was no consensus on the precise manner in which this general agreement could be worked out in institutionalized arrangements. This struggle over the establishment of social policy legislation became even more complicated by the fact that between 1895 and 1918 parliamentary politics were repeatedly beset by changes in representation and by differences between the first and second chambers, for example a progressive majority in the First Chamber being reined in by a conservative majority in the Second Chamber or vice versa. Consequently, the decisions of one regime often had to be implemented by one of a different ideological complexion.

The first social insurance act, the *Ongevallenwet* (Industrial Injuries Act), reached parliament on 25 April 1898. The proposal provoked vehement debates, both inside and outside parliament. The issue was not so much the idea of obligatory insurance as such, but its institutional and administrative setting. This issue would run as a leitmotiv through all subsequent Dutch debates on social insurance. The discussion on the *Ongevallenwet* highlighted social insurance as a key element in the relationship between state and society. The Confessional (Protestant-Christian and Catholic together) circles in particular offered strong resistance to an *étatist* option colouring the institutional and administrative setting of the Act. The control of the industrial injuries insurance scheme was assigned to the Rijksverzekeringsbank (State Insurance Bank) to the exclusion of all private initiatives. It was the leader of the Confessional power bloc, Abraham Kuyper, who formulated the principal objections against this option. He conceived his famous *Groot Amendement* (Great Amendment), which aimed to break the state monopoly and open the way for (private) industrial boards to administer and execute the scheme, 'in order to stimulate the self-reliance of the organs of social life'. The Confessional resistance was at that time hindered by the fact that neither the employers' organizations nor the trade unions, from their point of view the principal agents of self-reliance, were organized on a national level, and therefore there was no real option for 'self-government'. The discussion in parliament took ten days. In the final version of the act some room was left for a transfer of risks from public to private institutions, which opened some possibilities for private initiative. The law was finally promulgated on 2 January 1901 and came into effect on 1 February 1903.[7]

The second issue was the debate on old age and invalidity insurance, and more specifically the question of the legal basis for Dutch social insurance. Essentially this became the controversy over the *Staatspensioen* (state pension). Three principal positions were defended. Talma, the spokesman for the Confessional parties, defended the option of a compulsory old age and invalidity insurance, based on the existence of a labour contract and carried out under the responsibility of employers and employees. Talma was fiercely opposed to the idea of a state pension. 'The state pension is and will be an alms, even if the state provides those alms, and even if there exists a legal right to receive such a pension.'[8] The Social Democrats advocated the option of a limited (only to workers) state pension. They argued that workers had a right to all their wages, as these were too low to make savings for pensions possible. Since the employers refused to take responsibility, this would have to be taken by the state. Such a pension would be provided to all workers and funded by taxing capital. A third position was held by the Progressive Liberals, namely the Ministry of Agriculture and Industry that also included social affairs headed by M.W.F. Treub in the Cort van der Linden cabinet (1913–17). For him social insurance was not an integral part of the labour contract. There existed sections of the population that did not have the ability to insure themselves against loss of income. Treub regarded social insurance as a shared responsibility of employers, workers and the state. In the specific case of old age and invalidity insurance, he argued that the state, as defender of the interests of society as a whole, should take responsibility and provide all citizens with a state pension.[9]

In spite of these profound debates, the results in terms of social politics were anything but overwhelming in the period between 1888 and 1918 as there were alternating Liberal and Confessional cabinets. In the social insurance field only the *Ongevallenwet* (Industrial Injuries Act) of 1901 was finally implemented. Other laws, such as the *Ouderdoms- en Invaliditeitswet* (Old Age and Invalidity Act) and the *Ziektewet* (Sickness Insurance Act), both passed by parliament in 1913, were not implemented. However, some progress was made in the regulation of labour conditions (a new Labour Law in 1911), education (the Compulsory School Attendance Law in 1900), health care (Health Care Act in 1901), housing (Housing Act in 1901), employment activities (since 1902) and a revision of the Poor Law (in 1912).

The first decades of the twentieth century did witness some initial signs of the arrival of mass society and, in its footsteps, mass politics in the Netherlands. Employers' organizations and trade unions became more and more nationally organized and intervened as such in social politics. Dutch (mass) society became organized along its pillarized conglomerates of parties, social organizations, associative alignments, school systems, cultural organizations and mass media. In the socio-political debates, all principal aspects of social politics came together: a further colouring of the ideas on social ordering, pillarization and corporatism as dominant organizational principles within social politics, and finally the attempts of the different power blocs to obtain social and political hegemony. In terms of the ideas on ordering the newly emerging social relations, two positions attempted to dominate the scene. The Confessional social and political organizations formulated their ideas on the relationship between state and society along the principles of *soevereiniteit in eigen kring* (sovereignty in one's own circle) and *subsidiariteit* (subsidiarity). State and society had to constitute two distinct domains with separate responsibilities. The working and living conditions of the population were first and foremost the responsibility of employers and workers; health and education were the responsibility of denominational social organizations. The Confessional parties achieved power through parliamentary majorities in the periods 1888–91 and 1901–5. The extension of their influence at the end of the nineteenth century and the prospect of forming majority coalitions brought Protestant-Christians and Catholics closer together. Internal and mutual differences were overcome. They realized that a lasting political majority could only be reached through cooperation.[10] From a political-strategic point of view it was significant that the Confessional (Protestant and Catholic) elite succeeded in keeping a large section of the Dutch working class under control during the *Spoorwegstaking* (Railway Strike) of 1903. This was the first major clash between the working class and state power in the Netherlands and signified an important breakthrough where Confessional politics proved to be the obvious force to lead the Dutch working class into the new era of a modern mass society.

The second major option was propounded by Progressive Liberals and Social Democrats. The Progressive Liberals had called for state intervention in social politics ever since the first results of the state inquiries into working conditions were published in the 1860s. The first social legislation, the *Kinderwet* of 1874, the *Arbeidswet* of 1889 and the first social insurance law, the *Ongevallenwet* (Industrial Injuries Act) of 1901, were of liberal making. However, the impact of liberal politics, and especially its progressive element, declined in the first decades of the twentieth century. From the early twentieth century onwards, the Social Democrats and particularly the Social-Democratic trade unions took more and more of a role in the day-to-day formulation of Dutch social politics. Their position slowly moved towards a more *étatist* and interventionist one. As a result of the debates on the state pension, other forms of social insurance and the regulation of conditions of employment, social-democratic thinking came to regard the state as a major force in the organization of social politics.

Taken together, this initial phase of Dutch national social politics was characterized primarily by a kind of stalemate between the subsidiary and the interventionist lines of argument. Two blocs held each other in balance: on the one hand the Protestant-Christians and the Catholics, usually supported by the Conservatives, and on the other hand the Progressive Liberals and the Social Democrats. Even when the Confessional parties were strong enough to form the government (as in 1888–91,

1901–5 and 1908–13), they did not possess sufficient power to translate their ideological principles into concrete legislative measures. Only in the field of education and moral legislation did Confessional politics have some impact.

The Consolidation and Further Development of Social Politics (1918–45)

The elections of 1918 produced a major political landslide and ended the pre-First World War social and political stalemate. The Liberals lost their prominent role within Dutch politics and lost 25 of their 40 seats in the Second Chamber, while the Confessional parties and the Social Democrats bolstered their parliamentary position. As a result, the Confessional parties were able to gain a majority position, which was strengthened during the elections of 1922 and actually continued until the late 1960s. In this way, the Confessional parties formed the central axis of Dutch (social) politics and became the main force in coping with the consequences of the development of a modern mass society.

In a general sense, social politics immediately after the First World War were influenced by the revolutionary mood that flowed through Europe in the last months of 1918. More than ever, ruling elites showed a willingness to meet social objectives. The Netherlands was no exception. In response to the demands of the SDAP (Social Democratic Workers' Party) and the Nederlands Verbond van Vakverenigingen (Dutch Trade Union Association), the first Ruys de Beerenbrouck government of 1918–22 announced a whole series of reforms: changes to the old age and invalidity insurance, the introduction of the *Radenwet* (Law on the Labour and Insurance Councils), an extension of the industrial injuries scheme, a legal regulation of sickness insurance, the first national initiatives in the field of health care, the introduction of the legal eight-hour working day and women's suffrage. However, from the early 1920s onwards the economic tide turned. Employers and the political right started a campaign against the reforms of 1918 and 1919. The eight-hour working day especially came under fire, while new social initiatives, such as the proposed introduction of an unemployment scheme in 1921, were successfully opposed. Old controversies between left and right on the legal basis for social insurance and the question of the administration and control of the insurance scheme flared up again. This time they were settled definitively as a result of the changed social and political climate. Confessional social and political organizations, that is to say employers' organizations, trade unions and political parties, dictated the final outcomes.

Two other broader issues appeared in the debate on social politics during the interwar period. The first issue concerned the organization of the emerging industrial (mass) society. Progressive Catholics proclaimed that, although based on the subsidiarity principle, the responsibility of employers and workers to look after themselves should be respected, with the state taking care of interests that went beyond this. Protestant-Christian circles proclaimed the concept of the *corporatieve maatschappij* (corporative society), with the cooperative relationship between employers and workers being seen as the basis for the ordering of society. In that context, they pleaded for the introduction of industrial (branch) organization. The Social Democrats formulated the idea of public industrial communities of interest as their preferred option. To make this possible, they proposed that each branch of industry should come under the direction of a Bedrijfsraad (industrial council), which then had general supervision over the national economy. This debate on the ordering of society resulted in a series of legislative initiatives by Confessional governments in the 1930s.

Like the disputes over social insurance, the substantive outcomes of this debate on societal ordering developed along Confessional lines or, more specifically, along Catholic lines. Where Protestant-Christians were much more reluctant to increase the role of the state, Catholic social and political organizations accepted a stronger role for the state in regulating industrial relations within society. They opted for the idea of *publiekrechtelijke bedrijfsorganisatie* (public industrial organization), which combined the principle of subsidiarity with another major Confessional concept, that of corporatism. It is interesting that even Social Democrats, although arguing that the proposed legislation would not prove to be sufficient, supported the proposals brought forward in parliament by subsequent Confessional governments.

The second issue became part of the debate on social politics during the 1930s, especially with the arrival of the Great Depression, namely the fight against mass unemployment. This time social-democratic social and political organizations took the initiative with their plea for state intervention. They proposed extensions in compulsory education and work-time reductions, while at the same time pressing for an expansion of public works and public expenditure in order to create 200,000 new jobs within three years, the latter being seen as a means of providing a corresponding boost in purchasing power. These proposed measures were accompanied by more structural proposals to guarantee full employment and better public welfare, and proposals to order industrial production, to guide the expansion of economic activities and to control the cyclical fluctuations of the economy.[11] However, despite these suggestions from the left, social politics during the crisis under Confessional governance remained mainly reactive and defensive. In trying to deal with economic policy and the struggle against unemployment, successive governments held that in the long run only a restoration of international economic activities and trade could produce any economic recovery. As early as the budget debates of 1931/2, the third Ruys de Beerenbrouck cabinet of 1929–33 argued for a decrease in labour costs, more specifically a lowering of wages paid in the public and private sector. Further state activities, such as support for the unemployed, public works, as well as subsidizing private industry, were looked upon as hampering economic recovery. This remained the view of the Colijn cabinets after 1933.

The ideas of the Confessional bloc also dominated other areas of social policy. It was not until 1900 that compulsory education was introduced. The equal status of private (denominational) education was guaranteed in the Constitution Act of 1920, whereby the state shouldered all the costs for Confessional elementary education. The percentage of pupils in public elementary schools decreased from 75 per cent in 1880 to 69 per cent in 1900, 55 per cent in 1930, 38 per cent in 1940 and 27 per cent in 1950, and increased again to 32 per cent percent in 1985.[12] Before the Second

World War, hospitals were developed through Confessional initiatives and without public subsidy. There was no compulsory health insurance until 1941, when it was introduced under Nazi occupation. Voluntary health care insurance covered 39 per cent of the population in 1939.[13] Compulsory as well as voluntary health insurance was organized by a number of sickness funds (*Ziekenfondsen*), partly on a religious or class basis, partly by physicians reacting against the dependence of their German colleagues upon insurance funds.[14] Preventative health care, infant and maternity care and measures against TB all developed before the Second World War in the hands of so-called *kruisverenigingen* ('cross associations'), the non-denominational Green Cross, the Catholic White-Yellow Cross and the Protestant-Christian Orange-Green Cross,[15] and received only marginal support from public funds.

In general, the evolution of social politics was not only reflected in the extension of the risks to be insured (industrial injuries, sickness, old age and invalidity, and some provisions for the unemployed), but also by the increase in the number of insured persons and the growing share that social expenditure took within the total central government budget. The number of insured persons in the industrial injuries insurance scheme grew from 445,000 in 1903 to 1.2 million in 1922, up to 1.4 million in 1936 and 2.3 million in 1950. For the old age and invalidity insurance the figures show a similar pattern, from 1.4 million insured up to 2.5 million in 1950. This growth is also reflected in the breadth of the working population covered. The level of coverage within the industrial injuries insurance increased from 22 per cent in 1903 to 28 per cent in 1910 and 36 per cent in 1920, up to its pre-war peak of 52 per cent in 1928. During the crisis of the 1930s, the level declined to around 40 per cent before rising again to 57 per cent in 1950. For the old age and invalidity insurance the level of coverage is even higher: 52 per cent in 1920, increasing to 65 per cent in 1939 and the first years after the war. The unemployment provisions show the smallest level of coverage, with figures for the 1919–40 period varying between 9 and 18 per cent. In line with this, the size of central government expenditure devoted to social policy expanded, but not spectacularly. The share of social expenditure as part of overall central government expenditure grew from less than 10 per cent at the end of the First World War to about 30 per cent in the years between 1928 and 1935. As a share of gross domestic product, social expenditure slowly increased from 3.2 per cent in 1920 to 3.8 per cent in 1930 and up to 5.5 per cent in 1935. However, this general picture of increasing coverage should not be overestimated. The benefits paid by the social insurance schemes were usually too low to provide even the basic necessities of life. Furthermore, high unemployment from the late 1920s onwards led to quite selective practices within the unemployment provision schemes. Large numbers of the unemployed, as well as the elderly, became dependent on the old poor relief institutions. Thus up to the Second World War the old poor relief schemes had more beneficiaries than the 'modern' insurance institutions.

The broader social and political context for the evolution of modern social politics that had developed before the First World War became effective directly after the conflict. It was Abraham Kuyper who constructed the principal dividing wall between Confessional and non-Confessional (social) politics during the first decade of the twentieth century under the banner of the *anti-these* (anti-thesis), expressed in the

1905 Confessional electoral device 'Tegen de revolutie het evangelie' ('Against the Revolution the Gospel'). In this thesis, Kuyper provided the Confessional ranks with a clear strategy to establish their own identity and, at the same time, provided an ideological motivation on which to found their own organizational structures of political parties, trade unions, agricultural organizations, employers' organizations, mass-media and cultural institutions at a time when mass politics began to emerge. Patterns of differentiation and even growing contradictions within their own ranks were caught within broader societal conglomerates. This strategy of mass mobilization and integration resulted in a spacious network of Confessional organizations in both Protestant-Christian and Catholic circles.[16] However, these 'pillars' were not confined to the Confessional blocs. The same held for the Social-Democratic social, political and cultural organizations, and to a lesser extent also the Liberal ones. The final outcome was a 'pillarized' landscape in which two broader power blocs competed for social and political hegemony, or at least in theory. In reality, Confessional social and political organizations definitively obtained a hegemonic position from the 1920s onwards and actually dominated the evolution of Dutch mass society.

This was especially the case with the relationship between state and society where the principles of 'sovereignty in one's own circle' and subsidiarity held sway. In that context the Catholic subsidiarity principle clearly gained ground against the more restrictive Protestant-Christian principle of 'sovereignty in one's own circle'. The further institutional development of the social security system followed Bismarckian lines, mainly based on employee insurance schemes controlled by employers and employees. During the crisis, state intervention in the economy and the labour market was mainly of a defensive nature, concerned not to hinder an autonomous recovery of international trade and the economy.

The 'Golden Age' of the Welfare State (1945–80)

In the immediate aftermath of the Second World War an attempt was made to introduce some new, Beveridgean principles of social citizens' rights into the existing Bismarckian insurance principles. As early as 1943 the Social Affairs Minister of the government-in-exile in London, Van den Tempel, had appointed the Van Rhijn Commission to prepare for a new system of post-war social security. The report of the Commission was published in May 1945. Both central pre-war issues, the legal basis of insurance and the question of administration and control, formed a major part of the report. The Commission argued that the legal basis of the existing social insurance system, the labour contract, no longer constituted a sufficient basis. A new legal basis was formulated, namely: 'The society, organized by the state, is responsible for social insurance and freedom from want of all its members under the condition that these members take initiatives to provide that social insurance and freedom from want themselves.'[17] In that light, the Commission proposed a major extension and far-reaching organizational reconstruction of the existing system: from a Bismarckian system towards a Beveridgean system, that is to say a universal set of national insurance schemes (*volksverzekeringen*) based on the principles of citizenship and state responsibility for the well-being of all its citizens, and administered and controlled by public institutions. Although the existing principle of earnings-related benefits was preserved for some of the social insurance schemes, a strong plea was made for the introduction of overall minimum benefits, linked to a proposed minimum wage. However, the Confessional-cum-Liberal majority, including the Confessional trade unions, bluntly rejected the proposals of the Commission. The state had no duty to shoulder men's 'risks of life', that was the task of the people themselves and of social associations smaller than the state. This conception was not very conducive to welfare state expansion. Until 1947 more was spent on public assistance and private charity than on social insurance. By 1950 the Netherlands had the fourth lowest social security and public health expenditure as a percentage of GDP of thirteen countries of Western Europe, with only Norway, Switzerland and Finland having lower expenditures.[18]

During the immediate post-war years Dutch social and political relations remained dominated by the Confessional ordering principles, and more specifically the Catholic principle of subsidiarity. Social Democrats, although they participated in the so-called *Rooms-rode* (Roman-red) coalition governments between 1945 and 1958, never had a chance to realize their ideas on a centrally controlled economy and active state intervention in economic and social life. Although Catholics opted for a stronger role of the state immediately after the war, this was a purely pragmatic choice in order to reconstruct the economy and society after the years of the Great Depression and Second World War. As soon as economic and social relations normalized, the Catholics returned to the primacy of market relations and associative responsibility. In the field of social insurance, Confessional hegemony resulted, as already mentioned, in the late 1940s and early 1950s in the obstruction of a far-reaching reconstruction of the system as proposed by the Van Rhijn Commission, and as a consequence in the dominance of pre-war Bismarckian policy lines.

However, from the mid-1950s onwards the landscape of social politics in the Netherlands changed. That process started with the introduction of the *Algemene Ouderdomsverzekering* (General Old Age Pensions Act), the first Dutch social insurance act based upon the legal basis of citizenship – as proposed by the Van Rhijn Commission. From then onwards, through a long series of step-by-step changes, without explicit debates or clear policy fissures, Dutch social politics set under Confessional hegemony a course towards a more universalistic (Beveridgean) policy orientation. The Dutch state reached a high degree of 'welfare stateness'. The breakthrough towards general social insurance on the basis of citizenship made by the introduction of the *Algemene Ouderdomsverzekering* and the *Algemene Weduwen- en Wezenwet* (General Widow's and Orphan's Act) in the late 1950s was continued. First, another three *volksverzekeringen* were introduced: the *Algemene Kinderbijslagwet* (General Family Allowances Act) in 1962, the *Algemene Wet Bijzondere Ziektekosten* (General Exceptional Medical Expenses Act) in 1967 and the *Algemene Arbeidsongeschiktheidswet* (General Disablement Act) in 1975. Second, a rather generous scheme for the disabled, the *Arbeidsongeschiktheidwet*, was introduced in 1963. This new act was not based on the *risk professional*, as usual in most Western countries, but on the *risk social*. Third, the principle of a general subsistence minimum, in order to protect the income of families and single persons, emerged both within social insurance and wage structures. A major provision in that context was the *Algemene Bijstandswet* (General Public Assistance Act) introduced in 1963. Finally, the minimum benefits for breadwinners in the social insurance schemes, as well as social assistance, were equalized to the net minimum wage in 1975. Since that time, and certainly after the adoption of the *Wet Aanpassingsmechanismen* (Adjustment Mechanism Act), the level of all minimum social benefits became linked to the (general) evolution of wages.

In other social policy fields a corresponding line of evolution can be found. In the health system in 1941, under pressure of the German occupation authorities, a compulsory health insurance scheme was introduced for all employees and their families insured under the 1930 *Ziektewet* (Sickness Benefits Act). Subsequently, compulsory coverage gradually extended to certain categories of non-employees and the range of medical care steadily expanded. This process was largely completed with the introduction of the *Ziekenfondswet* (Health Insurance Act) of 1966 and the *Algemene Wet Bijzondere Ziektekosten* (General Exceptional Medical Expenses Act) of 1967. The latter law served initially to finance prolonged and expensive institutional care, but over the years it was extended to more and more aspects of prevention and health care, such as the work of the home nursing associations. The Dutch educational system is characterized by its pillarized structure. In 1920, after forty years of 'school struggle', the Primary Education Act established an equal status for private (i.e. denominational) and public education. Since then, private education has outstripped public education. Increases in the leaving age for compulsory education, higher birth rates and a growing demand for trained personnel led to an increasing number of pupils and students, especially after the war.[19] The educational system was reorganized through three important acts: the 1955 Nursery Education Act, the 1960 University Education Act (amended by the 1981 New University Act) and the 1964 Secondary Education Act. Post-war housing policies were characterized by a shift from the strong public regulation of house building to a more liberal approach. In the first years after the war a whole series of acts were introduced: the 1950 Reconstruction Act, establishing housing construction programmes, the 1950 Regional and Town Planning Act, regulating the planning of house building, and the 1950 Implementation for Rent Act, fixing rents and rent increases. This strongly centralized housing policy came to an end with the introduction of the 1960 Liberation of Rent Act. From then on a long period of relative liberalization started.

This programmatic and institutional evolution, in general quantitative terms, created an explosion in the size of the Dutch welfare state. In terms of GDP social expenditure rose at an annual growth rate of 7.1 per cent from 12.7 per cent in 1950 to 18.4 per cent in 1960, 26.9 per cent in 1970 up to 38.0 per cent in 1980, an expansion which brought the Netherlands from a rather second-class position to the top of the ranking of modern welfare states. Welfare recipients also showed a strong growth, from 718,000 clients (7.8 per cent of the population over 20 years old) in 1950 to 1.23 million (17.3 per cent) in 1960, 2.09 million (25.1 per cent) in 1970 up to 2.98 million (30.8 per cent) in 1980. Together with public servants and other employees directly dependent on the state, almost half the population received an income from the welfare state in 1980. That figure reveals the major character of the Dutch welfare state as a *transfer-state*, i.e. a state with few instruments to intervene directly in the labour market or the economy as such, but relying mainly on the payment of benefits and the subsidizing of other forms of social support. As long as the economic situation was good and unemployment remained low, the evolution of the welfare state hardly provoked any criticism. However, from the mid-1970s onwards the labour-market situation deteriorated. Until the early 1980s that decline had a rather contradictory impact on the evolution of the Dutch *transfer-state*. The number of beneficiaries grew rapidly and, coupled with the economic slowdown, the share of social expenditure as a proportion of GDP increased immensely.

In retrospect it could be argued that all the rather far-reaching proposals of the Van Rhijn Commission in 1945, strongly opposed and rejected in the late 1940s and early 1950s, were nonetheless introduced through a more or less incremental route and formed the basis for the emergence of the Dutch *transfer-state*. This evolution, as would be an obvious assumption, was not born out of compromises between the Confessional power bloc and any other social and political conglomerate of Social-Democratic or Conservative Liberal tailoring. It was incrementalism that was characteristic of Confessional social and political hegemony, combined with a stronger orientation on *universalistic* principles. The arrival of universalistic social politics and the explosive post-war expansion of the Dutch welfare state occurred against the background of enduring and solid economic growth, at least until the early 1970s.

Alongside the hegemony of Confessional social and political organizations, three more specific features of Confessional ideology and practice can explain this evolution, and more specifically the incremental arrival of universalism. First, the corporatist organization created a broad permanent base for the defence of existing social rights and for their expansion. Through the various bipartite organs of social security and through the post-war advisory bodies, the *Stichting van de Arbeid* (Foundation of Labour) and the *Sociaal-Economische Raad* (Social-Economic Council), trade union cadres and leaders became involved in all issues of social security. Thereby, the gainfully employed and their organizations became closely connected with those dependent on the welfare state. This prevented the isolation of these beneficiaries, in contrast to the Anglo-Saxon pattern where benefits are provided by the public administration and particularly targeted at 'the poor'. Second, the insurance principle based on the notion of a just or necessary wage was intrinsically sensitive to rises in the general wage level. To the workers below this wage level the compensation rate was high from the very beginning. The Industrial Injuries Act of 1901 paid 70 per cent of the applicable wage, which was raised to 80 per cent in 1930, together with the inauguration of sickness insurance. This had also to do with the absence of any serious preoccupation with incentives in Confessional social thought. Man was supposed to be governed by moral principles not by purely material interests. Finally, the idea and practice of self-governing social insurance produced a cost-led development of social expenditure. The branch organizations running the 1930 Sickness Insurance were allowed to set the premiums so as to cover their costs. This idea was carried over into the post-war period. Subject to the final acceptance of the Ministry of Social Affairs, premiums for social insurance were adjusted yearly to cover expected expenditure. In years of economic growth and inflation, this led to a constant tendency to push expenditure upwards.

The Reconstruction of the Welfare State (1980–)

From a more short-term economic perspective, the mid-1970s witnessed the end of a long period of extensive economic growth. Growing unemployment and increasing levels of disability aggravated the financial burdens of the welfare state. A reorientation of social policy became part of the political agenda. In the 1980s and 1990s this socio-economic and cultural setting was accompanied by some salient trends within social and political relations. Again, as in the earlier periods, Confessional politics played a crucial role. While they had moved towards a stronger universalist course until the early 1970s, from the early 1980s the newly formed Christen Democratisch Appel[20] (Christian Democratic Appeal, CDA) developed a more critical stance towards the role of the welfare state. In a general sense, the Confessionals argued that citizens who expressed growing expectations *vis-à-vis* the state were becoming more and more dependent on the state and had lost their willingness and capacity to take responsibility for themselves. The Confessional politicians argued for a reversal of this trend. State activity, especially in the field of socio-economic life, had to be restricted. On the basis of these statements, the more progressive wing within the party, which had backed cooperation with the trade unions and a stronger welfare state commitment to fighting unemployment and defending the position of the 'weak' in society, lost ground to the conservative wing. This shift was accompanied by a second one. Whereas for decades Christian Democrats had used corporatist structures and institutions in order to implement the general principles of social organization, they now shifted more and more into the realm of parliamentary politics. This was not without complications, not least because their electoral majority had been lost after the late 1960s and there were growing internal disagreements within the party. This relatively insecure basis for social politics forced Christian Democracy to make a second change regarding the orientation of their (social) politics. The core of Confessional (social) politics moved from a strong parliamentary focus towards the primacy of the governmental level. From the early 1980s, with the arrival of the centre-right, first Lubbers cabinet, the unity within Christian Democrat politics was driven by adherence to strict government legislative programmes which left hardly any room to manoeuvre for the Christian Democratic Party in parliament. This evolution probably constituted *the* major paradox of post-war Confessional politics: in order to maintain its social and political hegemony, Christian Democracy withdrew from its genuine field of politics, corporatism, and shifted its activities into parliamentary, and finally governmental, echelons.

This evolution had two important consequences. First, following on from the strengthening of the conservative/moderate wing of the CDA, Christian Democrats played a major role in the first attempts to reconstruct the Dutch welfare state. Social politics became dominated by slogans such as 'primacy to the market', 'the reduction of public debt' and 'lowering the public expenditure quota', resulting in a long series of retrenchments and downsizing of social programmes. This process started under the Confessional first and second Lubbers cabinets (1982–9) and continued under the Confessional/Social-Democratic third Lubbers cabinet (1989–94). Second, the loss of its central social position within the old corporatist structures in the long run eroded the parliamentary and governmental position of the CDA. In 1994 a 'purple coalition' of Conservatives, Liberals and Social Democrats under the command of the Social-Democratic leader Wim Kok (1994–2002) came to power. To some extent, at least for a period of eight years, this coalition proclaimed the 'end of ideology'. Under a favourable set of economic circumstances and using the slogan 'work, work and work again', Kok's cabinet claimed to have modernized the Dutch welfare state from a 'passive income-guaranteeing' welfare state into an active welfare state, successfully focused on high labour-market participation. However, while the market led to an unprecedentedly positive situation in terms of labour-market participation and low levels of unemployment, the 'purple' coalition was not able to use the momentum in order to come to a fundamental reassessment of the exhausted and outmoded social policy concepts of the twentieth century.

Conclusions

The twentieth-century welfare state, or more precisely social politics, played an important role in announcing the arrival of mass society in the Netherlands. The origins of this prominent position actually date back long before social politics became the core business of the national state. From the sixteenth century onwards, policy patterns emerged where ruling elites intervened in the labour market and in determining the living conditions of 'the masses'. Over a long period ruling elites developed their interventionist strategies, capacities and institutions, while at the same time the lower classes and their allies strengthened their counteracting forces. From the early nineteenth century onwards, the basic parameters of 'mass politics' developed within Dutch society. In the debate on *staatstusschenkomt* (state intervention) social politics again played a prominent role. Actually, it was substantial pressure from a large coalition of social organizations, employers, trade unionists, teachers, scientists, doctors and representatives from the churches that urged politics, and more specifically the national state and its representatives, to intervene in the fate of child factory workers, and subsequently other elements of the Dutch working classes. It was this first social movement that paved the way for modern methods of social intervention and, alongside that process, the arrival of mass politics. Political parties, trade unions, employers' organizations, as well as broader social movements, developed since then, in part as a response to these first large debates on social politics. And even more specifically, it was not merely 'mass politics' and 'mass society' that emerged from the debates on social politics during the second half of the nineteenth century and the first decades of the twentieth century. In the Dutch case it became a fairly characteristic, and to a certain extent even contradictory, type of 'mass society', a *pillarized* 'mass society', organized along its pillarized conglomerates of parties, social organizations, associative alignments, school systems, cultural organizations and mass media. And interestingly enough, it was social politics, and more specifically the institutions and organizations of the emerging welfare state, that formed a major basis for this 'compartmented (corporatist) mass society'.

The basic structure of this specifically Dutch version of 'mass society' remained largely intact until the early 1970s. Certainly, in some adjoining fields, such as higher education, youth culture, popular music and religious feeling, the first fissures of the dominant concept of control had already flared up from the late 1950s. From the 1980s onwards the 'compartmented (corporatist) mass society' broke apart under the pressure of global modernity, of 'depillarization' and growing individualization. For the first time 'mass politics' in its genuine contours flooded into Dutch society and demonstrated the obsolete character of the corporatist structures of the welfare state. The 1980s and 1990s witnessed traces of despair within the Dutch social and political elites. They were dislodged from their secure bastion of policy compromises, practices and institutional arrangements and became deprived of their traditional responses to emerging problems and new challenges.

Social politics under the newly emerged geopolitical context, and in a more and more rapidly transforming economic, social and cultural environment, will be confronted by challenges which will explicitly question the strong national and *étatist* social policy orientation of the twentieth century. First, as a kind of grist and at the same time counterpart of globalization, the decentral, i.e. the local level of social politics, gains importance as opposed to the central, i.e. the national level. That is not merely a case of competences and policy decisions. This trend also signifies that to a certain extent social policy gets more and more caught up in the everyday life of citizens. Where the national level treats citizens preeminently as objects and in an impersonal way, citizens act on a decentral level also as subjects, and thus a closer relationship emerges between (local) government and its citizens. Poverty, long-term unemployment, health problems, work and city life, as well as the multicultural society, constitute practical problems that politicians, policy-makers and civil servants are confronted with, and for which they feel obliged to take responsibility. Work, income and care in the broadest sense make up an inextricable bond. Such an entity demands an integral approach, which will lead to new contents and forms of social policy. It is beyond the scope of this chapter to elaborate on this connection, but one could think of a broadening of the 'participation' concept, new income-supporting measures, experiments with social activation and social empowerment, experiments with the obligation to apply for jobs, a local 'basic income', integral arrangements on work, income and care, an integral community approach, the development of 'client-for-client' trajectories (client self-help and the reinforcement of social networks), a higher level of own choice and responsibility for welfare-state clients *vis-à-vis* the public authorities and many other ideas.

This evolution has, second, important consequences for the relationship between public and private arrangements. Actually a re-evaluation of private initiatives and non-public social institutions is under discussion, not so much in terms of the old, strongly pillarized institutions, but mainly along new routes and initiatives at the 'civil society' level. The conservation and strengthening of the private character of provision and institutions can also be interpreted as a means of maintaining and encouraging forms of 'personal work', of alternative (social) production, of 'own' projects, self-help, voluntary work, community activities, as well as projects around spiritual themes. Seen from a broader perspective, this can be seen as creating the possibility of maintaining and encouraging social activities and institutions *vis-à-vis* the excessive impact of governmental bureaucracies and the 'public invasion' of the personal life of citizens. There is the possibility of building new forms of citizens' social choices and citizens' social responsibility. Social policy no longer only belongs to the state, but to a larger and larger extent to the direct social environment of modern citizens. This is a final move from the 'compartmented (corporatist) mass society' towards a 'modern mass society', in which globalization and a more direct sense of belonging go hand in hand.

Notes

1. See as an example the periodization of Christopher Pierson, *Beyond the Welfare State? The New Political Economy of Welfare* (Cambridge, 1991): the birth (1880–1914), consolidation and development (1918–40), the 'Golden Age' (1945–75) and contradictions and crisis (1975–).

2. H.F.J.M. van den Eerenbeemt, 'De Patriotisch-Bataafs-Franse tijd (1780–1813)', in J.H. van Stuijvenberg (ed.), *De economische geschiedenis van Nederland* (Groningen, 1979), pp. 157–62.

3. P.B.A. Melief, *De strijd om de Armenzorg in Nederland 1795–1854* (Groningen/Djakarta, 1955), pp. 194–200.

4. 'Geen burgerlijk armbestuur mag onderstand verleenen aan armen, dan na zich, voor zoveel mogelijk, te hebben verzekerd, dat zij dien niet van kerkelijke of bijzondere instellingen van liefdadigheid kunnen erlagen, en dan slechts bij volstrekte onvermijdelijkheid.' Melief, *De strijd om de Armenzorg*, p. 212.

5. A. Kerdijk, 'De wet op den Kinderarbeid', *Vragen des Tijds*, (1878), pp. 99–100; P.A. Diepenhorst, *De Nederlandsche Arbeidswetgeving*, vol. I (Utrecht, 1921), pp. 141–3.

6. *Staatsblad*, No. 130.

7. H. Amelink, *De sociale wetgeving* (Hoorn, 1939), pp. 15–17; F. de Jong, *Om de plaats van de arbeid* (1956), p. 51.

8. H. Amelink, *De sociale wetgeving*, pp. 52–3.

9. G.J.M. Veldkamp, *Inleiding tot de sociale zekerheid*, Vol. I (Deventer, 1978) pp. 66–8.

10. Abraham Kuyper, the famous leader of the Protestant-Christian forces in the last decades of the nineteenth century, opposed any alliance with the Catholics for a long period. However, in his *Deputatenrede* (Deputation Speech) in 1901 he told his audience: '[If] you exclude the catholics ... then Protestant ... Christianity is completely tied, and for ever delivered up to an unbelieving majority.' Without the 23 Catholics in parliament, said Kuyper, 'no one can ever believe that ... a majority on the right is possible'. W.J. van Welderen-Rengers, *Schets eener Parlementaire Geschiedenis van Nederland*, Part I (The Hague, 1950), p. 511; quoted by H.

Spoormans, *'Met uitsluiting van voorregt'. Het ontstaan van liberale democratie in Nederland* (Amsterdam, 1988), p. 137.

11. F. de Jong, *Om de plaats van de arbeid* (Amsterdam, 1956), pp. 244–7; H. Hoefnagels, *Een eeuw sociale problematiek* (Alphen a/d Rhijn, 1974), pp. 259–60; J.P. Windmuller and C. de Galan, *Arbeidsverhoudingen in Nederland*, Vol. 1 (Utrecht/Antwerpen, 1979), p. 65.

12. Ph.J. Idenburg, *Schets van het Nederlands schoolwezen* (Groningen, 1960), p. 112; Centraal Bureau voor de Statistiek (CBS), *Statistisch Zakboek 1986* (The Hague, Staatsuitgeverij, 1986), p. 121.

13. P. Juffermans, *Staat en gezondheid in Nederland* (Nijmegen, SUN, 1982), p. 169.

14. Ibid., pp. 122. and 152.

15. A. Querido, *De wit-gele vlam* (Tilburg, 1973).

16. M.B. ter Borg, 'Het confessionalisme en de sociale zekerheid', *Sociale Wetenschappen*, 29(3) (1986), pp. 200–1.

17. Commissie Van Rhijn, *Sociale zekerheid*, Vol. 1 (The Hague, 1945), p. 10.

18. P. Flora and J. Alber *et al.*, *State, Economy and Society in Western Europe 1815–1975* (Frankfurt, London and Chicago, 1983–7), Vol. I: *The Growth of Mass Democracies and Welfare States* (1983), p. 456.

19. C.T. Geerlings, *Zicht op het Nederlandse schoolwezen* (Meppel, 1978), p. 77.

20. Officially, the fusion of the three Confessional parties became a fact in October 1980, but since the mid-1970s the three parties have in reality acted as one party.

–5–

The Welfare State in Mass Society
Twentieth-century Britain

Pat Thane

Like Joop Roebroek, I believe that if we are fully to understand the relationship of states to the welfare of their populations in the twentieth century we need to understand the long pre-twentieth century histories of these relationships. There are striking similarities between the Dutch experience between medieval times and the nineteenth century, as Joop Roebroek describes it, and the experience in England. I stress *England* rather than Britain since the relevant administrative and legal structures have long been different in Scotland and Ireland from those of England. Wales has for centuries shared England's legal and governmental institutions despite important cultural differences, and there have been significant historical, cultural and economic variations within England. The diversity among the countries and regions of Britain was important at the beginning of the twentieth century and was, if anything, more important at the beginning of the twenty first, following the devolution in the late 1990s of a range of powers, especially those concerning social policies, to new elected assemblies in Scotland and Wales. What follows is an overview of the relationship over the course of the twentieth century between the growth of 'mass society' and of the 'welfare state'.

A major difference between Dutch and British societies over the century lies in the importance of religion and of faith-based political and voluntary organizations in Dutch society and their relative unimportance in Britain, especially in England. However, another instance of the differences within the British Isles is the intense and continuing importance of religion and religious-based institutions in Northern Ireland. Elsewhere in Britain religious groups exerted most influence over education policy through the first half of the century, successfully preserving state funding for denominational schools and compulsory religious education in all schools. In other respects religion played a very minor role in British politics, especially in the second half of the century. The overt Christianity of Prime Minister Tony Blair at the end of the century was widely regarded as aberrant and somewhat embarrassing.

The British state took on new welfare responsibilities in the first years of the twentieth century: free school meals for poor children (1906); improved Workmen's Compensation for industrial accidents (1906); medical inspection of schoolchildren (1907); improved protection of abused and neglected children (1908); the first state old age pensions (1908); a minimum wage for selected low-paid, mainly female, workers; the first state-funded unemployment agencies to assist unemployed people to find work (1909); National Health and Unemployment Insurance (1911). Together these changes marked a real shift from the centuries-old Poor Law tradition of minimal, punitive poor relief to tax-supported assistance which, while never generous, was not punitive in intent and sought prevention where possible.[1]

All of this legislation was passed by Liberal governments who were consciously responding to the mass organizations that were emerging, in particular the trade unions and the Labour Party, which was founded in 1900 and had its first significant successes in the general election of 1906 that brought the Liberals back to power after a decade in opposition. The Liberal Party depended upon the votes of large numbers of working men and felt threatened by the emerging working-class party. Its leaders were quite explicit that their social policy measures were designed to persuade working people to continue to support the party. Until 1918, however, 40 per cent of men and all women were excluded from the vote. Both leading political parties, the Liberals and Conservatives, were well aware that this situation could not long continue and, before the First World War, were making plans to appeal to the mass democratic electorate that was surely coming. If they had any doubts that mass democracy was on its way, they should have been dispelled by the militant women's suffrage campaigns of 1910–14. These, and more peaceable women's activism by such large organizations as the working-class Women's Co-operative Guild (31,000 members in 1914), helped to bring about the Liberal legislation that began to improve women's wages and the health and welfare of children.

This early welfare legislation was driven not only by the spectre of a coming mass electorate but also by other issues that forced politicians to think about the masses. A central concern at the beginning of the century was the size and fitness of the population. This was influenced by awareness of the steady fall in the birth rate, which, it was feared, would weaken Britain in relation to other countries, and by the discovery at the time of the South African war (1899–1902) that a high proportion of those volunteering to fight were physically unfit to do so. Together these were seen as evidence of the physical deterioration of the British population, which was attributed to the effects of modernization and, especially, urbanization in the most urban society in the world. This caused concern because it threatened Britain's capacity to fight against potential enemies in Europe and to defend her huge empire, the more so since Britain held on to her colonies in South Africa in the South African war with much greater difficulty than anticipated. The physical frailty of much of the population also threatened Britain's position in an increasingly competitive world economy. Men too weak to fight were also too weak to work productively. There is no evidence that the physical state of Britain's working class was actually worse than at any previous time, but the challenges faced by the nation were perceived to be greater than before. Pre-war measures such as those to improve the health and welfare of children were designed to improve the fitness of future adult generations.

Pre-First World War welfare legislation also performed another role, that of defining who was British. Since the early twentieth century, eligibility for state-funded welfare has been linked to citizenship, whereas poor relief and state education (the major pre-existing forms of state-funded welfare) were not. The first state pensions and national insurance benefits excluded residents who were not naturalized British subjects and also women who had been born as British subjects but had married non-naturalized 'aliens'. Those most immediately affected were the large numbers of Jewish immigrants who had come to Britain from Eastern Europe since the 1880s. Jewish protests led to modification of the law (e.g. the granting of pensions to the British-born widows and divorced wives of aliens) but the principle remained unchanged and continues to operate to the present.[2]

Unlike the Netherlands, Britain was directly involved in the First World War, which had a profound effect upon British society. The 'welfare' role of the state increased during the war as the state assumed unprecedented powers to regulate social and economic life, in particular to maintain food and other essential supplies. Renewed concern about the physical fitness of recruits to the services led to increased funding for health services, especially for young children. The population became accustomed to the state acting effectively to improve their lives. The war economy also brought unprecedented full employment and higher living standards for civilians, which raised expectations of post-war standards. Furthermore, war needs enabled the government to increase taxation, which remained at higher than pre-war levels after the war, enabling the funding of further welfare legislation.

Legislation such as this was thought necessary by the post-war Conservative-controlled government, which perceived 'the masses' as an imminent threat. Fears about the reactions of servicemen returning from the horrors of the war to unemployment and the poor housing which still characterized Britain's big cities, especially when they had the model of the Russian Revolution before them, drove the government to increase spending on house building and unemployment relief. Politicians also had to adapt to a great expansion of the electorate in 1918, when all men aged 21 and above gained the vote (and all younger men who had served in the war) and most women aged 30 and above. (Women gained the vote on equal terms with men in 1928.) The electorate almost tripled in size, from 7.7 million in 1910 to 21.4 million in 1918. A high proportion of the new male voters were working class, though not all were, since the peculiarities of the previous voting system had previously excluded numbers of unmarried middle-class men.[3] The Labour Party emerged much stronger from the war and formed governments in 1924 and 1929–31, though both were weak and without overall parliamentary majorities. Nevertheless, the party which claimed to speak for the mass of the population was stronger than ever before. Other parties – in particular the Conservative Party that dominated inter-war governments – had to take it very seriously. Labour also had growing success in local elections, especially in the larger cities, in the 1930s. From 1934 it controlled London. At this time local authorities had powers to levy local taxes to improve housing, education, health care and transport, of which Labour-controlled authorities took advantage.

Politics and society in inter-war Britain were dominated by high unemployment, which hit Britain earlier than other European countries (late in 1920) and continued to 1940. In some regions the economy revived and standards of consumption rose, especially in the south and Midlands of England in the 1930s, driven by the development of new mass production industries such as motor-car manufacture, but such industries only ever employed a minority of the working population. Elsewhere poverty and high unemployment continued.

Remarkably, this period of economic dislocation saw increased public expenditure on a growing range of provision for health, pensions, welfare, education and housing. Expenditure on social services formed 33 per cent of total government expenditure (central and local) in 1913 and averaged about 45 per cent through the 1930s.[4] In particular, the large numbers of the unemployed had access to benefits on an unprecedented scale. These were not generous, often administered in a stigmatizing fashion, and often denied to married women and always to those who could not prove themselves to be British subjects,[5] but they were a great deal better than ever before. Along with increased government expenditure devoted to welfare went a continuation and probable growth of voluntary action. Statistics for voluntary action are always uncertain, but much state expenditure at this time was channelled through voluntary organizations and sustained their activities.[6]

The high level of government social expenditure at this time is best explained by the increased political influence of the mass of the population once they had the vote, and the politicians' real fear of the danger of neglecting the unemployed. The new voters did not exert influence through mass protest. Between the wars there were fewer demonstrations, riots or colourful protests by radicals, trade unionists, women or other excluded groups than at any time in the previous century or more. There were demonstrations and marches during the brief General Strike of 1926, by the unemployed, especially in the 1930s, and by women in the 1920s for equal voting rights, but they tended to be more sober than before.

Perhaps this first generation to experience a mass right to vote believed that their grievances were best expressed through the ballot box. There is every sign that new voters, male and female, used their new civil rights. In the inter-war years women both joined political parties in large numbers and organized in single and mixed-sex associations as never before. As in the United States and Australia, the numbers of women's associations increased markedly when they gained the vote. In Britain there were broad organizations devoted to campaigning for gender equality on all fronts, and also to encouraging women to use their new civil rights, such as the National Union of Societies for Equal Citizenship and the National Council of Women; single-issue groups, such as the campaigners for improved pensions for women and the Abortion Law Reform Association, both founded in the 1930s; women's trade unions, such as the National Union of Women Teachers; faith groups such as the Union of Jewish Women, and many more. Though few women were elected to parliament in the inter-war years, organized women lobbied male politicians relentlessly. The passage through parliament of an unprecedented number of items of legislation (at least twenty between 1918 and 1930) for which women's organizations campaigned, most of them related to family law or the health and welfare of women and children, so soon after women gained the vote is unlikely to have been coincidental. Politicians were very uncertain about how to respond to the new female voters and anxious not to alienate them. Certainly very many female voters were less passive and conservative than they have sometimes been portrayed. In particular, they placed the welfare of women and children more firmly on the political agenda than before.[7]

Again during the Second World War the government took control of the economy and society, including the labour market. From 1940 to 1945 it was a coalition government, including all the major political parties. Labour Party ministers controlled the key home front ministries, while Churchill conducted the war. Their effectiveness, combined with the fact that voters identified the Conservatives with a failure to resolve the pre-war economic crisis, contributed to Labour's unprecedented success in the election of 1945. From 1945 to 1951, for the first time, Britain had a Labour government with a substantial majority in parliament.

Labour could now implement the policies the party had been developing since its foundation.[8] Its social and economic policies were closely linked. Labour's post-war social legislation owed much to the recommendations made by the Liberal William Beveridge during the war, though his proposals went further than Labour was prepared to go, for example his willingness to provide improved benefits for divorced and separated women. Beveridge's proposals and the structures put in place by Labour owed much to developments both in legislation and in the voluntary sector in the earlier part of the century and before.

Beveridge recommended universal, equal, welfare benefits. For the first time the whole population should receive the same amount of old age pension, sickness, maternity or unemployment benefit in return for the same rate of national insurance contributions, regardless of income. This, of course, took a higher proportion of the incomes of the poor than of the rich. Labour followed this recommendation and extended the principle of free and equal access to the newly nationalized health services and to an extended and improved state education system. Labour's education policy was based on the Education Act initiated by a Conservative minister, R.A. Butler, in 1944, which Labour supported. Post-war education policy expanded the system of mass education, which had been developing since the late nineteenth century, providing an improved basic education for everyone up to the age of fifteen. The 1944 Act instituted a meritocratic system of selection by examination at age eleven which sorted an academically able elite into grammar schools, a small number into technical schools and the great majority into 'secondary modern' schools designed to provide a basic education to age 15 but no access to the examinations which provided the escalator into elite occupations. Funding for university scholarships, to take further the training of the grammar school elite of intellect and expertise, was also increased. Theoretically this system offered equal opportunities for children of all backgrounds to enter the elite. In reality it became clear within a decade that it favoured middle-class males. There were fewer grammar school places for girls and they had to achieve higher examination grades than boys in order to attain places. At the same time, the parallel system of private education remained untouched, keeping in place the elite of money and birth. The class and gender order of British society was shifted very slightly at best.

Labour provided education and other services and benefits free to all British citizens, funded by a combination of national insurance contributions, paid by all workers, and taxation, which at this time fell relatively lightly on manual workers. Labour believed that this mildly redistributive universal welfare state would serve the important function of integrating and stabilizing society as a whole, diminishing social divisions by offering a common experience and equal opportunity to all. As the experience of education showed, this was overly optimistic.

Post-war pensions and other benefits were not generous; indeed they have never provided an income adequate for survival for anyone without a supplement from other income. The poorest pensioners have always had to rely on a means-tested state supplement. Beveridge advocated that the state should provide no more than minimum benefits, providing an income sufficient for survival, to eliminate severe poverty without providing 'comfort', in line with Britain's long Poor Law tradition. Supplements to provide higher living standards should be provided from family support or personal savings, accumulated, ideally, through voluntary, non-profit, mutual organizations, such as the long-established trade union and friendly society funds.

The Labour government provided the minimal benefits but failed to support friendly society and trade union welfare. Rather, it fostered the illusion that the state could provide for all welfare needs and that voluntary institutions belonged in the dustbin of history. These were probably weaker, among both men and women, in the immediate post-1945 years than at any other point in the century, though they did not disappear and strengthened as the weaknesses of the 'welfare state' became obvious from the 1950s onwards.

The leaders of the Labour governments believed, as leading members of the Labour Party and trade unions long had, that the key to 'welfare' was a strong economy and full employment, enabling working people and their families to provide for their own welfare needs. The government gave priority to investment in, and modernization of, manufacturing industries over welfare expenditure and private consumption.[9] Full employment was achieved, as elsewhere in Western Europe between the late 1940s and the early 1970s, although to what extent this was the outcome of government policy is doubtful. Labour's policy of restricting personal consumption (wartime rationing lasted into the 1950s) alienated middle-class voters, disrupting the social cohesion Labour aimed for.[10] As a result, Labour narrowly lost office to the Conservatives in 1951, following two closely fought elections. In both of these Labour won more votes than the Conservatives but, due to the peculiarities of the 'first-past-the-post' electoral system, fewer seats. The two elections of 1950 and 1951 also had the highest voter turnouts of the century, 85% and 82.5% respectively. The most striking manifestation of mass voting in the century showed the country deeply, and evenly, divided between two essentially class-based parties, the Conservatives and Labour.

Thirteen years of Conservative government followed. The Conservatives did not dismantle the post-war welfare state, but nor was this, as some commentators have suggested, a period of 'consensus' when Labour and Conservatives shared economic and social policies. There was strong pressure in the Conservative Party to shift welfare provision as far as possible from the public to the private sector, but they were constrained by the voters. Too many people, including large sectors of the middle class, had too much to gain from high quality state-funded health care and education to reject it. Few middle-class people in the 1950s could afford to provide for equivalent services from their own incomes.[11]

By 1951 Labour had been able to make only an incomplete start to both social and economic reconstruction after the war and the preceding Depression. Some aspects of social reconstruction were carried forward by the Conservatives, in particular a huge expansion of council-house building for poorer families. Labour had lost votes due to its failure to provide enough housing to meet the needs resulting from wartime bombing and the legacy of the poor pre-war housing stock. Quality living space had become an expectation in modern society. Labour's failure to meet this need was partly due to the diversion of resources into the rebuilding of industry, but also to its determination to build high-quality houses for working people. This they did but, due to the higher cost of spacious and comfortable houses, in numbers far too small to meet the need. The Conservatives built hundreds of thousands of houses that met the need in the short term, but they were of poor quality and created the problem housing estates of the latter part of the century. On other aspects of welfare, the Conservatives kept pensions low and encouraged private pension saving through private insurance companies. The popular National Health Service was improved through a much-needed programme of hospital building. There was no consensus of principle between the two major political parties on social policy, but there was enough common ground among the mass electorate to keep the essential features of the post-war welfare state in place.

In their approach to the economy, the Conservatives differed markedly from Labour. They rejected unpopular austerity and encouraged private consumption rather than focusing on industrial investment, gaining from the Europe-wide economic expansion of the 1950s. The Conservative prime minister, Harold Macmillan, encouraged private affluence, pointing out in 1957, in a much-quoted phrase, that 'most of our people have never had it so good'. He was quite right and Conservative optimism, compared with Labour's rather grudging approach to spending and pleasure, helped the Conservatives win three elections.[12] Leading Conservatives argued that the new affluence was eroding old social divisions. R.A. Butler, architect of the 1944 Education Act, argued in 1960: 'We have developed ... an affluent, open and democratic society, in which the class escalators are continually moving and in which people are divided not so much between "haves" and "have-nots" as between "haves" and "have-mores".'[13]

This redefinition of acute social divisions clearly did not appeal to all voters in a society in which one outcome of affluence was increasingly public challenges to traditional class divisions on the stage, in film and television and in literature. This public revolt against tradition was assisted by high-profile upper class scandals, such as the Profumo affair of 1963, which discredited the Conservatives, and by an increasingly assertive, large-selling popular press. Partly in consequence, from 1964 to 1970 Labour returned to office. It committed itself to renewed efforts to modernize an economy which was seen to be weakening internationally and to removing new as well as old social divisions by replacing the selective system of education introduced in 1944 with non-selective comprehensive secondary schools intended to provide equal opportunities, though not necessarily equal outcomes, for all children, regardless of background. Once again, though, private education remained untouched. Social expenditure increased by 1970. Also everyday life was liberalized in other respects. In a remarkable run of legislation between 1967 and 1970, tacitly if not always overtly supported by the Labour leadership, abortion was legalized, capital punishment abolished, homosexual acts between adult men were decriminalized, the divorce laws eased, equal pay between men and women encouraged by law, and racial discrimination outlawed. Behind most of these changes were determined, often long-established, pressure groups which gained unprecedented popular support in the 1960s. If civil society had been weak in the late 1940s, it had revived strongly by the 1960s.

But liberalization was not all pervasive. Labour continued the Conservative policy of restricting immigration from former colonies such as India, Pakistan and the islands of the West Indies, driven largely by public demonstrations of racism and the negative impact on Labour votes. If Britain had become a somewhat more inclusive society internally over the course of the twentieth century both culturally and politically, it erected higher barriers against those wishing to join the internal mass from outside. The right to British citizenship was gradually withdrawn from those born in what had been the Empire and the rights of non-citizens to the expanding range of welfare benefits continued to be restricted. Other serious social divisions remained within the British Isles. In Northern Ireland discrimination against Roman Catholics in the allocation of council housing, school provision and access to public-sector employment was a major trigger of the civil rights campaign of 1967, which brought to the surface the sectarian crisis which has never gone away.

Between 1970 and 1979 first a Conservative then a Labour government struggled with the crises brought on by the end of the long post-war boom and the coming of the 'oil shock'. Nevertheless, the Labour government of 1974–9 continued to increase spending on welfare and by 1979 British state welfare provision was at its most expansive and expensive ever. It was a complex, incoherent structure delivering the poorest levels of pensions in Europe and uneven standards of education and health care, with, on the whole, the poorest groups receiving the worst services, but it was better than anything previously provided by the British state, comparable with that elsewhere in Western Europe. An effect of affluence and improved education was that a population which was still in the late 1940s generally deferential to authority and expertise was by the 1960s increasingly inclined to be critical of medical and other professionals who were perceived not to deliver satisfactorily. People were assisted by an increasingly assertive mass media. Also the mass of the population now had higher expectations of health, education and quality of life. State welfare had always had weaknesses. A less deferential population was less willing to put up with them and more outspoken, though not necessarily always fair, in its criticism.

The discontents of the 1970s brought Margaret Thatcher to power in 1979 and the Conservatives to office for eighteen years until 1997. They governed Britain for 35 of the 55 years between the end of the Second World War and the end of the century. The real inadequacies of the welfare state, combined with the new popular assertiveness, enabled Thatcher's governments to chip away at it and to encourage people to believe that they were now affluent enough to pay for their own homes, health care and pensions and for the education of their children, as their parents had not been in 1945. Unless they were unemployed, of course, as at least 15 per cent of the workforce was by 1986. But the prime minister evidently recognized that the unemployed still formed a minority of the population and were unlikely to vote. And again, as in the inter-war years, the unemployed were not wholly neglected and excluded. Unemployment benefits were eroded but kept at a level that prevented total despair and alienation. In consequence, total government social expenditure fell hardly at all in the 1980s, despite the government's best efforts. In spite of an almost total cessation of council-house building, the erosion of education and health services and a decline in the value of pensions, the high costs of unemployment kept total expenditure at high levels.

Many people discovered, however, that they could not afford the high costs of private health care, education, pensions and other benefits, as well as expensive owner-occupied housing. The growth of owner occupation, from very low levels at the beginning of the century to 32 per cent in England and Wales in 1938 and around 70 per cent at the end of the century (levels of owner occupation have been consistently lower in Scotland), encouraged by Thatcher's sale of council housing at knock-down prices, is another significant difference between British and Dutch society. By the 1980s it was regarded as a popular norm. Providing personally for all these needs was too costly in relation to average incomes and voters placed limits on how far Margaret Thatcher could go in eroding the health care system in particular, as they came to realize why they needed a welfare state. This was one of the reasons why she, and ultimately the Conservative government, lost office.

The Thatcher governments encouraged voluntary action in place of state welfare. This served as a reminder that voluntary organizations remained important features of British society, though they were incapable of taking on the vast responsibilities of the modern state. Similarly, families bore an increasing proportion of the care of the old, young, sick and disabled as social services were eroded, for family cohesion remained strong in spite of all the prophecies that it was doomed to extinction in the mobile modern society.

The society 'New Labour' was elected to govern in 1997 was very different from that of 1945, let alone 1900. It was more affluent, more unequal, with a wider gulf between the richest and poorest than in the 1970s, perhaps more unequal than in the 1940s, probably not so different in that respect from Britain in 1900. It was less deferential, though still deeply class-divided in terms of life chances. These social divisions, after narrowing somewhat between the 1940s and 1970s, widened in the 1980s and 1990s and were perceived as more complex. The characteristics of class, as of other forms of social division, had changed; in particular, there were fewer workers in heavy industry and more low-paid service workers. The hope, often expressed in the 1960s, that working hours would shrink and that leisure rather than work would come to define social identity faded as hours of paid work increased, especially in the 1980s and 1990s and, for the first time, among higher business and professional as well as lower paid workers.[14] Britain seemed to be adopting American rather than European work patterns. In this respect also Britain in 2000 had more in common with 1900 than with the hopes of the 1940s. Many more women were in paid work at all levels, fewer women were dependent on male 'bread-winners'. More of them than in 1945 were single mothers on low incomes, though not more than in 1900 when there were comparable numbers of widowed mothers on low incomes. British society was far more multicultural than it had ever been, though this was more evident in some parts of the country than others; London by 2000 was a profoundly culturally diverse city. Ethnic minority groups varied considerably in terms of income, skills, education and social position. Devolution of powers, especially concerning social policy, to elected assemblies in Scotland and Wales from 1999 encouraged these assemblies immediately to develop different approaches, for example to the funding of higher education and health care, from those of the government at Westminster. There was much greater awareness than in 1900 or 1945 that British society was divided not just by class but by gender, race and region. By the end of the twentieth century Britain was perhaps as much, or more than ever, a cluster of mass societies as a single mass society.

Notes

1. Pat Thane, *The Foundations of the Welfare State*, second edition (London, 1996).

2. David Feldman, *Englishmen and Jews: Social Relations and Political Culture, 1840–1914* (New Haven, CT, 1994); Pat Thane, 'The British Imperial State and the Construction of National Identities', in Billie Melman (ed.), *Borderlines: Genders and Identities in War and Peace, 1870–1930* (London, 1998), pp. 29–46.

3. Duncan Tanner, *Political Change and the Labour Party, 1900–1918* (Cambridge, 1990).

4. A. Peacock and J. Wiseman, *The Growth of Public Expenditure in the UK* (Princeton, NJ, 1961), pp. 184–91; Thane, *Foundations*, pp. 153–210.

5. Laura Tabili, 'The Construction of Racial Difference in Twentieth Century Britain: the Special Restriction (Coloured Alien Seamen) Order, 1925', *Journal of British Studies*, 33(1) (Jan. 1994), pp. 54–98.

6. G. Finlayson, *Citizen, State and Social Welfare in Britain, 1830–1990* (Oxford, 1990); F. Prochaska, *The Voluntary Impulse* (London, 1988).

7. Pat Thane, 'What Difference Did the Vote Make?', in Amanda Vickery (ed.), *Women, Privilege and Power: British Politics, 1750 to the Present* (Stanford, CA, 2001), pp. 253–88.

8. Duncan Tanner, Pat Thane, Nick Tiratsoo (eds), *Labour's First Century* (Cambridge, 2000).

9. Ibid., Jim Tomlinson, 'Labour and the Economy', pp. 46–79.

10. Ina Zweiniger-Bargielowska, *Austerity in Britain: Rationing, Controls and Consumption, 1939–1955* (Oxford, 2000).

11. Harriet Jones, 'The Conservative Party and the Welfare State, 1942–1955', PhD thesis (University of London, 1992).

12. Anthony Crosland tried to persuade Labour to change: *The Future of Socialism* (London, 1956); L. Black, *The Political Culture of the Left in Britain, 1951–1964: Old Labour, New Britain?* (Basingstoke, 2003).

13. R.A. Butler speech at Conservative Political Centre Summer School, 8 July 1960.

14. Robert Taylor, *Britain's World of Work: Myths and Realities* (Swindon, Economic and Social Research Council, 2003).

Part III
Media

–6–

Media, Morality and Popular Culture
The Case of the Netherlands, 1870–1965

Frank van Vree

One of the most successful branches of Dutch exports over recent decades has been the audiovisual media industry. This may seem quite remarkable for an economic activity that usually depends heavily on language and cultural traditions. However, companies like Endemol do not export actual programmes but ideas and formats, the most spectacular of which has become world-famous: *Big Brother*. The programme was a huge financial success for its licensee and, at the same time, as the Dutch were soon to discover, proved an icon of the times during the political turbulences of 2002. These had many features in common with the television programme, such as the swinging moods and preferences of the public, the new 'frankness' (or should we say 'exhibitionism'?), the public confessions and ongoing conflicts in front of the camera.

Both *Big Brother* and these political developments may be seen as symptoms of a process of spectacularization of the public sphere, blurring traditional borders between the public and the private. This applies even more to some programmes that were, luckily for those outside the Netherlands, not made for export, like *Sex voor de Buch*, which means something like 'sex ahead', literally 'in front of the bow' – bow, in Dutch *boeg*, being phonetically similar to the surname of the programme's host, Menno Buch. The show, broadcast by a commercial TV station, was fully devoted to sex. The public was invited to participate – a call which many took up with wild enthusiasm, revealing their fantasies not only in words but put into practice right in front of the camera, just after prime time at about 10.30 p.m. The programme seemed to aim to demonstrate the literal truth of Jean Baudrillard's famous statement that today media and information have become all pervasive, even obscene and pornographic.

In contrast to television, the Dutch press is still a paragon of sobriety and sensibility. There is no equivalent of the *The Sun*, the *Daily Mirror* or *Bild Zeitung*. Compared to the yellow press in other countries, *De Telegraaf*, the daily with the widest circulation, although referred to as 'sensationalist' ever since the First World War, is a very moderate, informative and particularly 'decent' newspaper. The same applies to the local and regional press, which manages to keep up a relatively high standard in national and international news, economics and culture. Admittedly, these papers are going through hard times, struggling for subscribers at the bottom of their markets – youngsters, the less well educated and ethnic-cultural minorities, who all tend to turn away from the written media to television as their primary or even only source of news and information, and by television I do not mean documentaries or current affairs programmes, but infotainment and varied news magazines.

It may be argued that the relatively high standard of the Dutch newspapers and the absence of a yellow press are primarily a relic of the past. Until the late 1960s the Dutch media were firmly rooted in a society and political culture that were 'pillarized' (in Dutch, *verzuild*). Pillarization (*verzuiling*) is defined as the emergence of socio-political formations or, more precisely, the emergence of integrated complexes of social organizations along religious and ideological lines,[1] strictly separated and turned in upon themselves. At the same time pillarization may be conceived as the Dutch version of modernization.[2] Each of these 'pillars' or *zuilen* had its own media, moulding its identity, organizing its cohesion and defending its position within Dutch society; newspapers, magazines and broadcasting associations served its cause and were consequently supported not only by the pillarized organizations but also by the readers and listeners. These bonds of mutual loyalty fixed the position of the media in the market: in the 1920s and 1930s the number of subscriptions to newspapers amounted to more than 95 per cent of the circulation, which meant that there was almost no vending at newspaper stands or in the street. A yellow press could never have flourished amidst these serious, devoted political or religious newspapers, relying on a readership that considered its paper as 'a friend of the family'.[3]

If the serious and relatively sober character of the newspapers today can be considered as a relic, TV programmes like *Big Brother* and *Sex voor de Buch* should be regarded as antipodal to Dutch culture of the late nineteenth and most of the twentieth century – a culture or public sphere that was fully dominated by Christian and middle-class moral values, a culture in which, according to current historiography, there was virtually no room for dissenting voices, for rough emotions, for physical experiences, for the spectacle and sensations that are so characteristic of 'mass culture'. This brings us right to the main theme of this chapter, the highly problematic position of the emerging popular culture in the Netherlands since the late nineteenth century.

Mass Media and Popular Culture: Some Preliminary Remarks

Before moving on we should consider, at least for a moment, the nature of our research and its object as well as the terminology we are using. First of all, the preliminary, explorative character of this chapter should be stressed. Although Dutch media history has achieved considerable progress over the last decades, very little has been done to develop a more or less coherent perspective on the emergence and evolution of popular culture. Press historians, for example, may build on a solid base of institutional, economic and political research as well as works using a more integrated approach or method, such as contextualized content analysis, the development of the public sphere or journalism culture.[4] The same applies to the history of radio and television, which hardly existed a few decades ago but may boom in the coming years, now that the archives are being opened up and old programmes are becoming available through *streaming video*.

Until now, however, the history of popular culture has not received much attention.[5] Our knowledge in the field of popular film and, even more, music and magazines – to name only three important expressions of popular culture – is fragmentary and consequently this chapter cannot be anything more than an exploration. This immediately raises another preliminary question: the problematic status of the term 'mass' in relation to culture and media. There are good reasons to doubt whether one should stick to this expression. 'Mass culture' and 'mass media' invoke images of a vast audience comprising many thousands or even millions of individuals. This, according to John B. Thompson in his powerful study *The Media and Modernity*, may be an accurate image in the case of some media products, but definitely not all of them, either past or present.[6] The important point in this kind of communication is not the number of recipients, but the availability of its products.

Moreover, there is a second objection to the term 'mass' or 'masses', since it bears, as Henk te Velde has already mentioned, strong connotations to traditional criticism in cultural theory as well as the social sciences, steeped in prejudices concerning media and modern life. In this discourse the concept refers to a social phenomenon that was at the same time present and a future threat. The idea of 'mass' in relation to media suggests 'that the recipients of media products constitute a vast sea of passive, undifferentiated individuals'.[7] This kind of criticism, based on the idea of an 'almighty media', assumed that the rise of modern media did produce 'a kind of bland and homogeneous culture which entertains individuals without challenging them', killing their critical faculties and providing instant gratification.

These kinds of ideas and connotations related to the very concept of 'mass' seem to blur our view of the process that actually underlies all this, namely the growth of 'mediated interaction' in almost all areas of social life, in politics as well as sport, leisure and culture, a process in which traditional folk culture has been transformed into or even replaced by modern, i.e. *mediated*, popular culture. For all these reasons I prefer to define the subject of this chapter in terms of media and the rise and repression of modern popular culture. Thus I will confine myself to the period from the late nineteenth century to the 1960s, concentrating on magazines, newspapers, radio and television, film and music, and leaving aside, although not completely ignoring, non-mediated forms of popular culture like dancing, shopping and live-music. I would like to argue that from the late nineteenth century on, during the growth of the system of pillarization, manifestations of popular culture have been repressed, selectively tolerated and neutralized, at least from the point of view of the dominant religious and political groups within society. Nevertheless, in some areas popular culture did emerge, spreading among various social groups, particularly in cities like Amsterdam and, even more, Rotterdam in the 1920s and 1930s.

Old Vices, New Vices

In 1908 the city council of Rotterdam decided to put an end to a long-standing and legendary phenomenon: the city's annual fair or *kermis*. This decision was the outcome of a long political struggle dating back to 1892, when several thousand citizens petitioned for the abolition of the annual fair on the grounds that it had 'such a negative effect on moral and spiritual life, brutalizing the people, provoking prodigal behaviour, undermining people's health, disturbing religiousness, undermining authority and leaving misery everywhere'.[8] There had even been a painstaking inquiry to prove that fluctuations in the number of illegitimate children could be linked to the fair, a correlation that appeared impossible to verify, notwithstanding these efforts. Initially the abolition movement found its adherents mainly in orthodox Protestant circles, but gradually it also received support from some Catholics as well as right-wing Liberals, who were initially opposed to a more repressive policy. By 1908, however, political ideas and the balance of parties had shifted and a broad majority now voted in favour of abolition. A similar event took place just a few years later, when the council decided to tear down a whole quarter, famous around the world for its pubs, dance halls, gambling dens and numerous brothels.[9]

The campaign against traditional 'immoral' popular entertainment was not a typically Rotterdam phenomenon. On the contrary, the harbour city was slow to act compared to other municipalities such as The Hague, Delft, Groningen and even Amsterdam. Fairs, animal fights, dance halls, rough games were all targets, as local authorities everywhere tried to abolish or at least curb them, and councils became convinced of the idea of a *moral authority*, a moral government, an idea that was propagated by Calvinists and Catholics alike and was central to the formation of their political, social and cultural parties and the organizations that were to make up the orthodox Protestant and Catholic pillars around 1900. Moral issues appeared to function as an ideal glue, patching up social differences between and within the religious communities.[10] On the other side of the political spectrum, the socialist movement cherished quite different ideals and ambitions, originating from its very different analysis of society, but ultimately it also sided with the religious and conservative parties. The liberation of the working class and the edification of the people required discipline and moral superiority. Alcoholism, moral corruption, gambling, physical and spiritual excesses were the enemy, and socialism had been fighting them since the very beginning of its existence.

As a result, an unlikely coalition came into being, opposing traditional 'physically uncontrolled', 'unrestrained' and 'uncivilized' forms of popular culture, the use of alcohol and all kinds of moral excesses, while promoting a strong belief in the edification of the population. Although Catholics, Calvinists and Socialists held different views and even clashed on the nature and the ends of this cultural and moral edification, they could agree on a policy to raise a barrier not only against the living remnants of a pre-modern working-class culture, but also against the burgeoning modern popular culture. Together they could rely on a vast majority in electoral terms of more than three-quarters of the population, with far-reaching consequences that became particularly clear in the inter-war period.

Repression and Elevation

The rejection of nearly every aspect of modern popular culture by the dominant political, religious and cultural groups during the inter-war years found its expression in various ways, not only in speeches and writings but also in the emerging social sciences[11] and in the social and cultural policy of the period, in their own organizations and, of course, in the structure and character of the Dutch media. The history of Dutch cinema provides a clear example of this argument.

Viewed as an interesting and exciting but relatively harmless attraction during the first decades after its introduction, the moving image gradually developed into an established branch of entertainment that might be used for political and ideological ends as well.[12] For almost ten years the Dutch parliament discussed measures to control what was generally referred to as 'het Bioscoopgevaar', the danger of cinema. Numerous proposals were launched during the ongoing debate, containing measures to banish children from public screenings, to split up cinemas into two parts, as was common in some churches, putting the men on the left-hand side and the women on the right, and banning the dimming of the lights during the show. Censorship turned out to be at the core of the law that was finally passed in 1926, the *Bioscoopwet* (Cinema Law). A national board was established, consisting of representatives from the main political and religious groups. Its members, being well-known spokesmen for their own groups, took their job very seriously. Films with an explicitly erotic or violent character were forbidden, where definitions of 'erotic' and 'violent' were interpreted according to the very narrow standards of those days. Sometimes screening was allowed on the condition that the offensive scenes were edited out. The same happened to films with an undesirable political message; thus the works of all Soviet directors could not be given public screenings. Finally, all films that might offend the religious feelings of any group in society were subject to strict censorship. According to Hyacinth Hermans, a Black Friar and a leading member of the national board of censors, the Netherlands had the most rigid film regime of all the countries he knew of.[13]

Although it may be clear that the government and the political and religious leaders grossly overestimated the influence the media might have on its audience, their measures definitely had an immediate impact. Since the board of censors appeared to be quite strict with regard to piquant, sensationalist and violent scenes, cinema owners tended to show U-rated films. On account of the criteria used by the board, American films were more often 'victims' of censorship because of their violent content, whereas many French films could not escape censure because they contained risqué scenes. Even the 'better' German films, generally favoured by the board over US films, were subject to censure, mainly because of their portrayal of loose morals and improper relations.[14] Yet even this was not enough. At a local level, city councils and mayors continued to impose even stricter rules, as they had done before the national *Bioscoopwet* came into force. In the southern Catholic part of the country, city councils and local priests prescribed a separate inspection by the Catholic Board of Film Censors. In some Protestant areas, screenings on Sundays (or even late Saturday nights) were not allowed.

The mighty arm of censorship stretched overseas as well; in the Dutch Indies the rules were stricter still. Any scene that might undermine the image and position of Europeans in the eyes of the indigenous population had to be edited out. In 1934 film importers and cinema owners in the colonies sent a petition to the government, complaining that the screening of a large number of films had become virtually impossible. Due to the drastic number of cuts imposed, the audience was no longer able to follow the story line of many films.[15]

The history of Dutch radio resembles that of the cinema in many respects, as does the history of public libraries, education, sport and various branches of entertainment. Following the political rules and conventions of the pillarized nation state, based on pacification, mutual agreement and equal treatment of minorities, both national and local government issued enabling legislation that set the moral and political rules and supplied the judicial instruments to maintain these. In the field of radio broadcasting this policy resulted in a unique system that forms the basis of the Dutch public media to the present day. In 1930, after seven years of struggle between various commercial, political, religious and national interest groups, the *Zendtijdbesluit* (Broadcast Time Order) was issued, awarding the two Dutch radio frequencies to four broadcasting corporations, the orthodox Protestant NCRV, the Catholic KRO, the socialist VARA and the non-denominational AVRO. Some minorities and special groups, like the liberal Protestants, received airtime of from a few hours a week down to half an hour a month. Thus the radio was organized along the lines of the existing pillarized media landscape. The decree dealt a heavy blow to the AVRO, which had developed from a more or less commercial station into a 'neutral' corporation, aiming to keep the radio free from politics and religion and calling itself 'truly national' for this very reason. The other corporations heavily challenged the aspirations and claims of the AVRO, arguing that diversity was the most characteristic trait of the Dutch nation, and the AVRO saw its following gradually reduced to the non-orthodox, liberal and conservative middle classes.[16]

At the same time, censorship was introduced. All programmes were to be submitted to a committee that was entitled to prohibit their broadcasting or to demand changes in the text or even the music. According to the rules, all programmes that might possibly hurt the feelings of other groups in society or were too political were eligible for banning. The censorship committee used its power thousands of times during the 1930s, prohibiting lectures on Spinoza (too atheistic) and Erasmus (ridiculing monks) and thwarting not only programmes that were too political, especially of a socialist origin, but also radio plays and entertainment shows.

Although the general rules and infrastructure were set by the government, Catholics and orthodox Protestants as well as socialists tried to repress any expression of immorality and sensationalism within their own pillarized organizations in the field of education, housing, sport, labour unions, women's clubs and, of course, the media, radio, newspapers, magazines as well as publishing houses and film clubs. At the same time, the pillars aimed to promote more 'elevating' cultural practices Catholics and Protestants because they wanted to fight immorality, socialists because they were convinced that culture would contribute to the emancipation of the working classes. In everyday life this implied a full exposure to traditional 'high' culture as the real source of true civilization.

However, it gradually became clear that one could not simply stick to this policy of repression and refusal with regard to modern media and popular culture and that film, radio and entertainment or a more accessible style of journalism did not necessarily do any harm to religious feelings or political discipline, but might even be deployed to serve a higher cause, be it the word of God or socialist unity. As a result, Catholics and Protestants started to make movies on their missionary activities and founded cinemas for young people. There were even critics, like Janus van Domburg, once a member of the famous *Film Liga*, who were arguing that Catholic film-makers should follow the aesthetics of the Soviet avant-garde to improve the quality of religious cinema.[17] As mentioned above, the dangers of radio were counteracted by the foundation of their own organizations, broadcasting programmes that were easy to recognize and meant to reinforce the solidarity of the pillar. Sports were easier to incorporate: practising sport might contribute to discipline and keep youths away from dancing, street life and other bad (sexual) habits. At the same time, there were numerous notes of warning against 'sport madness' and professional sports.

And so popular culture trickled into Dutch society in a more or less domesticated form – a process that was reflected in the press during the first decades of the twentieth century. An exploratory analysis, based on research into six non-religious newspapers, demonstrated that modern popular culture was almost completely neglected during the first decades of the century.[18] Only sport received some attention, although the reports were very brief. Conversely, 'high culture', such as music, literature, painting, opera, theatre and museum exhibitions, appeared to be a natural subject for attention; the editors obviously went along with the elite and the middle class in their pursuit of the moral and cultural edification of their readers. The attention paid to traditional popular theatre, exhibitions, amateur plays and concerts performed by schools, clubs and associations fits in with this thesis. These activities were considered to be 'healthy' expressions of recreation and a sound base for cultural elevation. In the inter-war period new patterns became visible, at least with regard to the attention paid to particular fields of popular culture. From the 1920s onwards, sport received considerable attention in the press, appearing as a common and generally accepted 'neutral' activity, although Protestant newspapers refused to report on sports played on Sundays and Roman Catholic journals tended to focus exclusively on the achievements of Catholic clubs and sports that were considered to be popular among the Catholic part of the population, like cycling.

Less innocent, but nevertheless evident in the daily press, with the exception of the Protestant newspapers, was the cinema. The love of film, however, was never unconditional. Roman Catholic papers, for example, openly disapproved of films with an explicitly erotic or non-Catholic character and refused advertisements showing unveiled knees or shoulders, while some liberal newspapers opposed popular cinema, propagating the idea of film art instead and paving the way for the famous *Film Liga*, consisting mainly of journalists, artists and film-makers, including the literary critic and writer Menno ter Braak and film-maker Joris Ivens. Even in the papers that paid ample attention to all kinds of films one clearly senses an undertone of disapproval with regard to the glitter and glamour around them, or, at least, serious worries on the effect of the 'strong emotions' of the film on children and even adults.[19]

These tendencies may also be discerned in the socialist daily *Het Volk*, which had become the second largest newspaper in the Netherlands in 1931. The attention given to popular culture, particularly sport, radio and cinema, had grown considerably, but socialist ideology never fully disappeared from the reports and reviews. In the way the paper reported on these events and spectacles one may even see an effort to reconcile modern popular culture with both older popular traditions and progressive labour values. Nevertheless, the growing attention given to popular culture gave rise to concern, discontent and opposition among some elements within the socialist movement itself. Senior national and local party members especially complained about the 'unaesthetic look' of the headlines and the photographs printed in the paper, the sensationalism used by reporters and editors, and the 'amoral' stories. During the annual party congress and at the meetings of the national board of the Social Democratic Labour Party (SDAP), prominent officials complained that the paper was viewed as 'annoying' for 'decent people', because it was 'too vulgar, too cheap'.[20] Willem Drees, a member of the newspaper's Board of Commissioners, who was to become the legendary post-war prime minister, strongly disapproved of 'the craving to be the first to publish sensational news', the overwhelming attention given to crime and sport, particularly 'a crazy, ridiculous excess like the six-day bicycle race', where the paper had even offered a prize for the winner.[21]

There were other senior party leaders who were worried about the changing character of the socialist press and the rise of popular culture, among them Emanuel Boekman, Alderman of the city of Amsterdam until his suicide on the day after the capitulation of the Netherlands in May 1940, now viewed as the foremost ideologue of post-war cultural policy in the Netherlands.[22] Boekman propagated the elevation of the masses through the spread of high culture as a source not only of *aesthetic* but also, above all, of *moral* civilization. In his publications as well as his political work he advocated government intervention. Fellow socialists like the members of *Kunst aan het Volk*, an association founded in 1904 to uplift the masses through the arts, or the legendary Henri Polak, the 'rabbi of the Jewish proletarians' and founder of modern unionism in the Netherlands at the end of the nineteenth century, did not wait for government action and took numerous initiatives. Polak, for example, deeply embedded the idea of the aesthetic education of the working class into the policy, activities and publications of the labour unions and youth organizations he presided over during the first decades of the century.[23]

Although the views of Boekman and Polak on the elevation of the masses were widespread, no formal government policy developed, except at a local level such as in the social-democratic stronghold of Amsterdam. In particular the introduction of the eight-hour day in 1919–20 led to new initiatives when the SDAP included in its municipal programme a demand for the furtherance of 'popular development' (*volksontwikkeling*) by government support for libraries, museums, concerts and sport. Liberals as well as Protestants and Catholics did not consider cultural elevation as a public issue: government intervention should be limited to school education and some support for cultural institutions of national importance, the rest was to be the task of private initiatives. Thus, on that level pillarized organizations developed numerous more or less 'safe' activities in the field of education, culture and leisure.[24]

The Rise of Popular Culture

Apart from specific differences of opinion, for example on the role of the government, Dutch politicians, intellectuals and religious leaders of various denominations shared a common belief in the superiority of 'high culture', as well as a certain despair about the future of Western civilization. In the Netherlands, as elsewhere in Europe, Ortega y Gasset's critical observations in *La Rébelon de las masas* were welcomed, and this was even more the case with Johan Huizinga's lengthy essay *In the Shadow of Tomorrow*, published in 1935.[25] In this work, subtitled 'diagnosis of the spiritual distemper of our time', popular culture (radio, newspapers, film and sport) served as a vehicle for the vices of contemporary society. At the time there were very few people in the Netherlands who openly dared to cast doubt on the analysis of this famous historian.

The first time Huizinga had been confronted with modern popular culture in its full glory had been fifteen years earlier during his stay in the United States. At that time, he was above all 'surprised' by what he saw and heard; perhaps he did not realize that the rise of popular culture was an irreversible process that would ultimately reach the Netherlands as well. And it did, despite all the opposition and contempt shown to *le défit américain*. While the assumed corrupting effects of film and radio could be curbed, as we have seen, thanks to a strict policy of censorship and regulations – city life turned out to be a tougher battlefield. Rotterdam, for example, assumed the air of a dynamic metropolis, with modern bars, pavements, dance halls and clubs playing jazz, or cabaret and orchestras, with cineacs, illuminated news and advertisement trailers, more sensationalist newspapers, sporting contests, modern buildings – a modern city that resembled the description given by Vanessa Schwarz in her book *Spectacular Realities*.[26] It was also a city in which avant-garde and popular culture became closely connected, as was demonstrated some years ago at an interesting exhibition, 'Interbellum Rotterdam, Arts and Culture 1918–1940'.[27]

Table 6.1 Population, Public Entertainment, Media 1935–70 (1970 = 100)

	population	*radio sets*	*tv sets*	*cinema*	*sports events*	*professional theatre*	*concerts*	*museums per 1,000 people*
1935	65	21						
1940	68	40		140	30	152*	56*	14
1945	71	11		356	59	174	68	37
1950	78	52		265	120	128	108	44
1955	82	74	4*	271	112	130	97	59
1960	88	93	29	225	103	99	73	70
1965	94	95	78	151	106	108	91	86
1970	100	100	100	100	100	100	100	100

* 1956   * 1941 * 1941

The intertwining of modernity and popular culture found a clear expression in the Rotterdam press, in printing and book design as well as in local magazines and newspapers like the non-partisan *Rotterdamsch Nieuwsblad* and its socialist counterpart *Voorwaarts*. A particularly interesting case is *Groot Rotterdam*, a family magazine founded in 1923 that managed to attract more than 100,000 subscribers within a few years. It contained many illustrations, aerial photographs, pictures of modern buildings and public works, stories, prize contests, women's and children's pages, sport and comic strips. As a local magazine it showed no signs of nostalgia whatsoever – on the contrary, it clearly expressed its faith in the modern city.

The combination of modern style and more popular forms of journalism turned out to be very successful. There is no doubt that these successes had a slow but inescapable impact on the press in the country as a whole. In fact, we have already demonstrated this above: the complaints about the socialist daily *Het Volk* in the early 1930s were the result of a drastic restyling and reorganization of this newspaper after the model of the Rotterdam-based *Voorwaarts*. The operation was led by the director of the Rotterdam paper and appeared to be an overwhelming success. The circulation of *Het Volk* tripled within eighteen months to almost 200,000, making it the paper with the second largest circulation. The emergence of modern popular culture proves that wide social circles were receptive to it, at least in the main cities like Rotterdam and Amsterdam. On the basis of newspaper readership figures there are good reasons to assume that these circles consisted of non-religious or at least unorthodox elements of the middle and lower classes, including the more pragmatic socialists but excluding members of the conservative and liberal bourgeoisie. Following this line of reasoning, one may conclude that more than half of the city population, perhaps even 70 per cent, was receptive to modern popular culture.

Restoration and Cultural Revolution

The reform movement, drawing its inspiration from a deeply felt antipathy towards pre-war politics and the past experience of the Nazi occupation and aiming to 'renew' politics and society along political and social lines instead of religious principles, did not hold sway for long in the post-war era. Even in 1946, barely a year after the liberation, pillarized institutions had regained their position in society. The widely expected *Doorbraak* (political breakthrough) never took place, and during the late 1940s and 1950s the intensity of pillarization actually grew if measured in terms of the degree of organization. Yet this was not simply a restoration of the pre-war situation. There was more room for dissenting voices, experiments and renewal, not only in the field of the arts and literature but also in popular culture. The abolition of radio censorship, for example, clearly illustrates that the atmosphere had become at least a little less narrow-minded and oppressive.

Cultural criticism, however, endured until the very end of the 1950s, partly as a continuation of the mood of decline and despair that already existed before the Second World War, partly as a consequence of past experiences. A rather peculiar form of pessimism was ventilated by some young intellectuals, writers and artists, who felt the war had taken away the very bedrock of morality and belief in progress. Others pointed out that the war experiences, just like the cold war and the atomic bomb, had led to a widespread demoralization, particularly among the younger generation, which might have a negative effect on national culture.[28]

Yet this was not all, the war experiences were not the only source of cultural criticism and pessimism. Other circumstances, like the emergence of a more aggressive and independent youth culture and the spread of American popular culture, along with the settlement of thousands of US soldiers in Western Europe and the cultural programmes related to the Marshall Plan, had also contributed to the widespread feelings of discontent, raising new objections and leading to new lines of argument, particularly in relation to the 'mass youth' from the concrete jungle, which was considered to be uprooted, detached, materialistic, even nihilistic. Social scientists, then a newly established profession, trying to prove that this criticism was justified, played an important role in the debate on these issues.

The debate about television, reluctantly introduced by the Dutch government in 1951 in the face of objections from the four 'pillarized' broadcasting corporations and giving priority to the interests of Philips as an export industry, may be seen as a perfect illustration of widespread opinion on both the 'mass' as well as the media. A few months before the first programme was broadcast, *futurologist* Fred. L. Polak, a prominent cultural theorist, published an essay predicting that television would conquer the country as it had already in the US. The invention of this medium should be ranked with that of the printing press, at least so far as its impact is concerned, because on other points a comparison would turn out in favour of the press. Television, according to Polak, 'literally moves on the surface of the screen and will raise superficial, empty-headed people.' It would lead to addiction and new forms of illiteracy; in short, all the vices of 'mass culture' were projected on to the new medium.[29]

Secretary of State Jo Cals, in his speech on the occasion of the first broadcast, appeared a little more optimistic. Television might even be turned into a positive force and, in capable hands, contribute not to the destruction but to the distribution and advancement of culture.[30] That very month the government decided to install a Television Board to promote these aims. Its task was to report on the social, cultural and educational aspects of the new medium. From the research carried out by the board and others in the following years it appeared that the impact of the new medium was very limited, due to the fact that initially the number of television sets grew very slowly (from about 3 per cent in the mid-1950s to 25 per cent in 1960) and that there was only one station broadcasting for a few hours a day, as well as the innocent character of the programmes, which consisted mainly of music, drama, news and children's television. Moreover, social scientists reported that television appeared to reinforce family life instead of disturbing it and to increase social and political involvement.

It was only in the 1960s that the cultural and political climate was to undergo a dramatic change. However, when Jan de Quay in his first speech as prime minister in 1959 announced that it was about time that the nation's newly acquired material wealth should be used to morally and spiritually uplift the people, the first signs of a radical change were already visible. Since this theme will be discussed elsewhere, I will confine this analysis to pointing out some features of this process, brought about and fostered by developments in and outside the country: (1) the far-reaching innovations within the Roman Catholic Church and the new radicalism in the Protestant churches worldwide were developments that struck at the roots of pillarization; (2) the economic progress that paved the way for better education, housing and social welfare and, more generally, gave rise to a consumer society, creating new opportunities in lifestyle as well as social and cultural mobility; (3) closely connected with this, the emergence of popular culture, particularly among the youth, a process boosted by television and, above all, music. In this period of cultural, social and political change that began at the end of the 1950s and took off at the end of the 1960s, the blossoming of popular culture played a key role. It is no coincidence that the disintegration of the pillarized institutions took place quickly and dramatically in the fields of the media, music, youth culture, cinema and sports.

Conclusion

The last remark on the direct relationship between the rise of popular culture and the so-called 'de-pillarization' of Dutch society underlies another important observation. From the analysis given above of the controversies surrounding popular culture in the Netherlands during the years of pillarization, it may have become clear that the negative attitudes, opinions and policy towards popular culture were neither by-products of pillarization, nor just rhetoric, nor an expression of disgust by an elite for the masses. From their perspective, these writers, cultural critics, politicians, ministers and priests were certainly right when they argued that modern popular culture was threatening social stability and morality. Because of its predominantly mediated character and its orientation on the market and the taste of the consumer, modern popular culture bears an intrinsically a-political and a-religious character. In the case of these pillarized organizations, based on political and religious values, popular culture did constitute a threat because it would indeed create undisciplined and uncontrolled masses of individuals, following their own taste and emotions, and finally destroy their very solid and disciplined religious and ideological basis.

Notes

1. This definition, formulated by the early theorist of pillarization J.P. Kruijt, is still very valuable. It refers directly to the most distinctive trait of Dutch society and politics, i.e. the strong and highly integrated social and political formations based on religion. It was not the socialist movement but the vast and massive Roman Catholic and orthodox Protestant pillars that gave Dutch society, politics and culture its peculiar character. Cf. J.P. Kruijt, *Verzuiling* (Zaandijk, 1959); S. Stuurman, *Verzuiling, kapitalisme en patriarchaat* (Nijmegen, 1983); Frank van Vree, *De Nederlandse pers en Duitsland 1930–1939. Een studie over de vorming van de publieke opinie* (Groningen, 1989).

2. See Janneke Adema, 'Verzuiling als metafoor voor modernisering', in Madelon de Keizer and Sophie Tates (eds), *Moderniteit. Modernisme en massacultuur in Nederland 1914–1940* (Zutphen, 2004), pp. 265–83.

3. Van Vree, *De Nederlandse pers*, pp. 48ff.

4. Cf. Jo Bardoel, Chris Vos, Frank van Vree and Huub Wijfjes (eds), *Journalistieke cultuur in Nederland* (Amsterdam, 2002).

5. After the final version of this article had been prepared, Madelon de Keizer and Sophie Tates (eds), *Moderniteit. Modernisme en massacultuur in Nederland 1914–1940* (Zutphen, 2004) was published. Only a few contributions, however, deal with popular culture.

6. John B. Thompson, *The Media and Modernity: A Social Theory of the Media* (Cambridge, 1995), p. 25.

7. Ibid.

8. 'Rapport van de commissie voor de Kermis-Enquête', 21 February 1894, *Verzameling Gedrukte Stukken Gemeenteraad 1894*, pp. 51–98, Rotterdams Gemeente Archief (Municipal Records).

9. See also my article on the Rotterdam policy of 'civilization', 'De verlokkingen van de Zandstraat: vertier aan de zelfkant van een stedelijke samenleving', in D. Kalb and S. Kingma (eds), *Fragmenten van vermaak. Macht en plezier in de 19de en 20ste eeuw* (Amsterdam/Atlanta, 1991), pp. 25–42.

10. This is one of the key arguments in Stuurman, *Verzuiling, kapitalisme en patriarchaat*.

11. See, for example, the early social research into leisure, A. Blonk and J.P. Kruijt, *De besteding van de vrije tijd door de Nederlandse arbeider* (Amsterdam, 1936), or the research on the effects of television in the 1950s. Cf. L. Heerma van Voss and F. van Holthoon (eds), *Working Class and Popular Culture* (Amsterdam, 1988); A.C.J. de Vrankrijker, *Volksontwikkeling. Geschiedenis en problemen van het sociaal-culturele werk in Nederland* (Assen, 1962).

12. For the early history of Dutch cinema, see K. Dibbets and F. van der Made (eds), *Geschiedenis van de Nederlandse Film en Bioscoop tot 1940* (Baarn, 1986); A. van Beusekom, *Kunst en amusement. Reacties op de film als een nieuw medium in Nederland 1895–1940* (Haarlem, 2001).

13. H. Hermans, *Van mensen en dingen die mij voorbij gingen* (The Hague, 1945), pp. 188–9.

14. J. Berkhout, 'Filmkeuring in de jaren dertig. De representatie van maatschappelijke verschillen en de gevolgen voor de Amsterdamse filmvertoning', MA thesis, University of Amsterdam, 2004.

15. *Nieuwe Rotterdamsche Courant*, 14 September 1934; *Het Volk*, 22 September 1934.

16. H. Wijfjes, *Radio onder restrictie. Overheidsbemoeiing met radioprogramma's 1919–1941* (Amsterdam, 1988); H. Wijfjes (ed.), *Omroep in Nederland* (Zwolle, 1994); J.H.J. van den Heuvel, *Nationaal of Verzuild. De strijd om het Nederlandse omroepbestel in de periode 1923–1947* (Baarn, 1976).

17. Robbert de Witt, 'De katholieke reconstructie geprojecteerd op het witte doek', in de Keizer and Tates, *Moderniteit*, pp. 300ff.

18. The pilot was carried out by MA-assistant Paula van Dijnen and included three national papers and three regional papers: *De Telegraaf* (non-aligned), *Het Volk* (socialist), *Algemeen Handelsblad* (liberal), *Leeuwarder Courant* (liberal),

Rotterdamsch Nieuwsblad and *Haagsche Courant* (both non-aligned). The papers were analysed over a full week in March 1900, 1920 and 1935. Additional information was drawn from Frank van Vree, *De Nederlandse Pers*.

19. See, for example, *Haagsche Courant*, 9 March 1935, and 'Film en opvoeding' in *De Telegraaf*, 3 March 1935.

20. See Van Vree, *De Nederlandse Pers*, pp. 101ff.

21. Minutes, Board of Commissioners, 30 December 1932, inv. no. 2879. Archives of the SDAP, Internationaal Instituut voor Sociale Geschiedenis (IISG), Amsterdam.

22. E. Boekman, 'Overheid en kunst in Nederland', PhD, Amsterdam, 1939; T. Jansen and J. Rogier, *Kunstbeleid in Amsterdam 1920–1940. Dr. E. Boekman en de socialistische gemeentepolitiek* (Nijmegen, 1983); H. van Dulken and T. Jansen (eds), *Het leven als leerschool. Portret van Emanuel Boekman* (Amsterdam, 1989); J. Rogier and T. Jansen, *Kunstbeleid in Amsterdam 1920–1940* (Amsterdam, 1983); Ministry of Education, Culture and Sciences (ed.), *Cultuurbeleid in Nederland* (2002).

23. S. Bloemgarten, *Henri Polak, sociaal democraat 1868–1943* (Amsterdam, 1993).

24. Lex Heerma van Voss, 'The Use of Leisure Time by Male Workers after the Introduction of the Eight Hour Day', in L. Heerma van Voss and F. van Holthoon, *Working Class and Popular Culture*, pp. 173ff. Cf. Th. Beckers, *Planning voor vrijheid. Een historisch-sociologische studie van de overheidsinterventie in rekreatie en vrije tijd* (Wageningen, 1983).

25. Johan Huizinga, *In the Shadow of Tomorrow: A Diagnosis of the Spiritual Distemper of our Time* (London, 1964).

26. Vanessa R. Schwartz, *Spectacular Realities: Early Mass Culture in fin-de-siècle Paris* (Berkeley, CA, 1998).

27. At the Las Palmas exhibition hall in Rotterdam. Cf. M. Halbertsma and P. van Hulzen (eds), *Interbellum Rotterdam. Kunst en cultuur 1918–1940* (Rotterdam, 2001). A synthesis is presented by Marlite Halbertsma, 'Culturele arrangementen en stedelijke cultuur', in de Keizer and Tates, *Moderniteit*, pp. 149–64.

28. M.J. Langeveld, *Maatschappelijke verwildering der jeugd* (The Hague, 1952); cf. P. de Rooij, 'Vetkuifje waarheen? Jongeren in Nederland in de jaren vijftig en zestig', *Bijdragen en Mededelingen betreffende de Geschiedenis der Nederlanden*, 101 (1986), pp. 76ff.; H. Galesloot and M. Schrevel (eds), *In fatsoen hersteld. Zedelijkheid en wederopbouw na de oorlog* (Amsterdam, 1987); G. Tillekens (ed.), *Nuchterheid en nozems. De opkomst van de jeugdcultuur in de jaren vijftig* (Muiderberg, 1990).

29. F.L. Polak, 'Tele-visie en vrije-tijd', *De Gids*, CXIV (1951), p. 316; cf. J. Bank, 'Televisie verenigt en verdeelt Nederland', in Wijfjes, *Omroep in Nederland*.

30. R. Berends, 'Een staatscommissie en een luchtbel. De Televisieraad en de sociaal-culturele aspecten van een nieuw massamedium, 1951–1953', *Jaarboek Mediageschiedenis*, 2 (1990), p. 135.

The Devil's Decade and Modern Mass Communication

The Development of the British Media during the Inter-war Years

Kevin Williams

The years between the two great wars, especially 'the Thirties', have a particular place in popular memory. John Baxendale and Chris Pawling have examined how the decade has been culturally constructed.[1] The dominant motif is of the 'Devil's Decade' or the 'Hungry Thirties', in which British society was bitterly divided between the haves and have-nots, between classes and peoples, a nation at war with itself. Such narratives call forth images of hunger marches, unemployment, idleness, poverty, slums, ill health, the rise of fascism, class struggle in the civil war in Spain and appeasement. Revisionist historians challenge this recollection. John Stevenson and Chris Cook claim the decade was not a period of absolute misery and depression.[2] Unemployment and hardship, they point out, were unevenly spread, concentrated mainly in the old industrial areas of the North, Scotland and Wales, where the jobless rates were particularly high. For those in work the 1930s were not 'wasted years' but years of prosperity. Some people were 'enjoying a richer life than any previously known in the history of the world: longer holidays, shorter hours, higher real wages'.[3] Stevenson and Cook argue that British society was not as divided by social conflict as the popular recollection would have us believe. Using evidence from official documents, such as police records, as well as local and general election performances of the period, they suggest Britain was relatively stable and comparatively unified. They argue a consensus of values existed in British society between the wars.

The role of mass communication in the promotion of this consensus has been explored by a number of media historians.[4] Two basic approaches underpin these explorations. First, the mass media are seen as reflecting the need for escapism in the face of the problems of everyday life during the Depression years. George Perry believes British films in the 1930s helped to cheer people up by providing an 'escape from reality'. Perry's argument is summed up thus: 'times were difficult, but the cinema provided fantasy and escapism for a country beset by difficulty'.[5] Ralph Bond, a stalwart of the documentary film movement, describes mainstream British cinema as a 'dream factory' whose 'social purpose was clearly to act as a drug … to prevent people thinking'.[6] Brian Whitaker argues the British press provided a 'feel-good factor' in the face of rising tensions at home and abroad. He refers to pressures from advertisers to remain cheerful, citing as one example the *Daily Express* front page headline of 30 September 1938, which screamed 'There Will Be No War This Year Nor Next Year'.[7] The decline in the space devoted to public affairs stories in the 1930s is seen as another example of the desire to escape from the realities of politics and current affairs into a more comfortable world of gossip, entertainment and human interest stories.[8] The newsreels regularly shown in most cinemas in Britain in the 1930s 'were basically trivial in content and offered nothing to trouble the conscience'.[9]

The second approach emphasizes the role of the mass media in constructing the appearance of social harmony and stability. For sociologist Tom Burns, the notion of a united, stable nation was an illusion conjured up by the mass media. Burns argues the mass media were used to propagandize a particular image of British society. He talks of the 'imposed consensus of the 1930s', whereby the press, radio and cinema projected an image of national, social and cultural integration.[10] Roy Armes dismisses the idea of the cinema as a 'mere provider' of escapist entertainment, arguing that the films of the 1930s sought to 'organise the audience's experience in the sense of fostering social integration and the acceptance of social constraints'.[11] The British press deliberately downplayed the threat of war.[12] The editor of *The Times*, Geoffrey Dawson, wrote in 1937 that he did his 'utmost, night after night, to keep out of the paper anything that might hurt their (the German government's) susceptibilities'.[13] Newsreels painted a rosy picture of unemployment and its attendant problems, concentrating more on 'successes, at sport, in economic terms and in both domestic and international politics'.[14] The BBC constructed a particular image of political matters in the 1930s that amounted to a 'conspiracy of silence'.[15] Whether by sheer escapism or ideological construction, the media are seen as representing society as more unified and stable than it actually was.

This chapter explores the relationship between the mass media and the changes and transformations in British society during the inter-war years. Many of the characteristics of the modern mass media – today's old media – as well as their interaction with society were forged in the particular political, economic, social and cultural circumstances of the 1920s and the 1930s. These years were formative in the development of the British mass media. Traditionally, the last decade of the nineteenth century is seen as the 'birth' of mass communication. Asa Briggs identifies 1896 as an 'important date' in the history of mass communication and entertainment in Britain.[16] In that year Harmsworth founded the *Daily Mail*, Britain's first million-selling daily newspaper, Marconi first demonstrated wireless telegraphy and the first moving picture show took place at the Regents Street Polytechnic. While this date may represent the technological arrival of the modern media, it was the inter-war years that witnessed the embedding of the mass media in Britain. The reach of the media only developed to the extent it is possible to talk about communication that is 'mass' between 1919 and 1939,[17] and this can be expressed in stark quantitative terms. By the 1930s newspapers regularly sold in their millions. It was the 'defining decade for the direction of popular daily newspapers in Britain', with their 'greatest expansion in terms of sales and readers'.[18] Annual cinema attendances reached 903 million in 1934, with, on average, every man, woman and child in Britain visiting the cinema twenty-two times that year.[19] Annual attendances rose to over 1,000 million by the end of the decade, which led historian A.J.P. Taylor to describe going to the cinema in the 1930s as 'the essential social habit of the age'.[20] The wireless became 'an integral part of everyday life in Britain', with the number of households having wireless sets rising to over 9 million, reaching three-quarters of the British population by the end of the 1930s.[21]

The mass media became a matter of political and cultural debate in the 1920s and 1930s. Worries about the political influence of the press emerged in the early twentieth century. Concerns were expressed about the growing power of 'press barons' such as Lord Northcliffe, who, in 1903, could boast that 'every extension of the franchise renders more powerful the newspaper and less powerful the politician'.[22] By making the masses more visible, the popular press was seen as eroding the power of the ruling class. These concerns subsided during the 1914–18 war, when press proprietors such as Northcliffe, Rothermere and Beaverbrook joined the government. However, they were renewed in the war's immediate aftermath, accentuated by the emergence of new and what were perceived as more powerful media such as the wireless and cinema. Added urgency was provided by the coming of the age of mass democracy in 1918 with the extension of the vote to all men and to women over 30. Social unrest, including a police strike in 1919, fuelled official anxieties about the consequences of mass opinion for parliamentary politics. In 1924 Prime Minister Stanley Baldwin expressed his anxiety about the influence of the press when he declared: 'what proprietorship of these papers is aiming at is power, power without responsibility – the prerogative of the harlot throughout the ages'.[23] The Committee for Imperial Defence warned in 1921 that broadcasting had 'incalculable significance for political stability'.[24] The British state had to adjust to new problems of political, social and cultural management in the era of mass democracy. The media presented both an opportunity and an obstacle. They were seen as a potentially dangerous catalyst for growing political tension and a threat to the authority of the state as well as a means to manage public discourse and mould popular taste.

It was not only the political elite who feared the increasingly omniscient mass media. Moral reformers claimed the cinema destabilized the sexual and social order in Britain.[25] The intelligentsia debated the impact on cultural standards of popular newspapers, children's comics, popular women's weeklies and pulp fiction. The centrality of the mass media in social life in the inter-war years was reflected in popular culture. Novels, for example Aldous Huxley's *Brave New World*, satirized both the press and cinema.[26] The mass media were a theme of a number of films, including Hollywood's *The Front Page* (1931), the proto-typical newspaper film. Remade in subsequent decades, it helped to establish the stereotype of the journalist as a hard-drinking, street-wise and unscrupulous character who would do anything for a story.[27] Consideration of the media as the subject matter of literature, the arts and popular culture, as well as official concern about the power of the media, reflect the fact that political, social and cultural elites had to directly address mass society for the first time. The masses began to exert an influence on society by the expression of their preferences through the ballot box, the market and the media. Elites, fearing their position in society, sought to direct mass opinion in all its manifestations. Their response to the emergence of mass society varied; some attempted to reassert traditional values, some to educate the public to produce responsible citizens, while others sought to embrace the people in building a new social order. The result was a struggle over how to represent the masses and mass opinion.

Crisis of Representation

Understanding of the inter-war years is shaped not only by contemporaneous events but also by a 'complex crisis of representation' that beset the process of cultural production.[28] Baxendale and Pawling point out that inter-war Britain was not just a time of profound change in the society that was being represented but 'even more so in the status and situation of those who were doing the representing'.[29] They draw attention to the changes brought about within the intelligentsia by the arrival of the mass media. Intellectuals suffered a loss of group coherence and authority. The creation of new centres of cultural production in the press, cinema and radio led to a vast expansion and transformation in the cultural professions. Those describing themselves as 'authors, editors and journalists' increased threefold between 1891 and 1931, a rate of increase six times that of the whole population.[30] These cultural producers were a new breed, associated with the new industries of broadcasting and advertising and more dependent on corporate interests and the state. They were as likely to respond to their audiences' wants as impose their values from above. Previously intellectuals, predominantly upper middle and middle class, had had little contact with the culture and lives of working people.[31] Mass society presented a challenge to their cultural authority. Some retreated into cultural pessimism, while others tried to manage mass culture through education or censorship. There were those who sought to make some kind of commitment to working people, either through investigating or documenting working-class life or by directly allying themselves to the political struggles of working people.[32] Many of these had a sense of 'extreme urgency' in trying to bridge the wide gap between intellectuals and ordinary working people. They wanted to 'learn to communicate in forms and language clear and convincing to ordinary people'.[33] This engagement was as important as the economic crisis in bringing the conditions of the working class to the surface of British society.[34]

Many intellectuals saw the mass media as a means to reach, understand and radicalize the public.[35] George Orwell wrote about the 'immense educational possibilities in the radio, the cinema and the press'.[36] John Grierson, the founder of the documentary film movement, spoke of using the cinema as an 'instrument of education and propaganda to assist that process of reconstruction which our modern society must undergo'.[37] Reconciling the activities of the new cultural producers with the promotion of consensus values is an important aspect of understanding mass communication in the 1930s. Cultural producers between the wars, as Orwell said of the individual writer, could not escape the conditions they worked in any more than the corner shopkeeper could 'preserve his independence in the teeth of the chain-stores'.[38] They had to struggle to be free from vested interests, the most significant being business and the state. For those working in the mass media in the 1920s and 1930s, the context within which the struggle took place was shaped by developments in the mass media. This chapter seeks to highlight three crucial changes in the mass media in the inter-war years: convergence, control and centralization.

Convergence

Traditional historical studies of mass communication in the inter-war years emphasize the separate growth of different media. The present talk of the convergence of old media as a result of new technology reinforces this notion of separateness. Prior to the rapid technological changes in media technology of our own time, the most significant upheaval in media forms took place in the early twentieth century. Popular newspapers, cinema, the gramophone, photography and the wireless emerged at roughly the same time in a frenzy of invention between the mid-1890s and the First World War. Print, sound and visual communication collaborated, competed and clashed with one another in the years between the wars. Such interaction amounts to more than different media borrowing from each other. There was a convergence of various media forms. The coming together of the media industries in the inter-war years, in terms of processes and organizations as well as audiences and content, was significant.

The arrival of the BBC in 1922 initiated a debate over the social purpose of mass communication.[39] The institutional arrangements ultimately agreed for the delivery of sound broadcasting represented a new philosophy of communication – public service. The BBC was founded on a rejection of commercialism. Commercial interests had moved into the media industries on a large scale in the early twentieth century. The desire to maximize profits was a departure from the attitude of nineteenth-century media owners, who stressed the importance of social responsibility and political commitment as much as commercial returns. 'Fierce competition' in the newspaper industry between the wars saw a significant reduction in the number of newspaper titles as circulation mushroomed.[40] The intensity of competition in the film industry led to British film distribution, exhibition and production being swallowed up by American interests and ultimately having to be protected by state intervention.[41] The press barons' and movie moguls' search for commercial success was seen as undermining the mass media as a means of promoting religious, cultural, social and political enlightenment. By pandering to public taste and providing cheap entertainment to pack in audiences, the commercial media, it was argued, failed to give the newly enfranchised working class the necessary information and education to allow them to play a full part in the parliamentary process.

The BBC's first Director-General, John Reith, believed, like many others in the years following the First World War, that the commercial media were responsible for a fall in standards of public education and discourse. He accused the cinema, the popular press and the gramophone industry of pandering to the lowest common denominator by producing 'vulgar and hurtful' material. Reith believed broadcasting should lead, not follow, public taste, by providing people with material of a high moral and cultural tone. 'He who prides himself on giving what he thinks the public wants is often creating a fictitious demand for lower standards which he himself will then satisfy'.[42] The BBC firmly believed that the public service role of radio was to educate the audience by providing them with 'the best of everything'.[43] This mission was preserved in the institutional arrangements under which the BBC was established. The public financing of the BBC freed the Corporation from having to pander to the whims of the audience, and the BBC's monopoly of sound broadcasting in the United Kingdom ensured that there would be no competition that could result in the watering down of the public service mission to improve knowledge and taste. In this mission Reith and the BBC had no doubts as to what the public needed. Responding to criticism of the BBC's neglect of public tastes, Reith stated: 'It is occasionally represented to us that we are apparently setting out to give the public what we think they need, and not what they want, but often they do not know what they want, and very few what they need.'[44] The rationale of the new medium of radio as well as the way in which it was organized were strongly influenced by the perceived performance of the commercial mass media.

Graham Murdock[45] notes that, by privileging the needs of citizenship over the market, public service broadcasting helped to organize a new system of representation in the first half of the twentieth century. Public service broadcasting promoted a notion of citizenship that sought to embrace the man and woman in the street and establish their right to be informed and heard. Many of the BBC's efforts in this direction ended in unsatisfactory compromises. For many working people, the BBC was always part of the world of 'them' rather than 'us'.[46] However, the Corporation was central to initiating a debate about representation, and the broadening of representation became a feature of the mass media during the 1930s. Within the press, the *Daily Mirror* is credited with the development of a new style of popular journalism, ushering in a 'golden age' of the popular press in which '"the voice of the people" was truly heard via the mediation of independent journalism'.[47] In the cinema the documentary film movement attempted to capture the dignity of labour and the lives and problems of ordinary working men and women, while the photo magazine *Picture Post* represented the ordinariness of people's everyday lives.[48] The nature and extent of what some have called the 'democratization' of representation in the mass media in this period have to be seen in the context of the structural changes that took place in mass communication in the 1920s and 1930s. By the end of the 1930s there had been a shift towards more popular forms of representation, but what constituted the 'popular' was shaped by the developments within and outside of the mass media.

Convergence is apparent in the concentration of ownership of the media industries. The BBC's monopoly of sound broadcasting was increasingly mirrored in other media. The domination of media by a 'limited number of institutions which prospered by practising economies of scale'[49] has been documented in the histories of each mass medium in the 1930s. By 1937 five companies owned 43 per cent of daily and Sunday newspaper titles in the United Kingdom.[50] The Rank Organization had gained control of Britain's main film distributor and major film studios by the end of the 1930s, and with the successful takeover of the cinema halls of Deutsch and

Gaumont-British in 1941 the organization had attained unchallenged influence over the whole of the British film industry.[51] The British newsreel industry was dominated by five companies, all tied to a major film corporation: Gaumont, Pathe, Movietone, Paramount and Universal.[52] In the gramophone industry the merger of Columbia and the Gramophone Company into the Electrical and Musical Industries (EMI) in 1932 created a new company which, with its nearest rival Decca, exercised nearly total control of the British music business.[53] The economic conditions of the period facilitated the trend towards monopoly. Economic crises also hit the media industries in the 1920s and 1930s. For example, the collapse of the film industry in 1926 and 1938 not only necessitated further restructuring of the industry which centralized control in the hands of the larger corporations but also brought about government intervention to protect the industry. Similarly, a collapse in record sales in 1928 was a factor in the reorganization of the music industry. Industrial concentration was a feature of the British economy in this period. Britain had developed from one of the least concentrated industrial economies in 1914 to one of the most concentrated by 1939.[54] Through merger and amalgamation British industry was restructured into large-scale industrial combines and the mass media were no exception.

There was also an increasing involvement of media industries in one another's business. Cross-media ownership was a feature of the 1920s and 1930s. The publisher Cassell was sold to the press barons Kemsley and Camrose in the late 1920s.[55] Gaumont-British, before its takeover by Rank, had interests in a number of media industries. It set up the Bush Radio Company and bought Baird Television and the commercial radio station Radio Luxembourg, one of the BBC's overseas competitors in the 1930s, as well as the *Sunday Citizen* newspaper.[56] Parts of the newspaper industry recognized the potential of wireless technology. Lord Northcliffe was intimately involved in the early days of sound broadcasting.[57] His premature death in 1926, only months before the BBC was awarded its franchise, was a significant setback to press involvement in the new mass media. Convergence occurred in the exchange of personnel and practices between the media industries. As the BBC developed and had to cater to a broader range of social groups as well as compete with overseas radio stations such as Radio Luxembourg and Radio Normandie, personnel with experience of reaching a mass audience were brought in. A comprehensive review of BBC news provision resulted in the appointment of the editor of the *Westminster Gazette* in 1928 to run its news service. By the late 1930s a fully fledged BBC News Department was led by experienced Fleet Street journalists.[58] Camera workers for the newsreel companies often began as press photographers.[59] By the end of the 1930s it was common for people to work across a range of media. One prominent example was the novelist and playwright J.B. Priestley. Priestley's plays and novels featured in the output of the film industry – his best-selling book *The Good Companions* was turned into a film in 1933. He adapted stories and wrote scripts for the film industry, including *Sing As We Go* (1934) for box-office star Gracie Fields. He was a regular contributor to the BBC Talks Department and his Sunday night talks in the early days of the Second World War were listened to by 10 million people. The exchange of personnel between media led to a gradual sharing of the values, practices and techniques of media production.

One area where the interaction between media shaped the nature of the product delivered was news. The press, news agencies and newsreel companies sought to 'undermine radio's innate competitive advantage of immediacy'.[60] They attempted to prevent the BBC from becoming an 'independent provider of news'. Their pressure, however, gave BBC news a distinct brand in an already overcrowded marketplace for news and helped the Corporation to establish a reputation for authority and integrity. Sian Nicholas documents how restrictions on news gathering and processing determined BBC news.[61] BBC news was limited, with a ban in the early years on broadcasting news before 7 p.m. As a result, bulletins were short and sharp. Their brevity and clarity were accompanied by an impersonal style of news reading. Obliged to rewrite raw material supplied by the news agencies, the Corporation excluded sensational copy, presenting news in a factual, impersonal and accurate way.[62] By distancing itself from the sensationalism of the press and news agencies, the BBC enhanced its 'air of authority' as a news provider,[63] and by the end of the 1930s 'all but a small minority gave more credence to the political objectivity of the broadcast news when compared with the coverage of the press'.[64] The tensions between the BBC and the other news media assisted the development of the style, form and reputation of BBC news.

The effect of broadcasting on the content of the press is a matter of conjecture, but Fleet Street editors such as Wickham Steed and Hamilton Fyfe argued that wireless reporting helped to keep newspapers honest.[65] The BBC's focus on impartiality made the press more careful in its gathering and reporting of the facts. Newspapers in the inter-war years began to place more emphasis on the distinction between fact and comment. Stephen Tallents, BBC Public Relations Director, believed the arrival of radio made it more difficult for 'a newspaper with a private axe to grind' to 'invent or suppress news'.[66] Newspapers and newsreels, to compete with the immediacy of radio, were forced to extend the definition of news beyond that of the worlds of business and politics.[67] The rise of the human interest story in the British press in the 1930s is partially explained by the competition from other media. Radio and the cinema had an impact on the layout and presentation of newspapers. To compete, newspaper 'headlines became bolder, columns were doubled and articles … were frequently supported by photographs' with the 'stress on shorter sentences, concise paragraphs and bolder presentation'.[68] The tightly knit narrow columns of fine print that characterized the British newspaper at the end of the First World War gave way to the broader columns, larger headlines and lower density of print of the newspaper of the 1930s.

Matters of convergence in the inter-war years ultimately centred around the term 'middlebrow', a term specific to Britain in the 1920s and 1930s. Critical debates around the content and performance of the mass media in this period were conducted in the language of 'brows'. 'Middlebrow' was a specifically British term meant to distinguish between 'high culture' or 'high brow' and popular mass culture or 'low brow'. Its use reflected the 'anxieties over cultural distinction attendant on the explosion of the mass communication media'.[69] The mass media, and in particular the BBC, described by Virginia Woolf in her essay 'Middlebrow' as the 'Betwixt and Between Company', were seen as the main agents for the diffusion of middlebrow values.[70] Writers such as Priestley became 'chroniclers of middle class life and the apologists of middle class values'; popular newspapers increasingly tried to appeal to the middle classes and the BBC promoted 'middle of the road' forms of music and entertainment.[71] Such diffusion was seen by some as leading to the 'homogenization of taste', sapping both high and popular culture of their vitality.[72] For others, the middle-brow output of the mass media reflected the needs of those working in the industries to balance the political pressures from government and critics and the popular demands from audiences to be entertained and represented.

Control

The growing presence of the mass media in British life between the wars changed the nature of political journalism and the relationship of authority to journalism and the media. Political control of the press in the nineteenth century rested on a basis of shared interests and common understanding. The 'gentlemen of the press' had equal status with those who exercised political power in British society and 'derived their influence from personal involvement in high political circles'.[73] As a result, newspapers supported parties or political factions or individual politicians. Mass communication shattered this cosy world by bringing the voice of public opinion into the political arena, the result of which was the development of new and more sophisticated mechanisms to manage the flow of information in society. The government was able to lay down the framework within which the mass media represented and reported key events. The feature of this process was the way in which the media colluded with the means of censorship, propaganda and publicity which politicians and government officials deployed to adjust to the new world of mass communication.

Peter Hennessy, Michael Cockerell and David Walker describe how a system of information management was built in Britain from the late nineteenth century onwards.[74] They identify three pillars to the system: draconian legislation to restrict the flow of information, a political news cartel and the commercialization of information. These pillars were firmly cemented into place in the inter-war years. Direct censorship was a feature of mass communication in the 1920s and 1930s. The British Board of Film Censors (BBFC), established in 1913, had, by the coming of sound to the cinema in 1926, extended its control over film. It was able to vet scripts in advance and cut material from the finished product. The grounds on which films could be censored and banned were coded into a number of rules which, according to James Robertson, encapsulated the moral and social values of late Victorian and Edwardian Britain.[75] What was shown in British cinemas during the 1930s was so carefully controlled that the BBFC's president could boast in 1937: 'We may take pride in observing that there is not a single film showing in London today which deals with any of the burning questions of the day.'[76] The extraordinary thing about the board's operation was that it was a voluntary system. The BBFC had been set up by the industry and was financed by fees from the producers submitting their films. While the head of the board, the chief censor, was appointed by government, the BBFC had no legal status and producers were not obliged to submit their films. The success of film censorship in the 1930s was underpinned by the complicity of the film industry. Their cooperation is an example of what has been described as the 'British way of censorship', central to which is self-censorship and informal understandings between those in power and those in control of the media that some things are best not reported or represented.[77]

Self-censorship was a feature of all forms of media production in the 1920s and 1930s. The newsreels were very careful in what they reported. Pressure from government, politicians and local authorities reduced the capacity of the newsreel companies for independent, informed opinion.[78] The penalty for ignoring government sensibilities could be severe, as British Paramount found in 1934 when it covered a demonstration by hunger marchers outside the Home Office. Its very livelihood was threatened when it was subsequently denied access to report any official event.[79] While items were pulled or not shown, more often the companies simply sought to avoid controversy. Informal control over the newsreels was exerted through the close ties between the newsreel companies and the Conservative Party. For example, the general manager of *British Movietone News* was a leading member of the Conservative and Unionist Film Association and its editor-in-chief had been a Conservative candidate in the 1935 general election.[80] BBC Radio exercised similar caution. One incident that highlighted the Corporation's sensitivity involved William Ferrie, a communist trade union official. In a talk responding to a leading industrialist who claimed the conditions of the working class had improved considerably in the twentieth century, Ferrie departed from his agreed script and was immediately cut off.[81] The BBC also took great care in reporting international events: 'independent expressions of views' on the European situation on the wireless were discouraged.[82]

The press was also willing to cooperate with the censoring of news about controversial political topics. This cooperation resulted from its involvement in the lobby system. The system had its roots in the 1880s, when, following a Sinn Fein bomb in the House of Commons in 1884, public access to parliament was withdrawn. A list of accredited journalists who could enter the Members' lobby was drawn up. Political reporting was conducted under these terms until the 1920s, when in response to requests from correspondents the lobby system was set up.[83] This system created a news cartel by setting up a formal mechanism for the flow of information from government to press. Political reporting was conducted through this cartel. A system of weekly unattributable briefings, usually given by the prime minister's press secretary, a post created in 1931, was established, and in return for the regular supply of information members of the press accepted restrictions on what they could and could not report.[84] As Richard Cockett states: 'It was in the 1930s that the peculiarly English customs and habits that had governed the relationship between the government and press became institutionalized by Whitehall to the permanent advantage of the incumbent government.'[85] The system was seen as engineering press support for the government's policy of 'appeasement'. The close relationship between political correspondents, their editors and the government helped to keep criticism of the Nazi regime out of the newspapers and minimized any talk of war. Outspoken critics of appeasement, including Winston Churchill, were denied access to the press. Even

Liberal and Labour-leaning papers, such as the *Daily Herald* and the *News Chronicle*, often cooperated in such a policy.

Politicians, however, realized they could not simply depend on crude mechanisms such as censorship to effectively manage the mass electorate. Government and political parties, following the experience of the Great War, established an apparatus to 'sell' information it wanted released. Press officers, official spokespersons, public relations advisors and information officers became a feature of government in the inter-war years. The first ministry to set up a unit to perform this function was the News Department of the Foreign and Commonwealth Office founded in 1916. The Air Ministry was the first government department to appoint a press officer in 1919, with the Ministry of Health and War Office soon following its example. Until 1926 the peacetime press and publicity work undertaken by the government was modest in scope, but the establishment of the Empire Marketing Board (EMB) in 1926 marked the advent of a large-scale government propaganda and publicity machine. The EMB was primarily established to promote trade with the Empire but was also seen by some government ministers as a means to counter the expansion of socialism in Britain. Under the direction of Stephen Tallents, it was highly innovative in the area of publicity. Tallents appreciated the importance of advertising and 'translated the message of the advertising profession into a language of government service'.[86] The EMB took out advertisements in the British press and employed a press officer to inform the newspapers of its activities. It also appointed a representative of the BBC to its publicity committee and persuaded the Corporation to broadcast numerous talks on the Empire.[87] The board was most innovative in its use of film and created, under the leadership of John Grierson, a Film Unit which attracted many of the leading lights of the British documentary film movement. The unit moved with Tallents when he went to the General Post Office in 1934, where it produced some of its best work. From 1933 to the outbreak of the Second World War, the Post Office spent more money on publicity than any other government department.[88] It acted as a central body for official government publicity and, under Tallents, developed public relations activities to increase general awareness of government business.

Many of the techniques of modern political propaganda and campaigning were developed during the inter-war years. They were pioneered by the Conservative Party under Baldwin, who emphasized the need for 'unceasing propaganda' to maintain an educated democracy.[89] Baldwin and Neville Chamberlain quickly learned to master the techniques of appearing before the microphone and in the newsreels.[90] Baldwin was the 'first politician to demonstrate that radio required a conversational style distinct from that suited to platform oratory'.[91] He first used the newsreels in 1923, when they were still silent, and by 1930 showed himself to be a skilled performer in talking newsreels.[92] Baldwin also pioneered the 'sound bite': to counter newsreel editors selecting extracts from his speeches, he ordered his staff to prepare deliberately short speeches.[93] To get around the ban by commercial cinema chains on overt political propaganda, the Conservative Party had its own mobile picture show, with twenty-two vans touring the country during the 1931 general election.[94] The National Publicity Bureau spearheaded the publicity efforts of the government in the late 1930s. Set up by the national government in 1935, the bureau 'carried through the first modern, large scale propaganda campaign on a national basis in the history of British politics, yet it worked so unobtrusively and anonymously that few outside the ranks of the professional politician and organization men had any appreciation of its potency'.[95] The bureau, as a 'non-political' organization, was designed to bring about national unity on a non-partisan basis.[96] However, working closely with the Conservative Party, the main partner in the national government, the bureau utilized modern forms of mass communication to pioneer many innovative techniques of propaganda.

Centralization

The growing convergence of media forms in the 1930s together with the increased sophistication of state control mechanisms provided the basis for the final feature of the development of the mass media in inter-war Britain. Media industries at the start of the 1920s had a strong local dimension. By the Second World War media production had become largely centred on London and the south-east and highly 'national' in outlook. This process made the British media system one of the most centralized in the liberal democratic world. The regional press, especially morning papers, experienced a significant decline between the wars. Strong circulation growth was accompanied by a severe contraction in the number of regional titles. The number of morning regional newspapers fell from forty-one in 1920 to twenty-three in 1937.[97] Helped by the expansion of the railway network, the London press took control of the newspaper market in England and Wales, although Scotland was able to maintain its own national press.[98] Similarly radio broadcasting changed from a network of local stations serving the main conurbations of Britain into a large corporation serving the whole country from its base in London. The new system established by the BBC in 1930 distinguished between a National and Regional Service, but this relationship was not one of equality. The National Service was the senior partner and most of the new BBC Regions had little cultural coherence. London controlled production and the nature of regional programming was determined by what it wanted to do. Reith and London further eroded local autonomy throughout the 1930s by removing programme decisions from programme makers and putting them into the hands of a small elite of London-based administrators. Regional programming as a result ultimately became a 'chink in between what London devises and dictates'.[99] The redrawing of the map of the media industries was also apparent in the shift of film production to the south-east of England. The early days of British cinema located film-makers in Brighton, Yorkshire, Lancashire as well as London.[100] Regionalized production soon gave way to film production centred on London at Elstree, Pinewood and Denham.

The centralization of production was accompanied by a concerted effort by the national government between 1931 and 1937 to use the media to promote a sense of national unity and patriotism. In a fragmented society they decided that the sense of being British was the one force that could push aside economic, class and regional divisions. George Orwell said in his famous essay *The Lion and the Unicorn* that, while riven with divisions, the vast majority of Britons 'feel themselves to be a single nation and are conscious of resembling one another more than they resemble foreigners'.[101] Government sought to play on such sentiments by findings forms of representation that supported this common-sense notion of belonging to a single nation. Baldwin used the mass media to put across at every opportunity the common-sense notion of Britishness which presented a 'picture of a sensible and moderate people united behind their government, true to their historic traditions'.[102] Tallents, while at the EMB, published a pamphlet in 1932, *The Projection of England*, which listed 'fitting representations' of the country's institutions and values. He argued the British had a reputation for disinterestedness, justice, coolness, fair dealing, fair play and institutions such as Parliament, the Monarchy and the Armed Forces that were the envy of the world. The 'sympathetic and patriotic depiction of British institutions and British character' received general support in the media.[103] The press, film, BBC and newsreels promoted national unity, national character and national institutions, downplaying class, regional and other national identities within the UK.

The newsreels constantly contrasted the calm, comfortable and contented way of life in Britain with the tensions and divisions abroad. A Gaumont-British story from August 1936 is typical of the coverage. Originally scripted under the title 'Wonderful Britain', the newsreel told its audience, after a round up of events abroad, that 'in a spirit not of boastfulness but rather of gratitude we turn from these fitful scenes to fortunate Britain still, with its tradition of sanity, the rock of steadying influence amid the eddying streams of world affairs. British industries have shaken off the chains that kept them fettered in the aftermath of the world war'.[104] The BBC took its role as a *British* institution very seriously. The primary aim was to standardize the BBC's output around a particular notion of Britishness and national culture which cut across class, sectarian, local and social divisions. The decision to impose a standardized form of speech across the network was an example of the efforts of the Corporation to define itself as a 'central, national authority acting on behalf of the nation as a whole'.[105] National events such as the King's Christmas Day speech, the FA Cup Final, the Derby and the Boat Race were broadcast to bring together the British people to produce a sense of belonging. The aim was to manufacture that 'we-feeling' by 'making the nation real and tangible through a whole range of images and symbols, events and ceremonies, relayed to audiences direct and live'.[106]

Newspapers, in spite of their distinctive political platforms, increasingly projected themselves as national entities. *The Times* summed up this feeling when it described itself as a 'national institution conducted solely in the best interests of the nation and the Empire'.[107] Nearly all the major Fleet Street titles, with the exception of the *Daily Herald* and *News Chronicle*, were Conservative in their ideology and outlook and responded with enthusiasm to calls for more sympathetic and patriotic depictions of British institutions and the British character.[108] The main rhetorical theme of Britain's best-selling newspapers during the inter-war years, the *Daily Mail* and the *Daily Express*, was that of national unity and national purpose.[109] British cinema also resoundingly endorsed the 'national'.[110]

Centralization did not happen without some resistance. The efforts to project a common-sense notion of national unity and identity that appealed to everyone were problematic. Opposition to BBC centralization came from a number of sources. The Sheffield relay station fought strongly against its closure in 1928 with a local campaign bringing together the Chamber of Commerce, the press, trade unions and members of the public. Reith believed the campaigners were 'short sighted and irritating to take such a purely local view' and forced through the closure.[111] Reith's mission to replace local output with metropolitan programming, bringing local audiences into contact with national figures and national events, was opposed by several regional directors.[112] Peter Eckersley, who established the BBC's regional scheme in 1928, believed Reith's interpretation of the scheme was a betrayal of its original purpose, to reflect the diversity of culture of the United Kingdom. Eckersley was dismissed in 1929. Publicly his departure was attributed to his being a co-respondent in a divorce case, but he insisted that his attempt to organize a revolt of regional directors was the real reason.[113] Eckerlsey's dismissal did not quell the rebellious mood of regional directors.

Fractious relations between London and the regions characterized the BBC in the 1930s. Certain regions campaigned for greater recognition. The BBC's regional scheme reflected 'administrative, technical and economic considerations before any notion of what regionalism might mean in terms of people, places and cultural characteristics'.[114] Some 'regions' sought greater acknowledgement of their special characteristics. Most noticeable was the situation in Wales. The so-called 'Welsh Controversy' lasted until 1937, when a separate Welsh region was finally fully established. A bitter struggle was intensified by Reith's 'deep dislike for the Welsh'.[115] After one meeting with Welsh MPs and representatives, Reith wrote in his diary that 'they are the most unpleasant and unreliable people with whom it has ever been my misfortune to deal'.[116] The regional struggle culminated in the Siepmann Report in 1936. Charles Siepmann had been Head of Talks and a strong advocate of centralization. His review was in part motivated by the activities of the BBC Northern Region, which under its director E.A. Harding was pioneering many of the techniques of radio documentary and actuality we take for granted today. In doing so, Harding and his colleagues touched on sensitive subjects such as unemployment and ordinary people's views of their conditions. In a year of Charter renewal such activities caused consternation in the upper echelons of the BBC. Siepmann's report surprisingly came down on the side of the regions, but its recommendations were never acted on. The outbreak of war saw patriotism sweep aside regional concerns.

Tension between the regions and London appeared in other media. There were attempts in the press to stave off chain control, for example the abortive struggle inside Westminster Press to maintain regional newspapers favourable to the Liberal Party.[117] In the cinema, local identities were acknowledged on screen. Commercial needs demanded the production of pictures that represented life in working-class communities throughout Britain. The films of northern stars such as Gracie Fields and George Formby were box-office successes. Fields, 'Our Gracie', was Britain's highest paid film star in the 1930s.[118] A 'Lancashire lass', she retained her strong regional accent, and her 'ordinariness' and roots in the North were part of her appeal to the film-going public. However, she came to personify the spirit of national unity and cohesiveness that the government sought to promote and the mass media were willing to communicate. According to Jeffrey Richards,[119] her film career shows 'the process by which she was transformed from a working class hero into a symbol of national unity'. Her film *Sing As We Go* (1934) provided an anthem for the Depression and represented the subtle subversion of working-class discontent.[120] The film is set in the Lancashire cotton industry and unemployment is contextualized by the community pulling together and expressions of patriotic fervour in the face of adversity.[121] The film's writer, J.B. Priestley, is reported to have wanted to portray the problems caused by unemployment to a greater extent than he was allowed.[122]

While regional accents and class differences were represented in the British media in the 1930s, they were usually incorporated into the discourse of national unity and consensus. This consensus was constructed around a particular notion of the nation. The values and identity promoted by the national government were 'far removed from the series of multiple identities which could be said to exist in Britain at the time'.[123] The concept of Britishness was synonymous with Englishness and a class bias. The output of the mass media was predominantly middle class, middle England and middlebrow. The mass media's positive response to the government's desire to promote a national consensus in the inter-war years is often attributed to the 'instability of the times'. However, there are a number of reasons to explain why the media shared the government's vision of national life in the inter-war years. There were close connections between the media industries and political parties and politicians. Pushing Britishness was also a means by which to resist the growing threat to mass media and mass culture from the US. American commercial and financial interests were eating into the British media in the 1930s. This was most apparent in the film industry, but US influence was also found elsewhere in the magazine, popular music, newsreel and advertising industries. Projecting Britishness was seen as a device to ensure US values would not increasingly take over British audiences and threaten the product and output of the British media.

Conclusion

It is wrong to see the mass media in Britain in the 1930s as either providing escapist entertainment or constructing a particular ideological consensus. This ignores the interaction between the media, the state and British society which helped to shape the nature of mass communication in Britain. This chapter argues that three trends can be seen as shaping this interaction: convergence, control and centralization. These developments were not self-evident. Relations between and within the media, the state and society can be characterized by struggle. One crucial struggle was between those who worked in the media industries who placed a value, moral, political or artistic, on what they produced, and those who owned and controlled these industries. At the heart of this conflict was a clash over who best satisfied the needs and wants of the audience. Crucially, these struggles were forged in the conditions of crisis that characterized the 'Devil's Decade'. While it is true to say that the conditions in Britain in the 1930s were complex, confused and uneven, with circumstances varying significantly across the country, the perceptions of those in positions of power and in the media and cultural industries were shaped by the notion of crisis. They sought to respond to what they perceived as growing instability in society and the need to represent this crisis and those caught up in it. Media owners and government officials attempted to extend their influence and control over the media and promote messages of unity, whilst cultural producers aimed to represent working people and the plight and conditions that faced them. This played out in the notion of a 'consensus', or a 'fusion of the best of right and left' as one leading commentator of the 'middle way' suggested in 1938. The exact nature of this 'fusion' varied between media, but the way in which mechanisms were developed to achieve it had a lasting effect on the structures, nature, output and processes of mass communication in Britain.

Notes

1. J. Baxendale and C. Pawling, *Narrating the Thirties* (London, 1996).

2. J. Stevenson and C. Cook, *The Slump* (London, 1977).

3. Quoted in Stevenson and Cook, *The Slump*, p. 3.

4. Anthony Aldgate explores this argument in a number of articles on the British cinema: for example, 'Ideological Consensus in British Cinema: Feature Films, 1935–47', in K. Short (ed.), *Feature Films as History* (London, 1981); 'The Age of Consensus: South Riding', in A. Aldgate and J. Richards (eds), *Best of British* (London, 2002), and 'Comedy, Class and Containment: British Domestic Cinema of the 1930s', in J. Curran and V. Porter (eds), *British Cinema History* (London, 1977).

5. G. Perry, *The Great Picture Show* (London, 1974).

6. R. Bond, 'Cinema in the Thirties: Documentary Film and the Labour Movement', *in* J. Clarke, M. Heinemann, D. Margolies and C. Snee (eds), *Culture and Crisis in Britain in the 30s* (London, 1979), p. 245.

7. B. Whitaker, *News Ltd.: Why You Can't Read All About It* (London, 1981), p. 68.

8. J. Curran, A. Douglas and G. Whannel, 'The Political Economy of the Human Interest Story', in A. Smith (ed.), *Newspapers and Democracy* (Cambridge, MA, 1981).

9. C. Day Lewis cited in A. Aldgate, 'The Newsreels, Public Order and the Projection of Britain', in J. Curran, A. Smith and P. Wingate (eds), *Impacts and Influences: Essays on Media Power in the Twentieth Century* (London, 1987), p. 145.

10. T. Burns, 'The Organisation of Public Opinion', in J. Curran, M. Gurevitch and J. Woollacott (eds), *Mass Communications and Society* (London, 1977), pp. 63–4.

11. R. Armes, *A Critical History of the British Cinema* (London, 1978).

12. R. Cockett, *Twilight of Truth: Chamberlain, Appeasement and the Manipulation of the Press* (London, 1989).

13. F. Williams, *Dangerous Estate: The Anatomy of Newspapers* (London, 1957), p. 234.

14. K. Lunn, 'Reconsidering Britishness: the Construction and Significance of National Identity in Twentieth Century Britain', in B. Jenkins and S. Sofos (eds), *Nation and Identity in Contemporary Europe* (London, 1992), p. 93.

15. P. Scannell and D. Cardiff, *A Social History of Broadcasting* (Oxford, 1991), p. 87.

16. A. Briggs, *Mass Entertainment: The Origins of a Modern Industry* (Adelaide, 1960), p. 9.

17. R. Williams, *The Long Revolution* (London, 1980), p. 189.

18. M. Conboy, *The Press and Popular Culture* (London, 2003), p. 113.

19. K. Williams, *Get Me a Murder a Day! A History of Mass Communication in Britain* (London, 1998), p. 81.

20. Quoted in J. Richards, *The Age of the Dream Palaces* (London, 1984), p. 50.

21. Williams, *Get Me a Murder a Day!*, p. 88.

22. Quoted in D.G. Boyce, 'Crusaders without Chains: Power and the Press Barons', in J. Curran, A. Smith and P. Wingate, *Impacts and Influences*, p. 100.

23. J. Curran and J. Seaton, *Power without Responsibility* (London, 1999), p. 42.

24. N. Pronay and D. Spring, *Propaganda, Politics and Film 1918–45* (London, 1982), p. 13.

25. Williams, *Get Me a Murder a Day!*, p. 72.

26. Keith Williams, *British Writers and the Media 1930–45* (London, 1996).

27. H. Zynda, 'A Form of Low Life – How Films Portray Press', *Journalism Studies Review* (July 1981), pp. 6–12.

28. Baxendale and Pawling, *Narrating the Thirties*, p. 5.

29. Baxendale and Pawling, *Narrating the Thirties*, p. 3.

30. Ibid.

31. Clarke *et al.*, *Culture and Crisis*, p. 8.

32. For a discussion of the role of intellectuals in the inter-war years see Baxendale and Pawling, *Narrating the Thirties*, chapters 1 and 2, and F. Mulhearn, *The Moment of Scrutiny* (London, 1979).

33. Clarke *et al.*, *Culture and Crisis*, p. 9.

34. J. Klugmann, 'The Crisis in the Thirties: A View from the Left', in Clarke *et al.*, *Culture and Crisis*.

35. Williams, *British Writers*.

36. Quoted in Williams, *British Writers*, p. 233.

37. Quoted in P. Taylor, *British Propaganda in the Twentieth Century: Selling Democracy* (Edinburgh, 1999), p. 91.

38. Quoted in Williams, *British Writers*, p. 14.

39. See G. Murdock, 'Citizens, Consumers and Public Culture', in M. Skovmand and K. Schroder (eds), *Media Cultures: Reappraising Transnational Media* (London, 1992), pp. 17–42.

40. G. Murdock and P. Golding, 'The Structure, Ownership and Control of the Press 1914–76', in D.G. Boyce, J. Curran and P. Wingate (eds), *British Newspaper History* (London, 1977), p. 131.

41. S. Street and M. Dickinson, *Cinema and State: The Film Industry and the British Government 1927–84* (London, 1985).

42. Scannell and Cardiff, *A Social History of Broadcasting*, p. 7.

43. J. Reith, *Broadcast over Britain* (London, 1924), pp. 147–8.

44. Quoted in P. Scannell and D. Cardiff, *The Social Foundations of British*

Broadcasting, Supplementary Material Units 1–6 Open University Mass Communications and Society Course (Milton Keynes, 1977), p. 18.

45. Murdock, 'Citizens, Consumers and Public Culture'.

46. Scannell and Cardiff, *The Social Foundations of British Broadcasting*, p. 27.

47. M. Bromley, 'Was It the Mirror Wot Won It? The Development of the Tabloid Press during the Second World War', in *Millions Like Us: British Culture in the Second World War* (Liverpool, 1999), p. 5.

48. See A. Higson, 'Britain's Outstanding Contribution to Film: the Documentary-realist Tradition', in C. Barr (ed.), *All Our Yesterdays: 90 Years of British Cinema* (London, 1986); S. Hood, 'John Grierson and the Documentary Film Movement', in J. Curran and V. Porter (eds), *British Cinema History* (New York, 1983); S. Hall, 'The Social Eye of Picture Post', *Working Papers in Cultural Studies 2* (Birmingham, 1972); T. Hopkinson (ed.), *Picture Post 1938–50* (Harmondsworth, 1970).

49. D.L. Le Mahieu, *A Culture for Democracy* (Oxford, 1988), p. 11.

50. Murdock and Golding, 'The Structure, Ownership and Control of the Press 1914–76', p. 135.

51. Williams, *Get Me a Murder a Day!*, p. 87.

52. A. Aldgate, *Cinema and History: British Newsreels and the Spanish Civil War* (London, 1979), p. 23.

53. S. Frith, 'The Making of the British Record Industry', in Curran, Smith and Wingate, *Impacts and Influences*, p. 282.

54. T. Ryall, *Alfred Hitchcock and the British Cinema* (London, 1996), p. 36.

55. J. Feather, *A History of Publishing* (London, 1988), p. 203.

56. M. Chanan, *The Dream That Kicks* (London, 1980), p. 57.

57. S. Taylor, *The Great Outsiders: Northcliffe, Rothermere and the Daily Mail* (London, 1996), pp. 201–3.

58. P. Scannell, and D. Cardiff, 'Serving the Nation: Public Service Broadcasting before the War', in B. Waites, T. Bennett and G. Martin (eds), *Popular Culture: Past and Present* (London, 1982), p. 175.

59. Aldgate, *Cinema and History*, p. 37.

60. S. Nicholas, 'All the News That's Fit to Broadcast: the Popular Press versus the BBC, 1922–45', in P. Catterall, C. Seymour-Ure and A. Smith (eds), *Northcliffe's Legacy: Aspects of the British Popular Press, 1986–1996* (London, 2000), p. 142.

61. Nicholas, 'All the News'.

62. Nicholas, 'All the News', p. 131.

63. Nicholas, 'All the News', p. 134.

64. M. Pegg, *Broadcasting and Society 1918–39* (London, 1983), p. 150.

65. Nicholas, 'All the News', p. 138.

66. Nicholas, 'All the News', p. 137.

67. Le Mahieu, *A Culture for Democracy*, p. 23.

68. Pegg, *Broadcasting and Society*, p. 151.

69. L. Napper, 'British Cinema and the Middlebrow', in J. Ashby and A. Higson (eds), *British Cinema, Past and Present* (London, 2000), p. 111.

70. D. Cardiff, 'Mass Middelbrow Laughter: the Origins of BBC Comedy', *Media, Culture and Society*, 10 (1988), pp. 41–60.

71. Cardiff, ' Mass Middlebrow', p. 46.

72. Napper, 'British Cinema', p. 113.

73. D.G. Boyce, 'Crusaders without Chains: Power and the Press Barons 1896–1951', in Curran, Smith and Wingate, *Impacts and Influences*, p. 100.

74. P. Hennessy, M. Cockerell and D. Walker, *Sources Close to the Prime Minister* (London, 1984).

75. See J. Robertson, *The British Board of Film Censors: Film Censorship in Britain 1896–1950* (London, 1985); J. Robertson, *The Hidden Cinema: British Film Censorship in Action 1913–75* (London, 1989).

76. Quoted in Street and Dickinson, *Cinema and State*, p. 8.

77. P. Schlesinger, G. Murdock and P. Elliott, *Televising Terrorism* (London, 1984), pp. 110–11.

78. Aldgate, *Cinema and History*, p. 90.

79. N. Pronay, 'Rearmament and the British Public: Policy and Propaganda', in Curran, Smith and Wingate (eds), *Impacts and Influences*.

80. Pronay, 'Rearmament and the British Public', p. 75.

81. Scannell and Cardiff, *A Social History of Broadcasting*, pp. 290–1.

82. See Scannell and Cardiff, *A Social History of Broadcasting*, chapter 5.

83. A. Sparrow, *Obscure Scribblers: A History of Parliamentary Journalism* (London, 2003).

84. Sparrow, *Obscure Scribblers*; Hennessy *et al.*, *Sources Close to the Prime Minister*.

85. Cockett, *Twilight of Truth*, p. 2.

86. S. Constantine, 'Bringing the Empire Alive: the Empire Marketing Board and Imperial Propaganda', in J. MacKenzie (ed.), *Imperialism and Popular Culture* (Manchester, 1986), pp. 202, 204.

87. Constantine, 'Bringing the Empire Alive', p. 207.

88. P. Swann, 'John Grierson and the G.P.O. Film Unit 1933–39', *Historical Journal of Film, Radio and Television*, 3(1) (1983), pp. 19–34.

89. Taylor, *British Propaganda in the Twentieth Century*, p. 93.

90. J. Ramsden, 'Baldwin and Film', in Pronay and Spring, *Propaganda, Politics and Film 1918–45*.

91. M. Rosenbaum, *From Soap Box to Soundbite: Party Political Campaigning in Britain since 1945* (London, 1997), p. 43

92. M. Scammell, *Designer Politics* (London, 1995), p. 34.

93. Rosenbaum, *From Soap Box to Soundbite*, p. 93.

94. Scammell, *Designer Politics*, p. 35.

95. R. Casey, 'The National Publicity Bureau and British Party Propaganda', *The Public Opinion Quarterly* (October 1939), p. 624.

96. Casey, 'The National Publicity Bureau', p. 625.

97. Murdock and Golding, 'The Structure, Ownership and Control of the Press', p. 134.

98. S. Nicholas, 'Being British: Creeds and Cultures', in K. Robbins (ed.), *The British Isles 1901–51* (Oxford, 2002), p. 110.

99. K. Kumar, 'Public Service Broadcasting and the Public Interest', in C.

MacCabe and O. Stewart (eds), *The BBC and Public Service Broadcasting* (Manchester, 1986), p. 54.

100. Ryall, *Alfred Hitchcock and the British Cinema*, p. 36.

101. Quoted in Lunn, 'Reconsidering Britishness', p. 90.

102. Lunn, 'Reconsidering Britishness', p. 95.

103. Lunn, 'Reconsidering Britishness', p. 92.

104. A. Aldgate, 'The Newsreels, Public Order and the Projection of Britain', in Curran, Smith and Wingate (eds), *Impacts and Influences*, p. 151.

105. Scannell and Cardiff, *The Social Foundations of British Broadcasting*, p. 19.

106. Scannell and Cardiff, *A Social History of Broadcasting*, p. 277.

107. A. Marwick, 'Press, Pictures and Sound: the Second World War and the British Experience', *Daedalus*, 135 (Fall 1982).

108. Ibid.

109. T. Jeffrey and K. McCelland, 'A World Fit to Live in: the *Daily Mail* and the Middle Classes 1918–39', in Curran, Smith and Wingate (eds), *Impacts and Influences*, pp. 9–27.

110. For a discussion of British national cinema in the 1930s see J. Sedgwick, 'The Market for Feature Films in Britain, 1934: A Viable National Cinema', *Historical Journal of Film, Radio and Television*, 14(1) (1994).

111. Scannell and Cardiff, *A Social History of Broadcasting*, p. 319.

112. J. Davies, *Broadcasting and the BBC in Wales* (Cardiff, 1994), p. 42; Pegg, *Broadcasting and Society 1918–39*, p. 22.

113. Quoted in Davies, *Broadcasting and the BBC in Wales*, p. 42.

114. Scannell and Cardiff, *A Social History of Broadcasting*, p. 322.

115. Davies, *Broadcasting and the BBC in Wales*, p. 6.

116. Davies, *Broadcasting and the BBC in Wales*, p. 69.

117. P. Gliddon, 'The Political Importance of Provincial Newspapers, 1903–45: the Rowntrees and the Liberal Press', *Twentieth Century British History*, 14(1) (2003), pp. 24–42.

118. Richards, *The Age of the Dream Palaces*, p. 169.

119. Richards, *The Age of the Dream Palaces*, p. 177.

120. Richards, *The Age of the Dream Palaces*, pp. 169, 177.

121. A. Aldgate, 'The British Cinema in the 1930s', Open University course Unit 7, Block 2, *Popular Culture* (Milton Keynes, 1985).

122. Aldgate, *Cinema and History*, p. 268.

123. Lunn, 'Reconsidering Britishness', p. 92.

Part IV
Leisure

—8—

Leisure and Pleasure
Competing Ideologies and Strategies in the Netherlands

Theo Beckers

Leisure is not only the germinating time of art and philosophy, the time in which the seer attains glimpses of the values and realities behind ordinary appearance; it is also the opportunity for appreciation, the time in which such values get across into common experience. The quality of a civilization depends upon the effectiveness of transmission of such values. The widespread enjoyment is thus a matter of greatest moment, culturally as well as economically.

Ida Craven, 'Leisure', The Encyclopedia of the Social Sciences (1933)

Back in the days when unremitting toil was the lot of all but the very few and leisure still a hopeless yearning, hard and painful as life was, it still felt real. People were in rapport with the small bit of reality allotted to them, the sense of the earth, the tang of the changing seasons, the consciousness of the eternal cycle of birth and death. Now, when so many have leisure, they become detached from themselves, not merely from the earth. From all the widened horizons of our greater world a thousand voices call us to come near, to understand, and to enjoy. But our ears are not trained to hear them. The leisure is ours, but not the skill to use it. So, leisure becomes a void, and from the ensuing restlessness men take refuge in delusive excitations and fictitious visions, returning to their own earth no more.

Robert MacIver, The Pursuit of Happiness (1955)

Introduction

In modern, industrial nation-states leisure became a contested and disputed domain, claimed by many actors in civil society, state and market, with their competing value systems and modes of intervention. Leisure is an intriguing object for historical and social science research since its organization reflects the power structure of society and mirrors fundamental social and cultural changes in modernity. In this chapter I will explore the moral concerns about leisure as democratic participation in the benefits of the Enlightenment and leisure as consumption by taking two historical snapshots: the inter-war period (workers' leisure) and the late 1950s and early 1960s (mass leisure).

115

From around 1890 until the late 1950s, leisure was predominantly defined as a *vraagstuk*, a social problem, from two distinct ideological positions: moralism and rationalism. In the moralist position, with its rationale in tradition or the Bible, modern leisure was seen as conflicting with the codes of traditional, rural society and culture, being not in accordance with the ordinances of the churches and the Calvinist perspective on the world and social order. The rationalist position, based on the ideals of the Enlightenment, criticized the unreasonable, vulgar, commercial exploitation of leisure. The pillarized institutions of Dutch civil society tried to develop strategies to reduce the dangers of modern leisure and to promote their own alternatives. The state played only a minor role, on the local level. Commercial exploitation of leisure and consumerism did not fit with either of these ideological positions.

The national welfare state of the 1960s prepared for a future leisure society, embraced the rationalist approach, and defined leisure no longer as a problem but as an opportunity and a democratic right for individual development after work. This was embodied in paragraph 23 of the new Dutch constitution of 1983. Soon after this symbolic moment, the combined effects of increased affluence in terms of time and money became evident. Leisure time was no longer spent in the self-organized leisure institutions of the pillarized civil society or limited to participation in the public goods offered by the state but became mass consumption via the market.

To reconstruct the institutionalization of Dutch leisure and consumption we cannot draw, unfortunately, on an extensive range of source material. In contrast to Britain, a systematic economic, social and cultural history of twentieth-century leisure in the Netherlands has not been written. For a long time, the study of leisure as a separate subject was only of marginal importance in Dutch historical research. Johan Huizinga's *Homo Ludens* in 1938 did not herald the start of an academic tradition. In most cases the scarce historical work was done by non-historians and had a limited scope, dealing with topics in the history of popular culture, tourism, recreation and sports.[1] Leisure studies suffered badly from a lack of serious historical work. Only recently did leisure become more of an integral part of the academic and popular historical analysis of the late nineteenth and twentieth century, but a more comprehensive analysis of the development of leisure in the context of time-spatial dynamics, commodification, modernization and democratization is urgently needed. The history of Dutch leisure undoubtedly has a future.

More historical research on leisure in the Netherlands generates opportunities for cross-fertilization and cross-national comparisons between Britain and the Netherlands. For this chapter I could draw on a long and strong tradition in empirical leisure research in the Netherlands. Leisure belongs to one of the earliest themes in modern social science research, especially in sociography, sociology and human geography.[2] Scientific leisure research in the Netherlands started after the First World War. When the eight-hour laws were under discussion in the industrial nations in 1916 and 1917, the prospect of such an acceleration of free time led governments and social reformers to discuss fearfully the leisure 'problem' and the abuse of leisure. A small number of social scientists were invited to assess the nature of this new social problem. All over Europe, North America and Australia temperance societies prepared for increased drunkenness and attention was centred on the evils of commercial recreation as it prevailed in most large cities.[3] Today we still discuss hooliganism and the abuse of drugs, alcohol and sex, but postmodern and post-industrial cities are now embracing and promoting commercial recreation.

The extended twentieth century witnessed the birth, the growth and the decline of leisure as a civilizing project of the Enlightenment and its replacement by the pleasure principle of the multinational leisure industry. Even the Dutch language reflects this change in the political, cultural and economic meaning and valuation. The Dutch equivalent for both free time and leisure is *vrije tijd*. A more abstract notion of time and a split between personal time and time of the master were introduced in daily language in the last quarter of the nineteenth century, during the first stage of industrial development in the Netherlands. The adjective *vrij* (free) was no longer seen as just a characteristic of a person, but also of his or her time. The notion of *vrije tijd* began to be applied to the lives of Dutch industrial workers after the first decade of the twentieth century. The English word 'leisure' and the French *loisir*, derived from the Latin *licere*, are very close to the essential meaning after the rise of capitalism and the commodification of time: to be permitted, to have the right, to follow your own preferences, within certain political, social and economic constraints. The Dutch word *licentie* and the Flemish word *verlof* have the same root as leisure. We can also see a remarkable development one century later. In the Netherlands local politicians, developers and planners imported a new, foreign word to label the rediscovery of consumerism and pleasure: the English word *leisure*, mostly associated with time-spatial experiences or multifunctional *leisure* centres, integrating sports, shopping, entertainment, museums and popular culture. The term *leisure* partially replaced *vrije tijd*. Leisure became an instrument and function to revitalize urban and rural areas, as a characteristic of the commercial supply of entertainment and amusements. Leisure became pleasure in both wording and meaning.

Modern Times

The spread of industrial capitalism in the Netherlands, although occurring later than in Britain, had similar socio-cultural and economic consequences:

- temporal segregation: between work time and free time;
- spatial segregation: between places for work and production and for leisure and consumption and between rural and urban areas;
- class segregation: between the middle class and the working class;
- gender segregation: between male wage-earners and unpaid female labour at home;
- institutional segregation: between private and public sphere.

Since the start of modernity, the commodification and abstraction of time is a crucial phase in the structural development of the *longue durée*. The introduction of the mechanical clock is the symbol for modern times. Gradually the holy times of the Church, the natural times of seasons and day and night, the cyclical time of traditional culture and *rites de passage* were replaced by social times, constructed in a capitalist economy and supported by a puritan morality of ascetic behaviour, saving money, using time efficiently, and deferred fulfilment of needs. Time was no longer embedded in natural and super-national rhythms, directed by external, unpredictable forces, but became a man-made, calculable and measurable commodity, exchangeable on a market of production and consumption. During the development of capitalism and industrialism the relationship between natural and social times weakened. While time was increasingly valued as a scarce commodity, human life became detached from biorhythms and collective rhythms and cycles. The abstraction of time, the split between work time and free time and time–space distanciation are typical of the process of modernization.[4]

Technological development especially generated a new consciousness of time, space and speed and reinforced the notion that man is master of his own time, creating an awareness that every moment is unique and irreversible. Since the combination of modernity, industrial capitalism and technological development, the time-is-money principle invaded all vessels of our social and cultural life. Modern means of transportation and communication created a new sense of time and space between 1880 and 1918.[5] The introduction of the train, telegraph, telephone, automobile, bicycle, aeroplane, radio and cinema built the conditions for a new culture of time and for new modes of consumption. The social distribution of the impact of technological innovations was uneven. The telephone, for instance, disturbed and reduced the relevance of physical space and material distances, but initially increased the social space and symbolic distance between classes.

One century later, in the transition from industrial, Fordist to post-industrial, post-Fordist society, we witness a new phase in the process of modernization. In 1909 a uniform, synchronic national time system was introduced in the Netherlands.[6] Before that date, major rural areas and many cities still had their own times. The introduction and acceptance of the new time regime is an indication of both the breakthrough of industrial capitalism in the Netherlands and the development of the nation-state.

Workers' Leisure, Moral Panic and Rational Recreation (1919–40)

> It is not in the interest of modern society, unlike that of other forms of society, that workers should spend a disproportionately large number of hours daily in their place of work. Productive capacity has increased for the producers to become to an ever-increasing degree consumers. Society's very existence depends on the continuous creation of new needs for material goods. But society does not confine itself merely to the creation of purely material needs. It simultaneously creates intellectual and spiritual needs, which depend for their fulfilment both on the mode of production and on the opportunities existing for the utilization of leisure time.[7]

This quotation is from a 1938 article in the *British Sociological Review* on 'Leisure in the Totalitarian State', written by the Dutch social scientist Andries Sternheim, one of the pioneers of Dutch leisure research.[8] Sternheim presents a view on leisure after the introduction of the eight-hour day that was broadly shared by many liberal and socialist intellectuals and social leaders in the Netherlands and elsewhere. Between 1870 and 1948 the average annual working time for industrial workers was reduced from 5,000 hours to 2,500 hours. The average formal industrial working week went from 70 hours in 1870 to 60 in 1910, 45 in 1920, 48 in 1922 and 1950 and again 45 in 1965.[9] The number of national, religious and contractual holidays for workers increased from 7 in 1870 to 8 in 1910, 9 in 1922, 17.5 in 1950 and 21 in 1965. The most skilled and best-organized workers, such as the typographers and diamond cutters, acted as pioneers and trendsetters, being among the first workers who could enjoy a paid holiday.[10] In 1920 only 120,000 workers had received a guarantee of paid holiday in a collective agreement. This number increased to 338,000, or 87 per cent of the workers who had the benefits of a collective agreement, but only 17 per cent of the 2 million employees in industry, commercial and public services.[11] The National Socialist regime subsequently introduced a general right to paid holiday and a right to a holiday allowance in 1941 and 1942.

For enlightened intellectuals and policy makers in the inter-war period, mass productivity produced the economic and moral dilemmas of leisure and consumer needs.[12] Free time and mass access to goods were problematic because of an ideological legacy that had roots in the beginnings of industrialization. A dream of the Enlightenment was to liberate time from the necessity of work and to force the physical world to meet consumer needs. For most Enlightenment thinkers, general affluence and extensive individual freedom from work were as much moral problems as they were economic benefits. For some, leisure undermined the work ethos and created the anarchy of undisciplined time; for others it multiplied need and produced a work-driven society based on 'false needs'.

Rousseau provided one solution to these dilemmas in his critique of the multiplication of needs. Misery, he claimed, came not from deprivation but from the need for things. He offered a timeless community of self-sufficiency and self-imposed simplicity. Hume suggested a second solution: he justified emulation as the only means of assuring economic progress. His antidote to unrestrained vanity was self-control. Mill looked hopefully to a 'stationary state' where universal participation in work and population constraint would allow a new leisure society in which an elite, a learned class of educators, could counteract the egoistic commercial spirit. Affluence would allow greater autonomy and participation of workers in cultural and political life and would lead to democratic leisure. Marx also expected prosperity to be coupled with the reduction of work time for the self-discovery of authentic needs. With the end of capitalism the realm of freedom would replace the realm of necessity. Although Marx had different views on the relationship between work and leisure,[13] his analysis and views inspired trade unions and influential intellectuals both in the inter-war period and in the early 1960s. Leisure as a countervailing power and alternative social and cultural practice, from *ascole* and *negotium* back to the classical appreciation of *scole* and *otium*, the importance of education and leadership, democracy instead of commerce, those are the shared views of the proponents of the Enlightenment in the twentieth century. Significantly, their advocates often assumed the social predominance of a bourgeoisie that practised self-constraint. The inter-war period became a test for those ideas and ideals, constructed in the splendid isolation of intellectual minds.

The Labour Act of 1919 introduced the eight-hour day and a general right to leisure for male industrial workers. The law, introduced by Aalberse, was approved by parliament on 11 July 1918 with only three members voting against it. After the official vote an extraordinary ritual took place. Twenty members started to sing the 'eight hours hymn', then a larger number took over and sang the national anthem, the *Wilhelmus*, directed by Duymaer van Twist. This unusual event in the Dutch parliament illustrates the highly symbolic and moral importance of the introduction of the eight-hour day.[14] Dymaer van Twist was the same person who had led the social and political movement against attempts by the Labour leader P.J. Troelstra to provoke a socialist revolution. For the Conservative majority, support for the Labour Act was the price they had to pay to prevent a workers' revolution. For the Christian trade unions it was a strategy to counteract the emerging success of the socialist trade unions. In fact, the law did not last very long. During the recession of the early 1920s the maximum working week was again raised to 48 hours, instead of 45 hours. Nonetheless, this had created the precedent of a civil right to personal time, freed from the control of employers and with the freedom to choose from many new options. In 1931 the High Court decided that the intention of the Labour Act was not only to protect the worker against excessive fatigue, but also to offer him enough disposable time for individual development and relaxation in the interest of his family.[15]

New agents and types of control emerged. A small number of progressive employers like Philips adopted a Taylorist, Fordist strategy, thereby extending the company's influence beyond the workplace into the private lives and private territories of families, by developing leisure facilities and leisure programmes for their workers.[16] Religious leaders and socialist trade unions condemned this (successful) attempt at extending social control to the domain of privacy and individual freedom. The Catholic Church especially saw leisure in general as a huge danger and as a new and modern attack on the structure and the culture of the Church, on the nuclear family and on the harmonious relationship between the classes. Different strategies were developed to counteract this: blaming the individual, condemning the leisure practices and creating Catholic-based leisure institutions were the most common. However, this response of creating separate, safe and controlled leisure environments for 'vulnerable groups' like youth and workers and their families did not come only from the Catholic Church. During the inter-war years a fascinating and complex organizational social infrastructure developed, based on the different ideological and religious principles represented in the Netherlands: thus one could find a Protestant tour operator, a Catholic youth club, a socialist sports association and a general broadcasting corporation. In this way, it was not only elite culture or the pastimes of the middle class that became subject to pillarization, regulation and self-organization, but also the popular leisure pursuits of the masses.

Concurrently with the passage of the eight-hour laws, a number of European governments set up official commissions to study the problems of workers' leisure. In 1924 the International Labour Office in Geneva, initiated by its director Albert Thomas, devoted part of its sixth conference to a discussion of the problem on the basis of national reports.[17] The Arbeidsinspectie prepared the Dutch report, commissioned by the government. The report addressed a number of issues that epitomized the moral panic in those years. Did the reduction of work time result in higher consumption of liquor, more visits to pubs and more alcoholism? Which bodies in the field of popular education had been created since November 1919? Were programmes for adult education more frequented by workers? Did the number of allotment gardens decline or increase? Was it desirable to integrate and unite the different initiatives in local or regional committees, with the participation of the government? The report was reassuring.[18] Moral panic was misplaced. It proved to be difficult to make a direct causal connection between more free time and changes in behaviour. The general picture was positive: the workers followed the leisure pattern of the middle class. The 'resigned' worker was far more numerous than the 'rebellious' worker. The increased consumption of liquor was not seen as a consequence of more time, but of more money. There was a disappointing lack of interest in reading and education, but an increasing participation of workers in sport. The authors understood that many really preferred to remain in the open air and have freedom of movement as a reaction to industrial work.[19] More time for home and family was one of the positive outcomes from this investigation, based on personal observations of labour inspectors. The report ended with a plea for local leisure committees under the condition that they were initiated and guided by the workers themselves; the government and other 'good-willing persons' should limit themselves to the support of workers' initiatives.

This was totally congruent with the views of the pillarized organizations in Dutch civil society. A special case was the 'planning for freedom' initiated by socialist leaders and intellectuals. The introduction of the eight-hour day was not only a victory in the social struggle for the ownership of time, but it was also a challenge for the international and Dutch labour movements and workers' political parties. They now had to prove that the new freedom would not end in uncivilized, anti-social and irrational behaviour. In 1930 the first International Congress on Workers' Spare Time took place in Liège, under the auspices of the ILO. The second conference was held in Brussels in 1935. Since the divided labour movement in the Netherlands did not have a coordinating organization for workers' leisure, the only Dutch representative was Sternheim, then head of the Geneva branch of the Institut fuer Sozialforschung.[20] The labour movement expected the moral regeneration of the working class and wanted to promote rational recreation: adult education, libraries, playgrounds, allotment gardens and nature conservation – in fact, the popular version of traditional middle-class leisure. In 1919, after a conflict in the general Nederlandsche Reisvereeniging, the Nederlandsche Arbeiders Reisvereeniging was founded in order 'to promote the development and recreation of the working class by creating the appetite for travel by organizing tours in the Netherlands and abroad, and a variety of small trips in the neighbourhood of the city'.[21]

Initially, the objective of the labour movement was to develop an alternative workers' culture, with the Soviet Union acting as an inspiration for some. An example is the Arbeiders Jeugd Centrale (the Workers' Youth Association), founded in 1918 to develop a new socialist culture and to struggle against the banalities and bad taste of bourgeois leisure, against kitsch, commercial entertainment, the lack of self-control and the inability to create an alternative lifestyle, according to the standards of rational recreation.[22] A new workers' leisure culture was to include simplicity in dress and housing, the introduction of 'new' leisure forms such as folk dance, folk songs, folk theatre and the rediscovery of nature. While one part of the working class followed the leisure pursuits of the middle class, another part was stimulated to return to a romantic pre-industrial and pre-modern past which had never existed in real social and cultural life. At the end of the 1920s the discrepancy between idealism and realism became clear to the leaders of the labour movement and gave rise to the first empirical study of workers' leisure in the Netherlands. The initiative came from the Instituut voor Arbeidersontwikkeling (Institute for Workers' Development, IA), founded in 1924 by the NVV (the socialist trade union) and the SDAP (the Dutch Labour Party). The struggle against commercial mass leisure and the promotion of a workers' culture of decency and rationalism were the main objectives. In their free time 'workers live in a society driven by profit and the exploitation of the lack of civilization', in cinemas, pubs and cabarets. The main objective of the institute was to withdraw workers from the bourgeois 'entertainment industry' and to offer them special programmes in cultural and nature education. In 1928 the Nederlandsche Arbeidersreisvereeniging was integrated into the IA.

In 1932 an IA committee on education expressed the need for a more systematic, empirical and 'modern' study of workers' leisure. The committee was concerned about the lack of workers' interest in the rational recreation promoted by the institute. Why did they not participate in the leisure activities of the socialist pillar? What else did they do in their free time? One of its members, the sociologist Kruijt, was asked to do the study. The urgency increased during the economic recession. The general expectation was that more 'forced' free time for the unemployed would worsen the situation. Kruijt was impressed and influenced by the publication of a study by Marie Jahoda, Paul Lazarsfeld and Hans Zeisl entitled *Die Arbeitslosen von Marienthal*.[23] Kruijt and his colleagues primarily used the methodology of time budgets.[24] For the first time in the Netherlands, workers were directly interviewed on their leisure behaviour and asked to keep a time diary. No longer were 'experts', paternalistic spokesmen like police commissioners, mayors and priests, asked to give their biased view on 'the problem of leisure', but 621 skilled socialist workers. A combination of different methods made it possible to make a valid analysis of contemporary workers' leisure. The objective of the researchers was clear: to give educators a better perspective on workers' leisure in order to develop a more effective strategy to upgrade the cultural and moral standards of the working class.[25] The working class proved not to be a passive mass subject to the rules of commercial entertainment, but to obey the principles of the Enlightenment. Like the Arbeidsinspectie in 1923, the researchers came to satisfying conclusions: since the introduction of the eight-hour day, workers had assimilated to the leisure patterns of the middle class, so there was no reason for moral panic. Leisure was predominantly spent at home, in the safe haven of the family. The researchers noticed a more intensive engagement of fathers with their children, more active participation in educational recreation, reading newspapers, outdoor recreation, sports and voluntary associations. A major concern remained the lack of interest in arts and high culture, such as reading books, making music, painting or visiting museums. Those cultural forms had to compete with passive leisure practices: visiting the cinema, dance halls and games. The popularity of passive radio listening was seen as a special danger for decent and rational workers' leisure.

The emerging democratization of leisure during the inter-war years was not only a product of the efforts of the self-organized, pillarized civil society. Local governments in industrial cities started to design and plan rational recreation for their citizens. The quality of housing and public spaces improved after the passing of the Housing Act of 1901. In the 1930s new urban expansion included playgrounds, parks and sports facilities. The professional support and imagination of progressive architects like Berlage, Wils and Van Eesteren and the political support of the local labour parties in Amsterdam, Rotterdam and The Hague played a decisive role. There was a strong influence from abroad, especially Germany, the United States and Britain. From Britain, Dutch architects imported principles, quantitative norms and examples from the Garden City Movement (Ebenezer Howard) and the 'survey' as a scientific prerequisite for urban planning.

The international recognition of rational recreation as an essential component of urban and industrial development was expressed in the Declaration of Athens in 1933 by the Congrès International d'Architecture Moderne (CIAM). In the modern functional city, recreation was defined as one of the four main elements of urban planning and society. Local engagement with rational recreation in some cities became a prelude to the intensive intervention in leisure by the Dutch welfare state between 1955 and 1985. The codification and institutionalization of rational recreation and workers' leisure in the second half of the 1930s marked the provisional end of a crucial stage in the process of the democratization of leisure. Leisure proved to be a *gesunkens Kulturgut*: initiated by the elite or higher strata of the middle class, imitated by the middle class in the late nineteenth and early twentieth century and popularized for and by the working class during the inter-war years. Like other industrial nation-states, the Netherlands witnessed a successful downward diffusion process in sport, tourism, outdoor recreation and adult education. In many cases there was a strong direct influence from abroad, mainly from Britain. Typical of the Netherlands in the 1930s was the role of a pillarized civil society as the main agent for change and control. In totalitarian states, such as the Soviet Union, Italy, Germany, Spain and Portugal, the democratization of leisure was used as a political instrument to buy loyalty to the state.[26] In the United States leisure was transformed into consumption, and democratization took place via the market.[27] During the inter-war years Dutch civil society tried to develop a compromise between moralism and rationalism, between leisure as a danger and leisure as a hope for the liberation of rational man.

The Welfare State and the Making of a Consumer Culture (1955–65)

The tourist infrastructure along the Dutch coast had suffered heavily during the Second World War. The restoration and rebuilding of holiday accommodation and facilities was just one of the many problems the Dutch government had to solve during the period of reconstruction. At the end of 1946 a local businessman in the seaside resort of Zandvoort planned to build a holiday camp in cooperation with Butlins, an initiative coined by its opponents as 'the industrialization of leisure'. The local government and the department of *Wederopbouw* (Reconstruction) supported the plan, and the national bank for reconstruction, a national brewery and the British-based Butlins organization were prepared to invest the necessary money in the project. The ANWB tourist organization described the first holiday camp in Skegness, built on the other side of the North Sea in 1936, as follows:

> One of the secrets of its success is the fact that, for a low budget, a quasi luxurious and mundane atmosphere is created, which provides an uncritical audience with the illusion of living in a world like the one on the movie screen. The system is deliberately planned to prevent individuals having a moment to themselves and delivers a holiday on an assembly line, which renders superfluous, or even excludes, any individual initiative.[28]

Today Club Med and Center Parcs are considered to be pioneering, multinational companies, successful in satisfying the needs of leisure consumption. However, the Butlins concept never came to Zandvoort. An orchestrated national action led by various organizations and political parties took place, and in 1947 the British government started to discourage foreign tourism and to promote domestic tourism for economic reasons, a policy that forced Butlin to remove his financial support from the enterprise. Dutch companies were interested initially and started to develop holiday camps for their personnel, but in 1949 the provincial government of North-Holland refused to adapt the local physical plan for 'such a holiday camp'. Combined social pressure from confessional political parties, the Labour Party and the youth movement was decisive and prevented the introduction of the first 'leisure industry' in the Netherlands.[29]

A commercial Butlins camp did not fit in the cultural context of the time and was seen as being in competition with the leisure provision of its opponents. Immediately after the war, religious organizations, trade unions and youth associations had started to develop, restore or expand their own holiday centres, partly based on pre-war facilities. The more general ideological and institutional reconstruction of pre-war pillarized structures and moralist and rationalist values was reflected in the organization of leisure. The war experience offered a number of additional elements in the public debate on leisure and stimulated the national government to participate actively in the politics of leisure. The period between 1945 and 1955 provided the basis for the intensive involvement of the Dutch welfare state in leisure provision after 1955. The welfare state policies in turn generated a breeding ground for the expansion of leisure consumption and the pleasure principle in the last decade of the twentieth century.

Immediately after the Second World War a pre-war intellectual debate on mass and community, individual responsibility and leadership, nation-state and civil society continued to dominate public discussion. It was part of an international debate on mass leisure. Two remarkable books summarize the contemporary debate in the mid-1950s and contain opposing views on the destiny of the heritage of the Enlightenment:

Mass Culture. The Popular Arts in America, edited by Rosenberg and Manning White in 1957, and *Mass Leisure*, edited by Larrabee and Meyersohn in 1958.[30]

For a short while there was a concerted attempt to overcome the pillarized structure of Dutch society. For the proponents of cultural and political reconstruction, democratized leisure seemed to be an attractive and crucial instrument to reach that goal. One of the leading spokesmen was Van der Leeuw, who became the first Minister of Education, Arts and Sciences after 1945. In his book *Balans van Nederland* (Balance of the Netherlands), written during the war but published in 1946, he criticized the 'technical' and 'withered' state of leisure as part of culture, a prolongation of the pre-war debate on the 'massafication' of culture.[31] According to the dominant discourse, the majority overruled the individual, the mass seduced the defenceless individual and lowered the cultural level, exploited the simpler and rougher qualities, and totalitarian regimes stimulated this development and abused revenge and cruelty.[32]

Van der Leeuw accused technological and industrial developments of dividing daily life into two separated worlds: work and leisure. Work is essential for society but not connected to it in an organic way. Leisure as such has nothing to do with society, since every individual can use it in his own way, because it is his own time.

That is why we see a complete anarchy, the profits of cinemas and the popularity of football. That is why we see a pathetic phenomenon: the creation of an artificial type of nature, camping five minutes distance from our home, walking alongside the rail track and bathing almost naked in a so-called 'nature-pool'. Since we cannot live any longer in this world, we created a nature substitute and try to forget that the total holiday enterprise is nothing else than a type of industry.[33]

Van der Leeuw is a realist. We cannot return to a pre-industrial past. We have to live with the division in our life and since leisure will be even more important in the future, we should develop a strategy for 'socializing' leisure, making leisure an issue for society as a whole. We can no longer keep leisure for ourselves. Leisure has to strengthen individual and social development, with a crucial role for education and leadership. Like the influential German sociologist Mannheim,[34] then teaching in Britain, he proposes an active role for the state. That is why he created within his ministry a separate organization for the regulation and promotion of adult education, physical education, youth policy and outdoor recreation: Vorming Buiten Schoolverband (Education Outside School).

Van der Leeuw's elitist and activist view was supported by other proponents of a 'personalistic socialism' and an active nation-state beyond the ideological and political segmentation of the Netherlands. As long as the state failed to offer solutions by developing alternatives to commercial leisure, it was considered the collective responsibility of religious, cultural and youth organizations to counter the increasing influence of the entertainment industry. These organizations had to try to find an answer to questions like: is it possible to meet the needs of the masses in the cities without stimulating superficiality, and is it possible to give value-based guidance and leadership to the urban masses? As Carl Mennicke said: 'We believe that the right answer to those questions is not only crucial for the fate of society in the big city, but for society as a whole.'[35]

The 'problem of leisure' and the inability to spend leisure time in a 'proper' and 'useful' way were no longer matters just for the working class but were now acknowledged as a general problem for civilization. There are many examples of expression of this concern between 1945 and 1955, like the conference of the Nationaal Instituut (National Institute) in 1946 on 'The future of Dutch civilization' with prominent speakers (Baschwitz, Thomassen, DeVries Reilingh, Banning, Kruijt and Oldendorff). Three categories were defined as particularly vulnerable and deserving of special attention: industrial workers migrating from rural areas to the dangers and temptations of the industrial cities; anti-social families living in deteriorating parts of the inner cities, and the so-called 'mass youth' which had run wild during the war and been confronted with Allied soldiers and new types of consumption and popular culture. Sociological and psychological research on leisure in those years seemed to confirm the symptoms of a society in disarray.[36]

The dominant view blamed industrialization and urbanization for delivering a levelling of mass society. Social and spiritual roots and relations had been eroded. Culture had lost its foundation in the community. The citizen had become a mass consumer. The relations between cities and rural areas and between man and nature were disturbed. Work no longer gave fulfilment and meaning. The power of bureaucracies increased, as did the tensions between generations. The rhythm of time and life had accelerated. This process of supposed alienation reinforced the need for compensation during free time, satisfied by the tempting supply of commercial leisure. Two wars and a period of mass unemployment had shown, in the eyes of many intellectuals and social leaders, the fragility of the country's social and cultural foundations. For example, they were very disappointed and deeply concerned about the lack of moral resistance during the German occupation.

As Kaan said in 1948, 'the use of leisure is the test of civilization,'[37] and through leisure the weakness and the low level of civilization became evident. Traditional institutions like family, church or school were seen as unable to resolve the problem. New agents of change with new types of intervention entered the complex arena of leisure. The most alarming and worrying dimension of this was not the cultural level or the uncivilized nature of modern leisure, but the very fact that leisure is identical with individual freedom of choice, which was beyond the control of traditional institutions.

Ironically, the welfare state, while challenged by civil society to tackle 'the problem of leisure' for the sake of social control, accepted the principle of individual freedom of choice, defined leisure practices as collective goods, included access to and participation in leisure as a democratic right, and developed a new institutional framework and shaped the conditions for the expansion of leisure consumption. In a sense, leisure provision by the nation-state was the reward for the collective effort in rebuilding and renewing the economic, physical and social infrastructure, which had resulted in longer hours and low levels of private consumption, for maintaining the social peace and accepting the cultural standards of the elite. In other words, it represented a period of delayed gratification during the first decade after the Second

World War. In 1954 the Netherlands was the only country in Western Europe not to have experienced an increase in real wages since 1948, and in 1960 the purchasing power of wage-earners was still below the level of 1935. In the meantime labour productivity per capita increased from an annual rate of 4 per cent per hour between 1853 and 1963 to 6.2 per cent between 1963 and 1973. [38] In the first decade after the war, the growth in affluence was needed for collective purposes, to cope with the loss of Indonesia and to finance the rapid population growth from 9.6 million in 1947 to 11.5 million in 1960. The expansion of the industrial system, the struggle against the shortage of housing, the expansion of urban areas, harbours and motorways, the reclaiming of new land, the development of a social security and public health system, all absorbed the growth in national wealth. More free time and higher wages had a low priority in this socio-economic context. According to Broekman (1980), the growth of real wages for industrial workers in the Netherlands between 1870 and 1975 was 600 per cent, whereas the growth of weekly free time was only 30 per cent.[39]

Around 1960 the economic context of the debate on leisure and leisure policies changed radically. The price per unit time in work and leisure, both productivity and 'consumptivity', increased. The structure of free time changed after the introduction of the five-day working week in 1961, first in industry and soon in other economic and social sectors. Dutch employers and economists discovered what Ford had proposed in 1926: mass-production presupposes mass-consumption. The combination of more free time and higher wages would boost the market economy. In the same year the American Federation of Labor voted for a resolution in favour of the five-day working week. A free Saturday should create more time for re-creation (recuperation) and for recreation (commercial leisure). After a delay of 30 years the Netherlands embarked on the same course.

The gradual commodification of free time between 1955 and 1965 had far-reaching consequences, providing a shift from time-intensive behavioural patterns to capital-intensive leisure.[40] There was also a shift from family-oriented leisure, based on shared interests and values, to leisure based on individual preferences and tastes. Moreover, there was an increase in personal space, both inside and outside the home. For their leisure activities, citizens detached themselves from the pillarized social infrastructure and explored their own paths in time and space. Television sets, DIY, sports equipment, caravans, private cars, boats and second homes became the new play things for the *homo ludens*. Leisure was now a self-evident routine in daily, weekly and annual free time. Leisure was the big equalizer, a strong force for democratization, overcoming the barriers between classes and ideological denominations earlier than in the labour system, the school system, the health system and the social security system.

From the early 1960s time, money and technology provided Dutch citizen-consumers with the means to shape their own private realms of freedom. Again, the discrepancy between traditional public and intellectual discourse and daily social life became evident. The discourse itself started to change. Using the political and social consensus of the mid-1950s and taking advantage of the institutional and ideological heritage of civil society, the nation-state developed an active leisure policy, culminating in the creation of a separate Ministry for Culture, Recreation and Social Work in 1966. Public expenditure on leisure was 13.5 million guilders in 1946 (1.5 guilder per capita), 95.5 million in 1955 (9 per capita), 150.9 million in 1965 (37 per capita) and 2.7 billion in 1975 (199 per capita).[41] The physical planning of the modernizing industrial society was used to plan and realize spaces and places for outdoor recreation, tourism, sports and culture in a relatively short period of time. Together with the development of new motorways, the reclaiming of new land, the reconstruction of agriculture and the expansion of urban areas, the public provision of leisure developed as a by-product. Like the elite in the sixteenth and seventeenth centuries and the bourgeoisie in the mid-nineteenth century, in the mid-twentieth century common people got their perfectly planned recreation areas and went back to nature. The people reacted positively, wishing to demonstrate their newly acquired affluence, and left the cities on a massive scale. But now the 'mass' was no longer a moral problem but a technical problem which could be solved by rational planning and management.

The changes in leisure practices were supported and conditioned by a new cultural orientation. Leisure was no longer defined as a social problem, but as a positive contribution to the development of the self and as the hope for liberation. A future leisure society was predicted in which work would be reduced to a necessary economic function and leisure would become the real fulfilment of life. An optimistic view of the empowering role of technology and the possibilities for social engineering and a strong belief in the rationality and stability of socio-economic change seemed to bring Marx's realm of freedom within reach.

Influenced by modern sociology and modern methodology, a new generation of young social scientists (Heinemeijer, Wippler, Thoenes, Lammners) opposed the biased and normative views and moral concerns of the inter-war generation. What the welfare state in progress needed was objective, value-free, empirical knowledge on the state of leisure. A good example is provided by the two big research projects of the Central Bureau of Statistics (CBS) on leisure in the Netherlands, one on the period 1955–6 and the other covering 1962–3. The first study was partly inspired by Rowntree and Lavers' 'English Life and Leisure' (1952), by Helen and Robert Lynd's 'Middletown, a Study in American Culture' (1929) and by Lundberg, Komarovsky and McInerny's 'Leisure: a Suburban Study' (1934). The first study was designed to look specifically at the impact of the introduction of television on leisure and family life. The second was commissioned by the government to assess the impact of the introduction of the five-day working week on outdoor recreation. In both cases the research was to serve the needs of the emerging welfare state for the supply of leisure as a public good. From 1973 a new cornerstone of the welfare state, the Social and Cultural Planning Office (SCP), included the development of independent and longitudinal knowledge on leisure in its programme. In 1983 the democratic right of access to leisure, culture and sports was included in the revised Dutch constitution.

Conclusion

International historical research shows that the commodification of free time and the popularity of the pleasure principle have deep roots in the development of modern capitalism. Again and again, political, social and cultural forces tried in vain to neglect, suppress or eliminate this movement. In the history of Dutch leisure the term 'mass leisure' had, until the mid-1950s, an evil connotation and was seen as a potential danger to society and civilization, both from a moralist and a rationalist perspective. During the flowering of the welfare state, access to leisure became a democratic right. The massive use of this right changed the meaning of 'mass leisure' as a moral category into 'many' as a notion of quantity. The welfare state thus acted as a pioneer in paving the way for the expansion of commercial leisure over the last fifteen years.

Notes

1. W. Knulst, *Van vaudeville tot video. Empirisch-theoretische studie naar verschuivingen in het uitgaan en het gebruik van media sinds de jaren vijftig* (Rijswijk: Sociaal en Cultureel Planbureau, 1989); A. Hessels, *Vakantie en vakantiebesteding sinds de eeuwisseling* (Assen: Van Gorcum, 1973); T. Beckers, *Planning voor vrijheid. Een historisch-sociologische studie van de overheidsinterventie in rekreatie en vrije tijd* (Wageningen: Pudoc, 1983); R. Stokvis, *Strijd over sport. Organisatorische en ideologische ontwikkelingen* (Deventer: Van Loghum Slaterus, 1979).

2. T. Beckers and J. Mommaas, *Het vraagstuk van den vrijen tijd. 60 jaar onderzoek naar vrije tijd* (Leiden/Antwerpen: Stenfert Kroese, 1991).

3. P. Bramham, I. Henry, H. Mommaas and H. van der Poel (eds), *Leisure and Urban Processes: Critical Studies of Leisure Policy in Western European Cities* (London and New York: Routledge, 1989).

4. A. Giddens, *The Consequences of Modernity* (Oxford: Polity Press, 1990).

5. S. Kern, *The Culture of Time and Space 1880–1918* (Cambridge, MA: Harvard University Press, 1983).

6. H. Knippenberg and B. de Pater, *De eenwording van Nederland. Schaalvergroting en integratie sinds 1800* (Nijmegen: SUN, 1988).

7. A. Sternheim, 'Leisure in the Totalitarian State', *Sociological Review*, 30 (1938), pp. 28–42.

8. T. Beckers, 'Andries Sternheim and the Study of Leisure in Early Critical Theory', *Leisure Studies*, 9(3) (1990), pp. 197–212.

9. CBS, *Tachtig jaren statistiek in tijdreeksen* ('s Gravenhage: CBS, 1979).

10. H. Heertje, *De diamantbewerkers van Amsterdam* (Amsterdam, 1936).

11. T. Beckers, *Planning voor vrijheid*, p. 36.

12. G. Cross, *Time and Money: The Making of Consumer Culture* (London and New York: Routledge, 1993), pp. 16–17.

13. E. Corijn, *De onmogelijke geboorte van een wetenschap. Verkenningen van de ontwikkeling van de studie van de vrije tijd* (Brussels: VUB-Press, 1998).

14. L. Karsten, *De achturendag. Arbeidstijdverkorting in historisch perspectief* (Groningen, 1989).

15. A. Oldendorff, 'Enkele sociale aspecten der arbeidstijdverkorting', in *Prae-adviezen voor de 177ste algemene vergadering van de Nederlandsche Maatschappij voor Nijverheid en Handel* (Haarlem, 1960).

16. Historical research on the self-interested interventions of companies in workers' leisure in fascist Italy can be found in V. de Grazia, *The Culture of Consent: Mass Organization of Leisure in Fascist Italy* (Cambridge: Cambridge University Press, 1981) and for the US in B. Hunnicut, *Work without End: Abandoning Shorter Hours for the Right to Work* (Philadelphia: Temple University Press, 1988); both explore the roots of those efforts in Taylorism and scientific management.

17. T. Beckers, *Planning voor vrijheid*, p. 136.

18. Centraal Verslag der Arbeidsinspectie, *Het gebruik van den vrijen tijd door de arbeiders* ('s Gravenhage: Arbeidsinspectie, 1923).

19. A. Blonk, J. Kruijt and E. Hofstee (1936) *De besteding van de vrije tijd door de Nederlandse arbeiders. Uitkomsten van een enquete onder 621 arbeiders* (Amsterdam: Maatschappij tot Nut van 't Algemeen, 1936), p. 69.

20. Britain is represented by the Industrial Welfare Society, France by the Comité National des Loisirs, Mussolini's Italy by the Opera Nazionale Dopolavoro, Sweden by the Arbetarnes Bildungsforbund and the United States by the National Recreation Association. The latter organized the first international congress on leisure in 1932, at the occasion of the Olympic games in Los Angeles. A similar conference in 1936 in Berlin, initiated by Kraft durch Freude, was boycotted by the international labour movement. See T. Beckers, 'Andries Sternheim', p. 198.

21. H. Michielse, *Socialistische vorming. Het Instituut voor Arbeidersont-wikkeling, 1924–1940 en het vormings- en scholingswerk van de Nederlandse sociaal-democratie sinds 1900* (Nijmegen: SUN, 1980), p. 212.

22. G. Harmsen, *Blauwe en rode jeugd. Ontstaan, ontwikkeling en teruggang van de Nederlandse jeugdbeweging tussen 1853 en 1940* (Assen: Van Gorcum, 1961).

23. Beckers and Mommaas, *Het vraagstuk van den vrijen tijd*, p. 22.

24. To measure the leisure behaviour (of workers) via time budgets has a strong tradition throughout the twentieth century. The roots are the nineteenth century's money budgets, used by economists to calculate expenditures of (worker) families. So, money became time. The first application in modern social science research was at Columbia University, published in 1913 by the theologian George Bevans: *How Workingmen Spend Their Spare Time*. The project was supervised by Giddings, one of the founding fathers of North American sociology.

25. Blonk, Kruijt and Hofstee, *De besteding van de vrije tijd door de Nederlandse arbeiders*, p. 72.

26. A. Sternheim, 'Leisure in the Totalitarian State', p. 32; A. Sternheim, 'Het probleem van den vrijen tijd in den totalitaire staat', *Mensch en Maatschappij*, 15 (1939), pp. 25–39.

27. R. Butsch (ed.), *For Fun and Profit: The Transformation of Leisure into Consumption* (Philadelphia: Temple University Press, 1990); G. Cross, *A Social History of Leisure since 1600* (State College: Venture Publishing, 1990); G. Cross,

Time and Money: The Making of Consumer Culture (London and New York: Routledge, 1993).

28. ANWB, *Toerisme voor iedereen. En pleidooi voor meer ruimte* (The Hague, 1950).

29. The term 'industry' is not a coincidence, considering the discourse at that time comparing this type of leisure with the assembly line.

30. Although dealing with similar issues and themes, the split between 'culture' and 'leisure' is indicative. *Mass Leisure* consists of earlier essays of Mead, Huxley, Piaget, Russell, Veblen, Riesman, Dubin, MacIver, Lundberg and others.

31. After *Untergang des Abendlandes* Oswald Spengler published in 1931 his book *Der Mensch und die Technik: Beitrag zu einer Philosophie des Lebens* (Munich, 1931), in which he analyses the impact of *Vermassung* on the decline of culture, the on-rushing mass, which is the victim of the loss of traditional community and the link between work and leisure. Mannheim's *Mensch und Gesellschaft im Zeitalter des Umbaus* (1935) and Huizinga's *In de schaduwen van morgen* (1935), and also the work of Ortega y Gasset, with whom Van der Leeuw had regular contact, present similar ideas.

32. I. Schoffer, 'Weten we ze nog wel, die jaren dertig?', in P. Klein (ed.), *De jaren dertig. Aspekten van crisis en werkloosheid* (Amsterdam, 1979), pp. 209–27.

33. G. van der Leeuw, *Balans van Nederland* (Amsterdam, 1946), p. 114.

34. In two important publications (*Man and Society in an Age of Reconstruction*, 1940, and *Diagnosis of Our Time*, 1943) he developed the idea of planning for freedom, a third way between market capitalism and totalitarianism. 'Only where, on the one hand, the average person has enough leisure to sublimate his surplus energies, and where, on the other hand, there is a dominant cultural group, do there arise mutually adapted classes which create and assimilate culture. … Unless material advancement is combined with personal example and the persuasion exercised by the presence of intelligent standards for the use of leisure, it may end in boredom, neurosis and general decadence.' (K. Mannheim, *Man and Society in an Age of Reconstruction: Studies in Modern Social Structures*, London: Routledge and Kegan, 1940, p. 317). 'Democratic planning might greatly expand subsidized and non-commercial opportunities for valuable leisure-time activities and cultural pursuits.' (K. Mannheim, Freedom, Power and Democratic Planning, London: Routledge and Kegan, 1951, p. 271).

35. C. Mennicke, *Sociale psychologie. De algemene grondslagen en de toepassing daarvan op de maatschappelijke en politieke verschijnselen, vooral van de tegenwoordige tijd* (Utrecht, 1948), p. 109.

36. Beckers and Mommaas, *Het vraagstuk van den vrijen tijd*, p. 76.

37. A. Kaan, 'Het vrije-tijdsprobleem', *Tijdschrift voor Maatschappelijk Werk*, 2(18) (1948), pp. 285–8.

38. T. Beckers, *Planning voor vrijheid*, p. 152.

39. F. Broekman, *Beschikbare en benodigde vrije tijd. Een analyse van de betekenis van de vrije tijd voor het consumentengedrag in de korte en de langere periode* (Leiden/Antwerpen: Stenfert Kloeze, 1980).

40. T. Beckers, 'Van geld- naar tijdintensieve consumptie', *Tijdschrift voor Marketing*, 28(5) (1994), pp. 34–9.

41. T. Beckers, *Planning voor vrijheid*, p. 289.

–9–

'Mass Leisure' in Britain

Douglas A. Reid

The discourse of 'mass society' was invariably a critical one that emerged in Britain at the birth of the twentieth century, as the scale and pace of social life increased and the challenges to a bourgeois social order multiplied – by contrast, as recently as 1883 Gladstone had used the terminology of 'the masses' in a positive political sense.[1] As far as leisure was concerned, however, apprehensions about the activities of 'the masses' merely added an extra dimension to a long-developed critique of popular leisure-time activities which was older than industrialization – particularly in fulminations on the sins of 'idleness' – and which was signified in the nineteenth century by the largely bourgeois banner of 'rational recreation'. Fundamentally, this stood as a critique of any working-class recreation which threatened strict decorum and control in a public or semi-public place, and its upholders therefore objected to alcohol consumption, to unruly sports, to street-gaming, or to events (like fairs) which might encourage such activities; more generally, it sought to promote recreations that were sedate rather than sensual, or 'reasonable and innocent'.[2] When turn-of-the-century critics began to conceptualize leisure in terms of the implications of 'mass society', they initially fixed their attention on sport spectatorship, because they were alarmed by its scale and their presumption that it would undermine the critical faculties of the individual. Later on, after the First World War, as football spectatorship had lost something of its ability to shock and cinema attendance expanded, critics became particularly concerned with the question of passivity in recreation. By the 1960s television was added to their list of concerns. Yet, in each case, there were voices to the contrary, advising that there was no need for alarm, and – ultimately – democratizing tendencies in the social structure, in politics, and in the spirit of each succeeding generation, meant that the discourse of 'the masses' came to seem outmoded. The first part of this chapter will examine these responses, the second will examine the development of leisure as such, and the third will assess trends in the development of key 'mass' activities.

I

A number of Liberal-Radical political commentators and politicians drew attention to mass sports spectatorship in the early twentieth century, of whom one of the most influential was J.A. Hobson.[3] His analyses of the popular response to imperialism directly reflected Gustave Le Bon's alarmist diagnosis of 'the mind of the masses' from 1895 – drawing analogies between 'the idle excitement of the spectator' and the excessive patriotic enthusiasm displayed at the celebrations on the relief of Mafeking in 1901.[4] Le Bon's influence can also be seen in John Burns' deprecation of the 'spirit of the horde' in football crowds, in 1908, and in C.F.G. Masterman's portrait of their excitableness and anonymous 'menace' in 1909.[5] Yet if some feared the crowds, others were comforted that their ready absorption in the flow of play meant 'England need never fear revolution'.[6] By the 1920s, commentators and reformers generally operated under the heading of 'the problem of leisure' where former critics had extolled 'rational recreation', perhaps because the early twentieth century's 'psychological turn' betokened a weakening of confidence in the possibilities of rationality.[7] However, other reasons for this shift of focus from 'recreations' to 'leisure' were the arrival of the eight-hour day in 1919 and an empathetic realization of the burdensome surplus of *unwanted* 'leisure-time' represented by the mass unemployment of the slump and the Depression.[8] Certainly, British intellectuals were aware of pessimistic 'mass-society' analyses – represented, for example, by the Russian-American historian, Rostovtzeff, who asked: was not 'every civilization bound to decay as soon as it penetrates the masses?'.[9] Ortega y Gasset's *Revolt of the Masses* – containing his argument that they would supplant cultured minorities, both in politics and in the 'domain of pleasure' – had been translated within two years of its publication.[10] Some critics came from a left-wing perspective, fearing manipulation 'of the mob' by 'fun-bosses' whipping up 'storm[s] of popular delight' to make money from passive audiences (particularly in the cinema).[11] The popular novelist J.B. Priestley feared the evolution of a population 'entirely without ... any real desire to think and act for themselves' and (following a logic first teased out by Masterman in 1909) worried that they would be 'the perfect subjects for an iron autocracy'.[12] However, once again, a bluff (and cogent) empiricism could be employed to puncture excessive concern. Thus, the liberal-rational historian and philosopher Cecil Delisle Burns dealt briskly with Ortega – arguing that the 'supposed lack of individuality in modern conditions is an illusion of superior persons', for 'the more you know of common men, the more uncommon you find each to be'. Moreover, the qualities of crowds at leisure events put the activities of mobs into perspective; most, he argued, were harmonious, self-regulating and good-humoured.[13] Similarly, there was no trace of regret in the outlook of historian and reviewer H.M. Stannard, who argued that the inescapable popularity of the wireless and cinema had altered 'the tone of English life' in a 'democratic' direction, contributing to 'a new conception of the art of living; with leisure placed on a level with work'.[14]

Potentially, theorists of leisure had the greatest opportunity to influence its practical development through impinging on the consciousness of legislators. To what extent did the British state react? Given that the dominant nineteenth-century tradition was to regulate but otherwise to be unwilling to intervene, it was in keeping that street betting was controlled in 1906 (in a notoriously class-biased manner), and cinema safety stipulations were imposed in 1909. However, localized Sunday cinema opening was authorized in 1932 (to cut the Gordion knot created by the tussle of popular demand and Sabbatarian traditionalists).[15] Furthermore, the exigencies of war had encouraged positive intervention in the drink trade in the Carlisle state-pub experiment of 1915, and the approach of another war motivated the provision of physical fitness facilities after 1937.[16] Superficially, the Holidays with Pay Act of 1938 might appear to be affirmatively interventionist, but the reform had minimal cost to the state and was gestated by many years of labour movement pressure.[17] Otherwise, the central state did little before the Second World War: the expansion of parks, sports fields and swimming facilities had to rely on hard-strapped local authorities, or philanthropists.[18] However, 'education for leisure' programmes were devised for districts of heavy unemployment, and the need for industrial efficiency in the Second World War led to the extension of paid holidays.[19] The war was also important in prompting efforts to maintain national morale through the popularization of high culture; under the aegis of CEMA – the predecessor of the Arts Council of 1945 – classical music and drama were taken to the people.[20] It was the prospect of more democratization of culture in a 'mass-society' which stimulated T.S. Eliot to a notable defence of an elite of aristocratic guardians in 1948.[21] However, consideration of the expansion of the broadcasting system since 1922, held at arms-length from the state by the BBC and shaped by the rational recreational spirit of Sir John Reith, makes Eliot's stance seem extraordinarily anachronistic.[22] In any case, despite his apprehensions, in practice, economic austerity and the cautious British voluntaristic tradition meant that the post-war welfare state made leisure provision a low priority. Little was done beyond a 6d rate authorized for municipal theatres and other arts, and the National Parks Act of 1949 – the latter under pressure from the outdoor movement – although the parks were neither nationally administered or financed nor very effective in preventing inappropriate development.[23] Support for the 1948 Olympic Games and the Festival of Britain of 1951 constituted Labour's chief contribution to the gaiety of the nation in the immediate post-war era.[24]

By the 1960s, however, ambitions were developing among Labour politicians to extend the remit of the welfare state sustainedly to leisure, and Conservatives too felt pressures to develop more interventionist policies, in terms of planning and expenditure. The 'problem of leisure' was now seen as consisting in a surfeit of time, especially that possessed by newly affluent, but often imperfectly socially integrated, youth. The period saw a late flourishing of fears that 'mass society' would destroy 'civilization', but by the 1970s the realities of electoral politics and social change in the post-war era radically reduced the appeal of such sentiments.[25] Nevertheless, although the Conservatives claimed to be 'unequivocally on the side of more leisure', they proved unwilling to give that view institutional expression before 1964, whereas the succeeding Labour government established a Sports Council (1965) and a Countryside Commission (1967), and in 1975 issued a White Paper describing recreation as 'one of the community's everyday needs' and leisure services 'as part of the general fabric of social services'.[26] Significant expenditure on sports centres, community centres and arts centres followed – not least because of a new, EEC-conscious realization of how far Britain had fallen behind continental developments, particularly in the Netherlands.[27] There were many serious differences of emphasis in the politics of leisure in subsequent decades; however, the arguments were always within a broad framework which accepted that a responsibility for leisure planning was now a function of modern government, not least because recurring unemployment, especially youth unemployment, resurrected fears regarding dissident and delinquent groups, particularly following serious urban riots in 1981–2. This was despite the period of Thatcherite neo-liberalism, when the Countryside Commission was marginalized, the Arts Council impoverished and the Sports Council induced to search for business finance to replace state money. Yet the introduction of the National Lottery in 1994 by Thatcher's successor, John Major, created the means to restore the trajectory of leisure expenditure for social welfare. More than £2 billion was available to the arts and sport by 2000, vastly outstripping contributions from the Treasury, even though this funding was distributed through a bidding process which disadvantaged the less articulate and advantaged the already well-resourced. Major's government sought to rebuild a sense of national cohesion symbolically through promoting elite sports in its *Raising the Game* strategy of 1994; however, under 'New Labour' the accent shifted back to *A Sporting Future for All* (2000).[28]

The influence of the state on mass leisure was therefore increasing as the century progressed, principally through the provision of greater access to the arts, the open air and to sporting facilities, providing alternatives to the profit-driven imperatives of commercial operators. Mass leisure time itself owed little to the state, having been created, just as it was predominantly filled, by other influences – commercial and industrial or voluntary and communal, in an amalgam of history from above and below.

II

'Leisure', seen in historical perspective, was irreducibly a question of *time*, for free time was its indispensable condition. Equally, however, in a society in which most activities were commodified (increasingly enticingly), it was also a question of *money*. Accordingly, the economically inactive need to be considered separately: whether they were unemployed, retired or – reflecting the gendered nature of leisure – housewives. Overall, however, at the beginning of the twentieth century one of the key distinctions between the mass of the population – the working and lower middle classes – and its middle and upper sections was that the former had neither much money nor much leisure time. By contrast, the upper reaches of society had ample amounts of both, and hence constituted a 'leisure class' – in Thorstein Veblen's terminology – namely, one with a considerable capacity for and tendency towards conspicuous consumption in order to assert status.[29] As we shall see, that strong contrast was ultimately blurred by the spread of popular leisure time and prosperity, for both developed enormously in tandem with the dramatic rise in GDP per capita, especially in the second half of the twentieth century – so much so that Lord Beveridge quipped that the 1960s' working class could now almost be called a new 'leisured class'.[30]

Beveridge assumed that the financially disabling mass unemployment which had scarred the inter-war decades had been vanquished. British workers had been inured by their place in history to regard leisure as the obverse of and reward for labour, so long-term unemployment had been devastating for many (though mitigated to some extent by welfare benefits introduced after 1911 and 1918, by allotments and cheap cinema seats, and by supportive communities).[31] The resurgence of large-scale unemployment in the 1980s could, potentially at least, be filled by now ubiquitous television. However, it seems that it did not generally give sufficient meaning to youthful lives to compensate. Rather, by beaming in evidence of the varied and expensive leisure activities of their working contemporaries, alienation was increased – hence a search for excitement and oblivion through the use of recreational drugs (as well as alcohol), particularly in the mining communities devastated by pit closures.[32] Unemployed youth in inner cities and outlying estates found a similar release. In the same period, there was evidence of a more fashion-driven take-up of recreational drugs (and drug-related music) by their more fortunate work-rich contemporaries, who were the beneficiaries of the unprecedented purchasing power developed to some extent in the 1930s but particularly since the 1950s – although alcohol and cigarettes were by far the most important stimulants.[33]

At the other end of the age range, the latter stages of the century witnessed the growth of an increasingly healthy retired population (15 per cent of the total in the last two decades), some of whom at least had now reached a personal 'age of leisure' – spending a higher proportion of their household incomes on leisure goods and services than any other group.[34] Yet their contemporaries also included large numbers 'in bitter want and need', and others who slipped steadily into senility.[35]

The influence of gender on the possibilities and uses of leisure has rightly been much emphasized in recent decades. In 1908 W.H. Davies, the bard of leisure, noted how poor men's wives 'do hum like bees/About their work from morn till night'.[36] He was correct about the almost incessant labour in unmodernized households, although the rustic image hardly captures the grim reality of slum life in places like Bethnal Green or Salford before the 1950s, where often the only respite was gossiping at the door.[37] Contrast that with the (amusingly Italian) evocation of a London theatre audience, also in 1908:

> It is a mixed crowd, formed for the most part of small parties and courting couples. There are shopmen, clerks, and spinsters in pince-nez; but more numerous still are the shopgirls, milliners, dressmakers, typists, stenographers, cashiers of large and small houses of business, telegraph and telephone girls, and the thousands of other girls whose place in the social scale is hard to guess or to define, who avail themselves of the liberty allowed them by custom, and the coldness of the English masculine temperament, to wander alone at night from one end of London to the other, spending all their money in gadding about, and, above all, on the theatre.[38]

For theatre (or music halls) for the young female wage-earner in the early 1900s, read cinema or dance halls in inter-war Britain, pop concerts in the 1960s, discos in the 1970s, and pubs and night clubs in the 1980s and 1990s. The possibilities of women's leisure were signally shaped by their stage in the life-cycle, and the period when they came of age – and therefore, in both instances, by their financial resources.[39] Thus, the position of many married women was very different. For two-thirds of the twentieth century the 'marriage bar' on employment was strongly enforced, and, despite falling birth rates, looking after children was seen as a practical constraint on their ability to share a wider social stage, as mothers tended to define their leisure lives in terms of their responsibility and duty to their families.[40] From about 1950, it is true, a great many more married women were making their way back to paid work after having had their (smaller) families, but then they bore the 'double burden' related by a female delegate to the 1955 Amalgamated Engineers' conference who called for a forty-hour week – for 'the women she represented had two jobs to do … [as they] … returned to the washing, cooking and housework'.[41] A working man was 'a man of leisure compared with his working wife'.[42] And so, it is appropriate to look both at paid and unpaid work for women in assessing the extent of their leisure, though, for men, things were perhaps changing on the unpaid front, at least in the late decades of the century.

III

To analyse leisure as time it is necessary to begin with work time, as its largest single determinant. In 1900 a minimum of 54 hours constituted the standard working week for most manual workers (one-third of whom were female), which, potentially at least, meant they had a half-day off on Saturdays (though not the substantial numbers who worked 72 hours or even more). In the 1990s, by contrast, the average week of full-time manual workers had gone down to 44 hours, with Saturdays off. Similarly, although hard savings and careful management meant that increasing numbers of workers could afford to take themselves off for a week's holiday in the early 1900s – the leading example being the Lancashire 'wakes' – this was very much influenced by their stage in the family life-cycle and contrasted invidiously with the *paid* holidays accorded to clerical and non-manual labour. By contrast, again, in the late 1990s the vast majority had at least four weeks' holiday paid for by an employer, and manual/clerical status distinctions were substantially eroded. These were historic gains for those – until the 1980s the vast majority – who had the hardest, dirtiest and dreariest jobs. Nevertheless, late-twentieth century Britain was a long way away from the 'age of leisure' which had been predicted earlier.[43] Indeed, in a comparative perspective, British workers shifted from having a working week 5–10 hours *shorter* than that of their counterparts in Germany and France in 1905, to a working week 4–5 hours *longer* than the European (including the Dutch) averages in 1998.[44] Why did this situation arise? What was its significance for our understanding of the evolution of mass leisure?

Widespread twentieth-century advances in leisure time had begun in 1918–19, as part of a remarkable European-wide trend towards a 48-hour week. In Britain, wartime and immediate post-war full employment, and full wage packets, gave workers the confidence to threaten strikes to shorten their working hours, in fulfilment of a trade union campaign for an 'eight-hour day' first put forward internationally in the 1880s.[45] Irrespective of the need to relax and recuperate, there were good solidaristic arguments for unions to seek this, in order to reduce unemployment or to lessen its effect at the next cyclical downturn; equally, union members knew that a shorter standard week created the possibility of higher wages through extended overtime payments.[46] Nevertheless, insofar as the 48-hour week allowed a Saturday half-holiday, and was not disrupted through new shift-working systems or the increasing length of journeys to work, this was an historic shift in the amount and quality of recreational time.[47] Some wished to go further, calling for a 44 or 40-hour week – mostly unavailingly in this period. Yet, as Figure 9.1 suggests, there was a dramatic and historic downward shift in *actual* working hours in the aftermath of the war – which fell from 54 to 46 between 1910 and 1924. Despite subsequent fluctuations, the mean of actual working time never subsequently rose above 48 hours.[48]

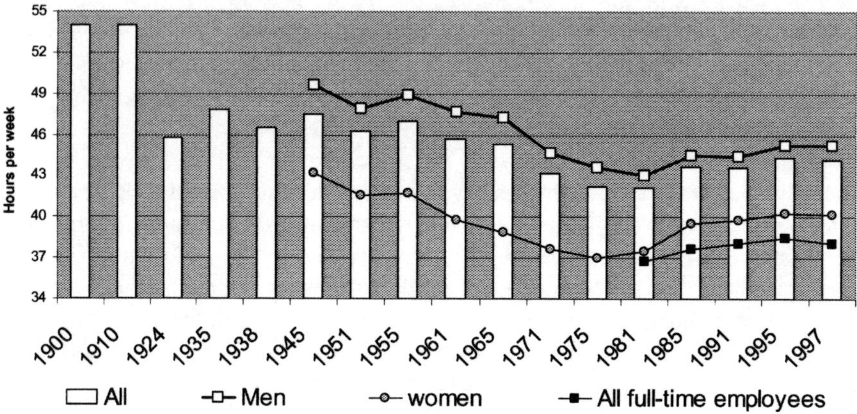

Figure 9.1 Average Actual Weekly Hours of British Manual Workers in Manufacturing 1900–97 (cf. all full-time employees 1979–97)
Sources: A.H. Halsey with J. Webb, *Twentieth-century British Social Trends* (Basingstoke, 2000), table 8.18, p. 306; 8.19, p. 307.

In the optimistic post-war period, women trade unionists proposed a 'Right to Leisure' Bill, so that 'full opportunity for recreation and physical and mental development … [might] be available for all'.[49] Although that initiative got short shrift, other trade unions were able to push simultaneously for the first large-scale development of paid holidays, which 1 million manual workers gained in 1919.[50] By 1922 an extra 500,000 had benefited in industries where 'Joint Industrial Councils' had been established to contain unrest.[51] The democratizing impact of that development was limited in scale but indubitable, dramatically so in the case of Robert Roberts' father – a Salford engineering worker – on his first charabanc touring holiday, for whom the condescension of the residential bourgeoisie in a Cheltenham hotel was enough to turn this erstwhile Liberal into a Labour voter for the rest of his life.[52] However, in the slump some employers retrenched on existing deals (not least the coal owners before the General Strike of 1926), and further aspirations to share work by decreasing the working week were frustrated by the Great Depression of the early 1930s – so that by 1936 less than 10 per cent of the total workforce had the paid holiday week.[53]

Yet the dream of holidays-with-pay had been implanted successfully, and labour organizations, industrial and political, national and international (in the form of the

League of Nations' International Labour Organization), revived the campaign in the 1930s, ultimately successfully (with a little indirect assistance from Hitler). Despite the severe, regionally concentrated unemployment which persisted throughout the inter-war years, real wages had risen substantially for the majority of workers across the period, as prices for food and mass-produced goods fell. More food, less exhaustion from work and the resultant vitality contributed to the notable inter-war demand for outdoor recreation which made holidays the topic of the day, and must have contributed to the sense that they ought to be a social right. The movement for outdoor, 'fresh-air' recreation (sponsored by religious and political organizations elsewhere in Europe) was built in Britain on the voluntaristic foundations laid by organizations like the Cyclists' Touring Club (1878), the Cooperative Holiday Association (1891), the Clarion Cyclists (after 1891), and by the numerous local rambling clubs (which federated nationally in 1905), the Camping Club of Great Britain (1905), the Boy Scouts (1908) and the Holiday Fellowship (1913).[54] These organizations had mainly benefited lower-middle-class and artisan sections of the population. However, cyclists and ramblers from the majority of the working class came into their own in the 1920s (a shift symbolized by the title of the Communist-led British Workers' Sports Federation of 1923) and were to some extent catered for by the foundation of the Youth Hostels Association in 1930 (on both CHA and German models).[55] The mood in the early 1930s was caught in *I'm happy when I'm hiking* – one of a rash of such popular songs – for hiking fitted well into the 1930s' vogue for sunbathing and 'keep fit' (37 per cent of the population told Gallup they hiked their way to health).[56] Nevertheless, when all was said and done, vastly more people were borne on trains to the ample bosoms of seaside landladies during 'wakes' weeks than went on walks, creating that distinctively raffish, pleasure-driven, consumerist, sensation-seeking escapism which was one of the working-class's distinctive contributions to British culture – even before widespread paid holidays.[57] From the 1920s, less active holiday-makers could achieve a little more fresh air and see the sights on enormously popular open-topped motor charabanc trips sponsored by workplaces, pubs and parishes (amongst others).[58] Stays at (tented) holiday camps by the sea also went back to the late nineteenth and early twentieth centuries, and a mixture of philanthropic, socialist and cooperative ventures, particularly on the Isle of Man and the east coast. They were expanded upon in the 1920s by commercial companies; however, the best-known entrepreneur, Billy Butlin, did not open his first camp until 1936 (when he astutely supported the lobby for a Holidays with Pay Bill).[59] Other sun and sand-seekers found places to stay in coastal shanty towns and caravan sites.[60] Yet, collectively, in 1937, across the country as a whole, only an estimated 15 million people took holidays away from home (a significant proportion of whom must have been from above the working classes). For some of the 31 million left in the cities and towns this was the great era for the development of glamorously modernistic municipal 'lidos', with their 'promiscuous democracy of age, class, bodily shape and temperament' contrasting significantly with their segregated, often somewhat utilitarian, predecessor Victorian indoor 'swimming-baths'.[61]

Taken together, these developments proposed the desirability of facilitating holidays more widely, especially as substantial economic recovery set in by the mid-1930s. Both unions and progressive employers saw the Holidays with Pay Act of 1938 as 'a measure of social justice' – for workers themselves and for the housewives and mothers who 'contribut[ed] … to their efficiency' through running their homes for them.[62] Leading employers and government ministers also saw the force of the argument that the intensiveness of what it has become fashionable, if controversial, to call 'Fordist' assembly-line production created a need for relief for 'the human factor in industry'.[63] Yet, it cannot be emphasized too strongly that the Act was actually more effective in its gestation than in the scope of its powers – the latter being limited mainly to securing holidays in the minority of government-regulated industries. Its real significance was in pushing the bulk of employers to act, to accede minimally to a week, to try to pre-empt the TUC's call for ten days or a fortnight. Thus, in the year between the inception of the investigative Amulree Committee and its report in 1938, the numbers with a paid week's holiday rose from less than 2 million to nearly eight (representing 40 per cent of the workforce).[64] By the outbreak of the Second World War the total had risen to 12 million workers (60 per cent), though hardly at a propitious moment. The war effort stimulated the sacrifice of weekly leisure (and bank holidays) to enormous amounts of overtime, but with ex-union boss and Coalition Minister of Labour Ernest Bevin convinced of the folly of overwork and encouraging the extension of paid holidays, they encompassed thirteen to 15 million workers by 1945.[65] Restrictions on southern and eastern coastal visits, and on rail travel, meant that people were encouraged to spend their holidays locally – an extensive 'holidays at home' programme was created, involving circuses, concerts, dances, fairs, opera in the parks and much else besides. However, the desire to get away was very strong indeed, and surprisingly large numbers achieved it, giving the Blackpool holiday industry a very good war.[66]

The post-war period can be roughly divided into two phases, cognate with the strength (and then weakness) of trade unionism, and reflecting prosperity and relative depression in the national economy: from 1945 to the 1970s, during which substantial gains were made in both working hours and the length (and variety) of holidays in an age of increasing prosperity and optimism, and from then to the end of the century, when inflation hit and unemployment rose, and there was a much more mixed picture.

Immediately after the war, the unions had the political wind behind them and got the pre-war 48-hour 'standard week' down to 44 or 45 hours, as well as achieving pay for bank holidays. Surveys suggested that well over half of the population spent some time away from home in their annual summer break after the war, compared with only one-third beforehand.[67] Billy Butlin, camp-proprietor extraordinaire, came into his own in this period and claimed 1.6 million visitors by 1949. Though holiday camps as a whole constituted less than 10 per cent of the market, their extensive facilities were particularly attractive to families with young children.[68] In the economically expansionary early 1950s a trade union push meant two-thirds of workers gained a two-week holiday – including farm workers, despite their employers' leader's condescending regret that 'so many … did not know how to use their existing week's vacation happily'.[69] By 1955 a fortnight was well-nigh universal – though in the process white-collar workers pushed up to three weeks to preserve their superior status.[70] Characteristically, for both social and economic reasons (workers' friend-ships and family links and firms' supply chains) the holidays were clustered. Thus, at the beginning of the holiday fortnight in 1955, of an estimated 850,000 Birmingham workers, 110,000 left with their families by 220 special holiday trains, 24,000 went with one coach company alone (uncounted thousands went by motorbike and sidecar, and automobile), while a mere 1,000 flew abroad. 'Workers seem to like the holiday spirit supposedly generated by crowds,' it was reported, 'going to the same boarding house every year, arranging to meet the same friends – often those they play darts with at home.'[71]

Yet, if there is no doubt that leisure in the form of holidays was valued, the sur-prisingly small numbers who travelled from Birmingham, plus a national rise in weekly working hours by the mid-1950s (see Figure 9.1), may testify to a simulta-neous desire to garner wages as well as holidays while the economic sun shone. Attractively advertised consumer products (and hire purchase schemes) were inducing workers and their families into a new world of material plentifulness (espe-cially by comparison with the hardships experienced before the war), and it is not sur-prising that many put money above time at this stage. By the 1960s, however, prosperity appeared to be more embedded, and the average *actual* working week began to fall (from 47 hours in 1955 to 42 in 1981). This phase began with a large number of trade unions agitating for a reduction in the formal, or 'standard', week to 40 hours, on the grounds, neatly summed up by one, of 'productivity, capacity and social necessity'.[72] The movement gradually but surely achieved a 40-hour week by the mid-1960s, and thus the indispensable condition of a *whole* Saturday free from work. However, perhaps the most striking gain in the 1960s and 1970s was the dou-bling of paid holidays, as trade unions pressed for permanent benefits for their members in the context of a generally tight labour market and rising real incomes.[73] Three-week holidays were phased in during the late 1960s for well over half the workforce, with the additional benefit that differentials between manual workers and clerks were to some extent eroded.[74] By 1981 over 85 per cent of workers had paid holidays of four weeks or even more, though small differentials remained between men and women and between manual and non-manual workers (prompting 'staff har-monization' policies to reduce these).[75] The creation of a May Day Bank Holiday at the behest of the TUC in 1978 symbolized this era of trade union achievement in making England a merrier place, although increasingly people preferred to spend their holidays abroad – 10 million in the following year and more than 20 million by 1987, with Spain the chief beneficiary – 'as the real cost of package holidays plum-meted'.[76] British seaside resorts accordingly entered a testing period.[77] By 1998 rising living standards meant that the number of holidays spent overseas overtook the number spent at home for the first time.[78]

Yet, the Thatcherite final decades of the century were also characterized by de-industrialization, casualization, deregulation, the near-halving of trade union mem-bership, and thus an economic and political climate unfavourable to union ambitions – announced in 1979 – for a 35-hour standard week.[79] Indeed, between 1981 and 1985 actual hours for manual workers *rose* from 42 to nearly 44; female manual workers suffered the largest increases, but the trend hit *all* workers, for whom there was nearly a further hour's increase by 1995.[80] Working hours data for the entire workforce covered a wide range, from low-paid service workers to City 'yuppies' on the way to burn-out – and all these averages concealed a vast increase in 'flexible working' (which brought uncertainty and anti-social hours to some) and the development of temporary, part-time, sub-contracted and self-employed labour. Overall, the trend was towards increasing inequalities in leisure time, matching those in income, though at least some longer working hours were undoubtedly driven by a desire to earn more to try to keep up with mortgage repayment costs, which steadily increased in relation to income in the following decade.[81]

The century ended with an episode which threw the contrasting elements of the story into high relief, particularly the relative contributions of trade unions and government. In the 1880s socialists had insisted that progress in the campaign for a fair reward for labour was most securely achieved through international cooperation by trade unions, though they were not averse to legislation if they could get it. At the close of the succeeding century unions operating in a hostile national climate welcomed with open arms the European Union's 'Employment Time Directive' of 1993, which sought a statutory guarantee of a limited working week and four weeks' holiday, thus overriding Britain's *laissez-faire* tradition. This was no bad thing from the point of view of those not covered by 'terms of service' agreements, who constituted half the national workforce by the late 1990s. All in all, when the Directive was enacted in Britain in 1998, 6 million workers had their holidays increased, 2 million of whom had not been entitled to paid holidays previously.[82] Characteristically, however, the 'New Labour' government allowed employers to count bank holidays within the 28 days (some of whom took the opportunity to do that) and negotiated an opt-out from the maximum 48-hour week – with the result that just over a fifth of UK workers (a mixture, on the one hand, of career-driven professionals and managers and, on the other, of plant and machine operatives in poorly paid industries orientated towards overtime) worked as much as 60 hours per week – twice the proportion who did so in other EU countries.[83]

It was not altogether surprising, perhaps, that dissatisfaction was frequently expressed in the 1990s about the balance between work and leisure. The root of this appears to have been twofold. Work was concentrated into fewer households, as dual-career families grew. Secondly, the reorganization of work – in manufacturing in the 1980s and the public sector in the 1990s – made for greater intensity, the sense of which carried over into complaints about the pace of life. The latter was increasing anyway because of technological developments in transport and electronics and, paradoxically, simply because there were more leisure activities to choose from. Dual-career parents, in particular, began to regard themselves as 'cash rich, but time poor'. 'Having it all', as the phrase went, turned out often to be a temporal high-wire juggling act.[84] Actually, their lives were made easier when Sunday shopping was legalized in 1994, admittedly at the expense of the leisure of 1.3 million service workers. Yet, of course, virtually *any* Sunday activity undertaken by the 'average household' necessitated the existence of service workers, of whom there were already 8 million. Such employees were compensated (or not) for Sunday work to the extent that they were unionized or self-employed.[85]

Sabbatarian influence on public opinion and leisure activities had begun to fail well before 1914 with the advent of Sunday cycling and motoring, golf and boating, and – after a long-fought campaign – the opening of the British Museum in 1896.[86] But entrance-fee entertainment and competitive sport were another matter. Commercial Sunday cinema was only permitted after 1932, on a local-option basis, which meant that in 1954 a third of English cinemas were still closed on a Sunday and very few were open in Scotland or Wales.[87] 'Sunday can be a dreadful day in our big cities', opined a reporter in July 1962, struck by the desultory life in Manchester's Piccadilly Gardens, where the only entertainment was 'the sound of recorded hymns'.[88] The Football Association set its face even against amateur Sunday matches until 1960, but by 1974, in a period of falling attendances, the financial advantages for the professional clubs came to seem overwhelming.[89] The Bishop of Coventry, a 'Sky Blues' patron, showed the way 'establishment opinion' was moving: 'When one sees young people mooching around the streets on Sunday afternoons, is it not better for them to watch a football match?'[90] Motor-racing had already finessed its way around the Sunday Observance Act, and professional cricket introduced a Sunday league in 1969.[91] Sunday cinema was legalized without exception in 1972, as was theatre; Sunday horse racing and betting were allowed in 1994; only dancing and casinos remained controlled (though the law regarding dancing was frequently flouted).[92] Britain thus slowly embraced what, in its insular way, it called, often inaccurately, 'the Continental Sunday' – though public opinion polls suggested that many continued to see Sunday as a day with a special emphasis on family activities.[93] To that extent, at least, the calls to 'Keep Sunday Special' were heeded.[94]

Yet, although no conclusions about leisure time can be drawn across the twentieth century unless working hours are considered, evidence regarding *unpaid* work to do with the household or family must also be taken into account, in order to measure the precise amount of residual time which is the ultimate definition of leisure – namely, time one could call one's own. Fortunately, 'time-diary' research from 1961 to 1995 allows account to be taken of family and household tasks, such as child-care and shopping. Unpaid activities of this sort were recorded as having increased, with the development, for example, in the 1990s of the 'school run' and car-borne Sunday trips to giant supermarkets – whereas time devoted to cooking and cleaning decreased. All in all, time-diary research suggested that leisure as residual time had certainly increased across the last four decades of the century – but only by a surprisingly small seven minutes per day for men. A key reason for this was that they were now playing a greater part in family life. Thus, although, 'in absolute terms', women still had 50 minutes less daily leisure than men, women's residual weekly time had increased by 41 minutes across the decades.[95] Furthermore, across the whole century there was also something of a convergence between high and low social status groups, both male and female, not least because of the flight from domestic service since the First World War. In the second half of the century high social status was increasingly indicated by busy-ness (as was suggested by the response to the 1998 Working Time Directive); more widespread leisure lessened its utility to those who wished to assert their difference from the commonality – standing Veblen's *Theory of the Leisure Class* on its head![96]

IV

Thus the extension of weekly leisure time and the making of weekends and holidays in twentieth-century Britain were complex processes, dependent on a mixture of trade union campaigns (based on underlying economic trends), employers' strategies, the lead given by voluntary social organizations, inducements offered by leisure entrepreneurs, and popular aspirations for more interesting lives. Quite often those aspirations, and their limited means, led people into crowded situations, to gather literally *en masse* at places such as football stadia, the pier at Blackpool or in public parks, in densities which contrasted with those experienced during the more privatized leisure of the later twentieth century.[97] Thus, 'mass leisure' may function as a label to signal the most numerously followed and therefore the most economically and, possibly, the most politically, culturally and socially significant leisure activities. Yet, there is a danger that the use of the label will mislead the historian into supposing that there was a uniformity of attitude and response from these audiences and spectators. After all, who were the masses? They were divided by gender, so that football was always dominated by men and cinema by women. They were divided by youth and age: as in the cinema and – for much of the first half of the century – in the pubs. Dance halls were the preserve of the young.[98] Seaside holiday crowds re-created the entire social pattern of inland towns in some resorts, notably Blackpool, but were otherwise extraordinarily differentiated.[99] On the face of it, the most standardized holiday experience was offered by holiday camps, if only because of their economies of scale. Their historians demonstrate that not the least of their attractions was that the pleasant fantasy world of luxury and escape that they created was such a contrast to the standardized existences of many of their clientele at work and home, yet, at the same time, it was precisely that background which made them work – 'knobbly knee competitions' and all![100] Nevertheless, the concept of 'mass leisure' overlooked the social specificity of much popular leisure, such as the regional and occupational cultures which gave rise to canary fancying or pigeon flying, for instance.[101] Equally, as we have seen, many people broke away from commercialized 'mass leisure' and sought country air through hiking, cycling and youth hostelling. Observed closely, the 'mass audience' fragmented into different sections. Moreover, there were other substantial but differentiated mass leisure pursuits, in the sense of being very wide and 'of the people', such as angling, which involved over 4 million people by the end of the twentieth century but which had very little impact on the rest of society.[102] Popular leisure was in significant ways not 'mass' at all. The leisure of many of 'the masses' took place at the street level, in local neighbourhoods, in playgrounds and on street corners. Thus, although a study of early twentieth century youths in Birmingham found that their 'greatest single interest' was football, and their 'greatest formative influence' was the cinema – followed by the music halls and by 'penny dreadfuls' and 'halfpenny comics' – it was amusement, stimulation and sensation which they sought, and these could also be found, to an extent, for free on 'the Street' – where there were also girls to parade with.[103]

In attracting the support of such boys, and their elder brothers and fathers, Association Football had witnessed an astonishing growth since the 1880s, especially in Sheffield, the Midlands, Lancashire and industrial Scotland, and from the 1890s in London, becoming the pre-eminent spectator sport. Against these industrial and urban backgrounds, it provided an exciting physical and psychological focus for the competitive (and territorial) instincts, and an activity that anyone could play, or watch in satisfying collective warmth, and comment or gamble upon. Between 1888 and 1908 spectatorship grew by a factor of ten, increasing to 6 million per annum, at this stage being composed principally of the upper working class and, to some extent, lower middle-class men and older youths. Attendance doubled again by 1914, and then rose through the 1920s and 1930s, consisting by now of a much broader swath of the working class, as the semi-skilled layer began to get better off and, after 1918, had the half-holiday. It reached its apogee in the 1945–7 seasons after the war, when purchasing power was high and many well-established modes of leisure enjoyed a boom (including dog-racing and cinema).[104] Thereafter it declined steadily for a mixture of inter-locking reasons, until there was a recovery very late in the century.

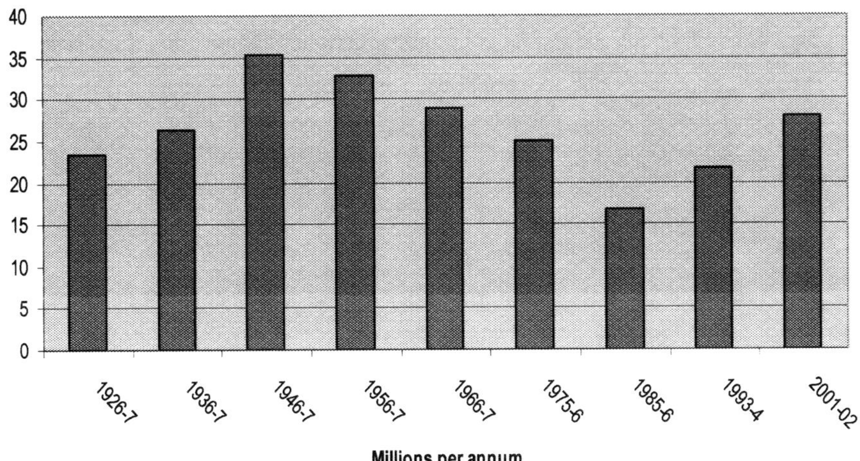

Figure 9.2 Football League Attendances 1926–7 to 2001–2
Source: Statistics are drawn from Stephen Dobson and J.A. Goddard, 'Performance, Revenue and Cross-subsidization in the Football League, 1927–94', *Economic History Review*, LI, no. 4 (1998), table 1 and http://european-football-statistics.co.uk/attn/totengall.htm re. 2001–2.

Alternative methods of spending time and money (such as motoring and the Do-It-Yourself boom in the 1950s) dissipated support at one level; in the 1960s and 1970s the erosion of jobs in heavy industries like mining and shipbuilding (from which many of the most loyal supporters were drawn) affected another.[105] As adult men were drawn away, the old self-regulating sense of discipline which had impressed observers as far back as the first Wembley Cup Final of 1923 – the 'White Horse Final' – began to collapse, and the phenomenon of usually youthful, attention-seeking 'football hooliganism' arose in the 1960s, which exacerbated the situation – especially with the advent of armchair spectatorship (*Match of the Day* began in

1964). Yet television also helped to save football, as the fees it generated allowed clubs to pay for greater policing and the reconstruction of their increasingly antiquated stadia, allowing a new sort of (often middle-class) spectator to share the experience (and, sometimes, the excitement) of live games.[106] Football had always been a sport with an appeal which went far beyond its players and its spectatorship, above all because of its ability to evoke strong feelings of local (though also national) identity. In the later twentieth century its appeal now stretched well beyond the working-class areas which had sustained it for most of its history: to some extent television and the marketing efforts of the wealthiest clubs created supporter networks which transcended localities (especially with regard to Manchester United), albeit often to the most intense scorn of the majority of supporters of opposing teams whose loyalties remained rooted in their home areas.

Even so, cinema, the inception of which can be dated precisely to 1896, was the mass entertainment *par excellence*. Such was the appeal of its (initially flickering) realism, and the emotional engagement achieved by its often melodramatic storylines, that by 1914 approximately 7 million tickets were sold *per week* (compared with 9 million football tickets *per annum*). Despite a certain amount of 'carriage trade' at Oxford Street 'picture palaces', attendance at this stage was overwhelmingly proletarian and young, catering for working-class neighbourhoods, which enjoyed the warm fug and audience-centred ambience of the early venues.[107] New levels of popularity were achieved during the First World War (particularly among women) as a result of the upheavals in previously settled routines, the thirst for news and diversion, and the desire to see the new stars, Charlie Chaplin and Mary Pickford – and cinemas became the most 'popular indoor amusements' in London.[108] However, as Nicholas Hiley has shown, a temporary slump followed the imposition of Entertainment Duty, which lasted until 1924. Its abolition for the cheaper seats produced an immediate boost to 20 million ticket sales per week (there were said to be 15 million regular attenders), but even the arrival of the talkies in 1928–9 did not encourage audiences up to 20 million again until 1940.[109] Declining audiences at small working-class cinemas which could not afford to be wired for sound had not yet been replaced by the new audiences attracted to the more expensive, very large, glitzy city-centre venues (with their additional inducements of dance halls and cafés to attract a more up-market audience). However, a core of approximately 15 million people (out of 45–46 million) sustained the cinema as frequent attenders: they were overwhelmingly working-class, female, unmarried and young. (Men, and the over-40s, went much less frequently.) The fundamentally working-class nature of cinema-going meant that cinema attendance was strongest where the working-class population was most concentrated, in the (often overcrowded) towns and cities of the north, the Midlands and Scotland, where cinemas acted as a luxurious contrast with, and escape from, home, as well as a source of entertainment and pleasure. Far from being a habitual, rather unthinking, passive activity, then, cinema-going involved choices which defied any monotonous 'mass-culture' stereotypes. Similarly, there were distinctly regional tastes in film to match.[110]

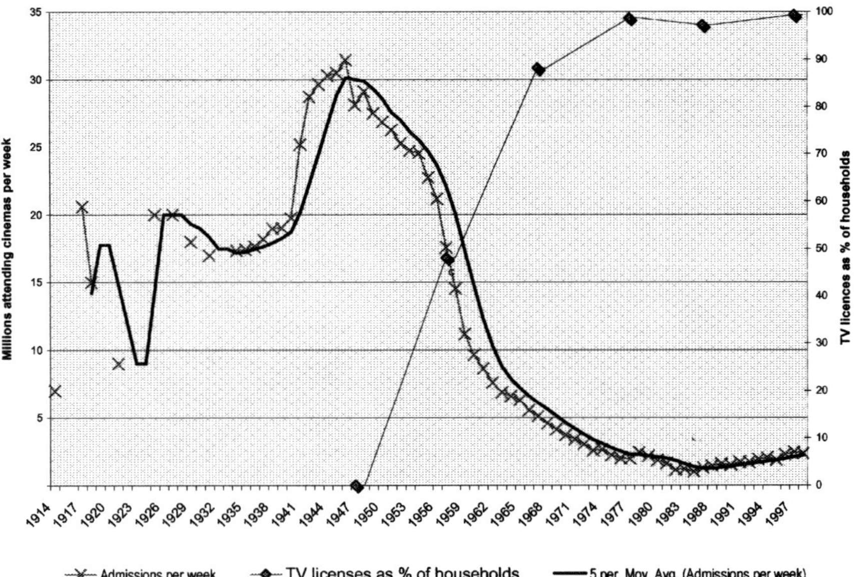

Figure 9.3 British Cinema Attendances per Week (Millions) and TV Licences as a Percentage of Households
Sources: Nicholas Hiley, '"Let's go to the pictures": the British Cinema Audience in the 1920s and 1930s', *Journal of Popular British Cinema*, 2 (1999), pp. 40–2, 46; Browning and Sorrell, 'Cinemas and Cinema-going in Great Britain', in A.H. Halsey with J. Webb, *Twentieth-century British Social Trends* (Basingstoke, 2000), p. 134, tables 18.8 and 18.10; *Annual Abstract of Statistics* (2003), table 12.3.

As the chart demonstrates, the greatest age of cinema attendance was in fact between 1940 and 1956, reaching its peak of 29 million people in 1948. Impressive as this was, it was still the case that, taking all in all, in 1943 the British public was divided roughly into one-third who went frequently to cinemas, slightly more than one-third who went less than once a week, and slightly fewer who never went at all (including 70 per cent of all pensioners).[111] We might deduce that, for a great many people, most of the time, even in the mid-twentieth century, leisure was already 'a home and family-centred affair'.[112] There was much truth in that and, from the 1920s onwards, domestic comfort was enhanced by new standards in private housing (and in much council housing – before the era of 'system build'), increasing the attractions of home. Gardening, do-it-yourself and 'hobbies' all increased as popular leisure activities in this period.[113] Radio broadcasting, from 1922, had a similar effect, as people rearranged their social and voluntary lives around particular broadcasts; by 1939 there were 9 million licences in a country of 11 million households.[114] The dramatic impact of television on cinema attendance, especially from the inception of ITV in 1955, is indicated in Figure 9.4. Television quickly established a central position in people's increasingly comfortable homes, fragmenting audiences into family groups (by contrast with cinema), though the idea of mass manipulation only made sense if it was assumed that people were indeed sitting there totally passively. Moreover, the time-budget evidence suggested that the amount of time devoted to watching television as such hardly changed across the period 1975–95, and, by the 1980s, the 'mass television audience' was further fragmented by the rise of video-recording, satellite broadcasting, and hence alternative channels, and the rise of home computers and CD players.[115] Thus, 'mass' publics were not necessarily very stable and, despite the fact that up to 33 hours per week were devoted on average to 'home entertainment' in 1985 (five times more than the time spent on gardening), the later history of the mass entertainment industry could be interpreted as querying the contention that 'mass society' created a 'mass audience' lacking individuality (and, by implication, lacking taste and discrimination). Nevertheless, the success of the BBC's *Royle Family* acting out their family dramas on the sofa in front of 'the telly' was piquant.[116]

In 1964 Mark Abrams reported that few now left the family hearth in the winter, except for the young.[117] Some, at any rate, of these young people were to play an important part in the sphere of mass leisure which historically had the greatest criticism directed towards it, namely alcohol consumption and the role of one of the most enduring, albeit changing, leisure institutions, the public house. As Figure 9.4 shows, alcohol consumption fell quite dramatically in the first third of the century – partly as a result of wartime taxation and the introduction of the afternoon break in public house hours, and partly as a result of a new generation being seduced by the cinema *et al.* Consumption then rose again during the Second World War, as other opportunities for the expenditure of full wage packets were limited (and, no doubt, for psychological reasons), then fell back in the 1950s and early 1960s as new consumption opportunities emerged. However, it then rose dramatically from the 1960s to the end of the 1970s. This was a reflection partly of demand – the coming of age of the post-war baby boomers with their ambitions to break the old behavioural barriers – and partly of supply – because Retail Price Maintenance was removed from alcoholic drinks in 1966 and supermarkets began selling at a discount, with great publicity.[118] The brewers were not far behind, setting up pub discos and issuing eye-catching advertisements, for example inviting the youth to 'Join the Younger set' and get 'a Younger taste … for life'. Even though beer consumption peaked in 1979, the profile of heavy drinkers continued to reduce in age – justifying the brewers' strategy. The result, in the mid-1980s, appeared to be the 'lager lout', who too frequently turned Friday and Saturday nights in British towns and cities into rowdy, disorderly, unpleasant places.[119] It was true that frequently violent drunken disorder had also been a feature of the low-consumption 1930s in Bolton and Blackpool, and a careful survey of several towns in the 1990s, backed by cross-national comparisons, suggested that it was rooted as much in the conditions in which drinking took place as in the drink itself, and in (age-old) male group dynamics – in which excitement and status were achieved through fighting.[120] Thus, the 'lager lout' joined the 'Teddy boys' of the 1950s, the 'Mods and Rockers' of the 1960s and the punks of the 1980s as 'folk devils' creating moral panic, though that might have been small comfort to anyone unwillingly caught up in the uncivil potential which lay at the core of their reputations![121]

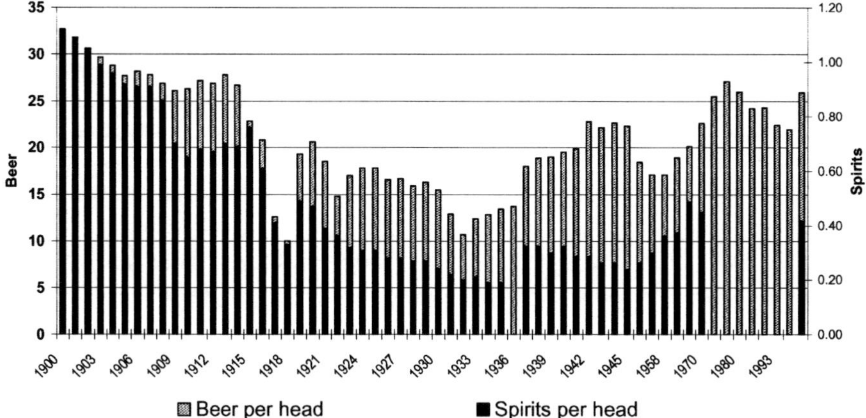

Figure 9.4 Beer and Spirits Consumption: Gallons per Head 1900–2000
Sources: G.P. Williams and G.T. Brake, *Drink in Great Britain 1900–1979* (London, 1980), pp. 354, 380, 383; John Burnett, *Liquid Pleasures: A Social History of Drinks in Modern Britain* (London, 1999), p. 137. It should be emphasized that there are problems of comparability between the data used in the chart, but then its purpose is only to be broadly indicative.

V

In conclusion, clearly, the history of leisure in twentieth century Britain was one of growth and sometimes dramatic development. In terms of time, there is no doubt that there was progress, albeit unequally distributed – especially just after the First World War, during the later 1930s, the later 1940s and the 1960s, and, so far as holidays were concerned, by the increase in living standards and the falling price of air travel. By the end of the twentieth century the British spent more on leisure and tourism than on food, rent and their community taxes combined.[122] The forces of change were above all market-driven (whether in terms of demand or supply), with government (national government at least) playing a limited and reluctant role in expanding opportunities for leisure time, although the welfare reform agenda established after 1945 eventually took leisure within its remit in as far as community facilities were concerned. Initially prompted by democratization, such facilities were also seen as palliatives for disaffected youth. Nevertheless, fears that 'mass society' would bring about a mind-numbing standardization which would destroy the civilization of the rich were overdrawn (visits to stately homes were up, visits to Blackpool were down).[123] It is true that late twentieth-century experience of the popular press did not altogether deny the proposition that the 'engineers of amusement', unchecked, had a capacity to debase the public taste by lowering the threshold of acceptability for profit.[124] Yet the notions of the mass-leisure pessimists were called into question not least because they overestimated the staying power of mature industrialism and the democratization of education and society more generally.

Notes

1. *The Times*, 29 June 1886; Asa Briggs, 'The Language of "Mass" and "Masses" in Nineteenth Century England', in David Rubinstein and David Martin (eds), *Ideology and the Labour Movement: Essays Presented to John Saville* (London, 1978), pp. 62–83.

2. Alexander Paterson, *Across the Bridges* (London, 1911), p. 217; Peter Bailey, *Leisure and Class in Victorian England: Rational Recreation and the Contest for Control, 1830–1885* (London, 1978; second edn 1987); Hugh Cunningham, *Leisure in the Industrial Revolution c. 1780–c. 1880* (London, 1980), pp. 90–2, 99–107, 110–11.

3. Michael Freeden, 'Hobson, John Atkinson (1858–1940)', *Oxford Dictionary of National Biography* (Oxford University Press, 2004) [hereafter *OxfDNB*]; G.K. Peatling, 'Rethinking the History of Criticism of Organised Sports', *Cultural and Social History*, 2(3) (2005), pp. 362–3ff.

4. Gustave Le Bon, *Psychologie des Foules* (Paris, 1895); *The Crowd: A Study of the Popular Mind* (London, 1896), pp. xv, xvii, xix; J.A.Hobson, *The Psychology of Jingoism* (London, 1901), pp. 6–12, 17–20, 29–32; J.A. Hobson, *Imperialism: A Study* (London, 1902), p. 226.

5. *The Times*, 9 June 1908; C.F.G. Masterman, *The Condition of England* (London, 1909; seventh edn, 1912), pp. 103, 105, 107, 113–14, 116.

6. *Commonwealth*, 1902, cited in R.J. Morris and Richard Rodger, *The Victorian City: A Reader in British Urban History* (London, 1993), p. 332; Leonard Hobhouse, *Democracy and Reaction* (1909), cited in Peatling, 'Rethinking the History', p. 364.

7. *The Times*, 17 Sept. 1929; Henry Durant, *The Problem of Leisure* (London, 1935).

8. For an excellent account of the complainants of the inter-war period see Gary Cross, *A Social History of Leisure since 1600* (Philadelphia, 1990), pp. 167–72.

9. M. Rostovtzeff, *Social and Economic History of the Roman Empire* (Oxford, 1926), cited in J.L. Hammond, *The Growth of Common Enjoyment* (Oxford, 1933), p. 14.

10. José Ortega y Gasset, *[La] rebelión de las masas* (Madrid, 1930); *The Revolt of the Masses* (London, 1932), p. 13. See the useful discussions of Rostovtzeff and Ortega in Patrick Brantlinger, *Bread and Circuses: Theories of Mass Culture as Social Decay* (Ithaca, 1983), pp. 44–7, 186–98.

11. Robert Sinclair, *Metropolitan Man* (London, 1937), pp. 116–17.

12. J.B. Priestley, *English Journey* (London, 1934), p. 405. For an excellent dissection of Priestley's outlook see Chris Waters, 'J.B. Priestley 1894–1984: Englishness and the Politics of Nostalgia', in Susan Pedersen and Peter Mandler, *After the Victorians: Private Conscience and Public Duty in Modern Britain* (London, Routledge, 1994), pp. 208–26.

13. C. Delisle Burns, *Leisure in the Modern World* (London, 1932), pp. 28, 166–7.

14. *The Times*, 3 May 1935.

15. David Dixon, *From Prohibition to Regulation: Bookmaking, Anti-gambling, and the Law* (Oxford, 1991), chap. 4; *The Times*, 28 May 1932. For class bias and regula-

tion see also Callum G. Brown, 'Sport and the Scottish Office in the Twentieth Century: the Control of a Social Problem', *European Sports History Review*, 1(1) (1998).

16. M.E. Rose, 'The Success of Social Reform? The Central Control Board (Liquor Traffic) 1915–21', in M.R.D. Foot (ed.), *War and Society: Historical Essays in Honour and Memory of J.R. Western, 1928–1971* (London, 1973), pp. 71–84; G.P. Williams and G.T. Brake, *Drink in Great Britain 1900–1979* (London, 1980), chap. 4; *The Times*, 5 Feb., 13 May, 15 Sept., 3, 6 Oct., 11 Nov. 1936, 8 Apr. 1937; Greenwood in *Parliamentary Debates (Hansard) House of Commons*, 5th Series, vol. 321 (1936), col. 599 [hereafter, references to Parliamentary Debates are rendered as *HL* or *HC Debs*, year (vol. no.), column number(s), with the name of the speaker in parenthesis]; *HC Debs* 1937 (322), 205–7 (Stanley); Tony Mason, 'Introduction', and Jeremy Crump, 'Athletics', in Tony Mason (ed.), *Sport in Britain: A Social History* (Cambridge, 1989), pp. 2, 68.

17. For details of the Holidays with Pay legislation see below.

18. See, for example, Henry W. De B. Peters, *The London Playing Fields Society … Centenary History, 1890–1990* (London, 1990), and cf. Stephen G. Jones, 'State Intervention in Sport and Leisure in Britain between the Wars', *Journal of Contemporary History*, 22(1) (1987), esp. pp. 166–7.

19. Andrzej Olechnowicz, 'Unemployed Workers, "Enforced Leisure" and Education for "The Right Use of Leisure" in Britain in the 1930s', *Labour History Review*, 70(1) (Apr. 2005), esp. pp. 34–6.

20. F.M. Leventhal, '"The Best for the Most": CEMA and state sponsorship of the arts in wartime, 1939–1945,' *Twentieth Century British History*, 1(3) (1990), pp. 289–317; Nick Hayes and Jeff Hill (eds), *'Millions like us'? British Culture in the Second World War* (Liverpool, 1999); Peter Mandler, 'Two Cultures – One – or Many', in Kathleen Burk (ed.), *The British Isles since 1945* (Oxford, 2003), pp. 129–31.

21. T.S. Eliot, *Notes towards the Definition of Culture* (London, 1948), pp. 16–19 *et passim*; Brantlinger, *Bread and Circuses*, pp. 199–210.

22. Paddy Scannell and David Cardiff, *A Social History of British Broadcasting, vol. 1: 1922–1939, Serving the Nation* (Oxford, 1991), esp. chap. 1; D.L. Le Mahieu, 'John Reith, 1889–1971: Entrepreneur of Collectivism', in Pedersen and Mandler, *After the Victorians*.

23. *The Times*, 5 Feb. 1948; *HL Debs* 1960 (221), 677 (Hailsham); 'Country Passport', *The Times*, 24 Sept. 1949; 'Shadow across the National Parks', *The Times*, 8 Dec. 1962. See also Ian P. Henry, *The Politics of Leisure Policy* (Houndmills, second edn, 2001), pp. 17–18.

24. Jeffrey Hill, *Sport, Leisure and Culture in Twentieth-century Britain* (Basingstoke, 2002), p. 149; Becky Conekin, '"Here Is the Modern World Itself": the Festival of Britain's Representations of the Future', in B. Conekin, Frank Mort and Chris Waters (eds), *Moments of Modernity: Reconstructing Britain 1945–1964* (London, 1999), pp. 228–46; Becky E. Conekin, *'The Autobiography of a Nation': The 1951 Festival of Britain* (Manchester, 2003).

25. This sentence refers to a debate in the House of Lords on 'the problem of leisure', and specifically to the speeches of Baroness Ravensdale (Curzon's daughter) and Lady Birdwood: *HL Debs* 1960 (221), 710–11, 726. I hope soon to publish a full

analysis of these debates in an essay entitled '"The Problem of Leisure" in 20th Century Britain".

26. *HL Debs* 1960 (221), 670 (Hailsham); *The Times*, 1 Mar. 1966, 11 Nov. 1967; Department of the Environment, *Sport and Recreation* (Cmd. 6200; London, 1975).

27. *The Times*, 27 Aug. 1963, 6 Jan. 1966, 6 July, 21 Nov. 1972, 27 July 1973, 6 Nov. 1974; John F. Coglan and Ida M. Webb, *Sport and British Politics since 1960* (London, 1990), pp. 69–70, 84; Henry, *Politics of Leisure Policy*, pp. 16–24. The number of indoor sports centres rose from 12 to 449 during 1971–81.

28. Peter McIntosh and Valerie Charlton, *The Impact of Sport for All Policy 1966–1984* (London, 1985), p. 156; Coglan and Webb, *Sport and British Politics*, pp. 86–8, 222–5; Barrie Houlihan, *The Government and Politics of Sport* (London, 1991), pp. 96–100; Henry, *Politics of Leisure Policy*, pp. 72–95; Kenneth Roberts, 'Leisure Responses to Urban Ills in Great Britain and Northern Ireland', in J. Sugden and A. Knox (eds), *Leisure in the 1990s: Rolling Back the Welfare State* (Eastbourne, 1992), pp. 9–14. For earlier proposals for a national lottery: *The Times*, 17 Apr. 1934 and 18 June 1949, *HL Debs* 1964 (258), 236 (Willis), and *The Times*, 3 Feb. 1965 (private member's Bill).

29. Thorstein Veblen, *The Theory of the Leisure Class: An Economic Study in the Evolution of Institutions* (London, 1899), esp. chap. 3. Veblen is excellently summarized in Jonathan Gershuny, *Changing Times, Work and Leisure in Postindustrial Society* (Oxford, 2000), chap. 2.

30. The essence of an enormous literature has recently been clearly and conveniently drawn upon by John Benson, *Affluence and Authority: A Social History of 20th Century Britain* (London, 2005), pp. 4–11. See also Jil Matheson and Carol Summerfield (eds), *Social Trends 30* (Great Britain: Office for National Statistics, 2000), p. 82; *HL Debs* 1960 (221), 688 (Beveridge). Productivity growth followed from reductions in the working week by more than 12 per cent after 1919, and 28 per cent after 1947: *HL Debs* 1964 (258), 240–1 (Burton).

31. Ross McKibbin, *Classes and Cultures: England 1918–51* (Oxford, 1998), pp. 151–60.

32. *New Statesman*, 1 Mar. 2004; *Sunday Telegraph*, 7 Mar. 2004; *Guardian*, 25 Feb., 12 July 2004.

33. M. Plant, *Drugtakers in an English Town* (London, 1975), pp. 67–8, 252–9; R. Yates, *If It Weren't for the Alligators: A History of Drugs, Music and Popular Culture in Manchester* (Manchester, 1992); Howard Parker, Judith Aldridge and Fiona Measham, *Illegal Leisure: the Normalization of Adolescent Recreational Drug Use* (London, 1998), Chs 1–3; L. Williams and H. Parker, 'Alcohol, Cannabis, Ecstasy and Cocaine: Drugs of Reasoned Choice among Young Adult Recreational Drug Users in England', *International Journal of Drug Policy*, 12 (2001), pp. 397–413; David Fowler, 'Teenage Consumers? Young Wage-earners and Leisure in Manchester, 1919–1939', in Andrew Davies and Steven Fielding (eds), *Workers' Worlds: Cultures and Communities in Manchester and Salford, 1880–1939* (Manchester, 1992), pp. 148–50; David Fowler, *The First Teenagers: The Lifestyle of Young Wage-earners in Interwar Britain* (London, 1995), pp. 7–41; Mark Abrams, *The Teenage Consumer* (London, 1959), pp. 9–11; discussion around Figure 9.4 below.

34. A.H. Halsey with Josephine Webb (eds), *Twentieth-century British Social Trends* (Basingstoke, 2000), table 2.20, p. 75; *Social Trends 30*, table 6.8, p. 108.

35. *HL Debs* 1960 (221), 687–88 (Beveridge), 728 (Chorley). See also Pat Thane, *Old Age in English History: Past Experiences, Present Issues* (Oxford, 2002), esp. chap. 20.

36. 'Money-O!', in W.H. Davies, *Nature Poems and Others* (London, 1908), p. 11.

37. Constance Harris, *The Use of Leisure in Bethnal Green: A Survey of Social Conditions in the Borough 1925 to 1926* (London, 1927), p. 33; Andy Davies, *Leisure, Gender and Poverty: Working-class Culture in Salford and Manchester, 1900–1939* (Manchester, 1992), pp. 55–61; Mass-Observation, *Bulletin*, 42 (May/June 1951), 'The Housewife's Day', pp. 3, 5, 13.

38. Mario Borsa, *The English Stage of Today* (London, 1908), pp. 4–5; cf. Catriona M. Parratt, *'More than Mere Amusement'. Working-class Women's Leisure in England, 1750–1914* (Boston, 2001), p. 1.

39. Selina Todd, 'Young Women, Work, and Leisure in Interwar England', *Historical Journal*, 48(3) (2005), pp. 789–809.

40. Claire Langhamer, *Women's Leisure in England, 1920–1960* (Manchester, 2000); see also Catriona M. Parratt, 'Little Means or Time: Working-class Women and Leisure in Late Victorian and Edwardian England', *International Journal of the History of Sport*, 15 (1998), pp. 22–53.

41. *The Times*, 27 Apr. 1955.

42. F. Zweig, *Women's Life and Labour* (London, 1952), p. 141.

43. Dennis Gabor, *Inventing the Future* (London, Secker and Warburg, 1963), esp. pp. 9–10; Anne Barrett, 'Gabor, Dennis (1900–1979)', *OxfDNB* (2004); *HL Debs* 1964 (258), 655 (Earl of Arran); cf. projections of 'a vast surplus of leisure time', *Spectator*, 21 May 1921, p. 641, cited by Olechnowicz, 'Unemployed Workers', p. 28.

44. E.H. P[helps] Brown and M.H. Browne, *A Century of Pay: The Course of Pay and Production in France, Germany, Sweden, the United Kingdom and the United States of America, 1860–1960* (London, 1968), pp. 48, 67; *Social Trends 33* (2003), pp. 74, 88; Halsey and Webb, *Twentieth-century British Social Trends*, pp. 632–3. Late-twentieth century figures refer to full-time workers: J. Kodz *et al.* (Institute for Employment Studies), *Working Long Hours: A Review of the Evidence, Volume 1 – Main Report* (London, 2003), p. 100. http://www.dti.gov.uk/files/file11543.pdf? pubpdfdload=03%2f1228

45. For an analysis of the evolution of leisure hours from 1830 to 1950 see D.A. Reid, 'Playing and Praying', in M. Daunton (ed.), *Cambridge Urban History of Britain, vol. 3* (Cambridge, 2000), pp. 746–57. In 1918–19 the engineering and shipyard workers achieved a 47-hour week, the railwaymen a 48-hour week: *The Times*, 3 Dec. 1918, 25 Mar. 1919.

46. As J.H. Thomas complained some of his members were doing: *The Times*, 7 Mar. 1919. For similar complaints regarding engineering workers see *The Times*, 3 Apr. 1960 (men working in their third week's holiday). For the debate about unions' motives see M.A. Bienefeld, *Working Hours in British Industry: An Economic History* (London, 1972); Gary Cross, *Time and Money: The Making of Consumer*

Culture (London, 1993), pp. 87–9, 92 and 239 nn. 37–42, 241 n.58; K. Hinrichs, W. Roche and C. Sirianni (eds), *Working Time in Transition: The Political Economy of Working Hours in Industrial Nations* (Philadelphia, 1991), pp. 95–6, 122–4; Stephen G. Jones, *Workers at Play: A Social and Economic History of Leisure 1918–1939* (Manchester, 1986), pp. 15, 23–6. Cf. the shipbuilders' case for a further reduction to 40 hours to reduce unemployment: *The Times*, 28 Feb. 1934.

47. London School of Economics, *New Survey of London Life and Labour* (London, 1930–5), vol. I, pp. 19, 116–18, 294; vol. IX, pp. 3–4.

48. Halsey and Webb, *Twentieth-century British Social Trends*, table 8.18, p. 306. The Factory Act of 1935 which brought the maximum hours of women and young persons down from 60 or 55.5 (in textiles) was therefore following rather than leading: *The Times*, 3 Feb. 1937; for the practical implications of a 55-hour week see *HC Debs* 1937 (321), 242. A 48-hour average could encompass working weeks as long as 70 or even 80 hours a week by people such as page boys, van boys and messengers: *The Times*, 7 Apr. 1937.

49. *The Times*, 7 and 17 Feb. 1919.

50. G.C. Cameron, 'The Growth of Holidays with Pay in Britain', in G. Reid and D. Robertson (eds), *Fringe Benefits, Labour Costs and Social Security* (London, 1965), p. 277, n.1, pp. 282–4; Jones, *Workers at Play*, pp. 17–20, 27–33, 77–8; Alice Russell, *The Growth of Occupational Welfare in Britain: Evolution and Harmonization of Modern Personnel Practice* (Aldershot, 1991), p. 66. See Robert Fitzgerald, *British Labour Management and Industrial Welfare 1846–1939* (London, 1988), *passim* for previous grants of paid holidays. Many unions sought a fortnight but accepted a week. The printers did best with six days, plus pay for the six bank holidays: *The Times*, 13 Jan., 10 Feb., 25 Mar., 9 Apr., 26 June 1919.

51. Gary Cross, *Time and Money*, p. 81 n.14.

52. Robert Roberts, *A Ragged Schooling: Growing up in the Classic Slum* (Manchester, 1976), pp. 185–6. For another example of this kind of confrontation, even before the war, see John K. Walton, *The British Seaside: Holidays and Resorts in the Twentieth Century* (Manchester, 2000), p. 51.

53. Cross, *Time and Money*, pp. 88–9; Russell, *Growth*, p. 68.

54. H. Taylor, *A Claim on the Countryside: A History of the British Outdoor Movement* (Edinburgh, 1997), *passim*; R. Snape, 'The Co-operative Holidays Association and the Cultural Formation of Countryside Leisure Practice', *Leisure Studies*, 23(2) (Apr. 2004), pp. 143–58; John Lowerson, 'Battles for the Countryside', in Frank Gloversmith, *Class Culture and Social Change: a New View of the 1930s* (Brighton, 1980), pp. 258–80.

55. Malcolm Wallace, *Single or Return: The History of the Transport Salaried Staffs' Association* (London, 1996), chap. 18; Benny Rothman quoted in Jones, *Workers at Play*, p. 65; Taylor, *A Claim on the Countryside*, chap. 7.

56. Ralph Butler and Raymond Wallace, *I'm Happy when I'm Hiking* (London, c.1931). See also their *Hike Yourself into Jolly Good Health!* (London, c.1932). Robert Graves and Alan Hodge, *The Long Weekend* (London, 1940/1), pp. 274–7; Julie Anderson, 'Fowler, Eileen Philippa Rose (1906–2000)', *OxfDNB* (2004); Prunella Stack, *Zest for Life: Mary Bagot Stack and the League of Health and Beauty* (London,

1988), pp. 38–40, 59–62, 69, 99–142; Jill Julius Matthews, 'They Had Such a Lot of Fun: the Women's League of Health and Beauty between the Wars', *History Workshop*, 30 (1990), pp. 22–54; Robert J. Whybrow, *Britain Speaks out, 1937–87: A Social History as Seen through the Gallup Data* (Basingstoke, 1989), p. 2.

57. John K. Walton, *Lancashire: A Social History 1558–1939* (Manchester, 1987), p. 295.

58. Alan Delgado, *The Annual Outing and Other Excursions* (London, 1977), pp. 139–52; for a terrific evocation of the charabanc trip to the seaside see Richard Hoggart, *The Uses of Literacy* (Harmondsworth, 1957), pp. 146–8.

59. J.A.R. Pimlott, *The Englishman's Holiday: A Social History* (London, 1947; Hassocks, 1976), pp. 79–84, 144–9; Su Barton, *Working-class Organisations and Popular Tourism, 1840–1970* (Manchester, 2005), pp. 146ff.

60. Dennis Hardy and Colin Ward, *Arcadia for All: The Legacy of a Makeshift Landscape* (London, 1987), chaps 3 and 4; Walton, *British Seaside*, chaps 1 and 5.

61. Elizabeth Brunner, *Holiday Making and the Holiday Trades* (Oxford, 1945), p. 3; see also for Bolton Gary Cross (ed.), *Worktowners at Blackpool: Mass-Observation and Popular Leisure in the 1930s* (London, 1990), pp. 40, 47–51; *The Times*, 27 Jan. 1938; Ken Worpole, 'The Pleasure Beaches of East London: Swimming in the City', *Rising East: The Journal of East London Studies*, 4(3) (n.d. [2001]), pp. 172–81; http://homepage.ntlworld.com/oliver.merrington/lidos/lidos1closed.htm. For sunbathing and seaside lidos see Walton, *British Seaside*, pp. 100–1.

62. House of Commons, *Report of the Committee on Holidays with Pay* (Cmd. 5724, Apr. 1938), pp. 27–8.

63. F.B. and L.B. Gilbreth, *Measurement of the Human Factor in Industry* (n.p., 1917); B. Seebohm Rowntree, *The Human Factor in Business* (London, 1921); Russell, *Growth*, pp. 83–5; cf. Jones, *Workers at Play*, pp. 30–3; *The Times*, 14 Sept. 1935 referred to 'the pervasive and deadening influences of mechanised life'. For a critical note on the meaning and extent of 'Fordism' see Fitzgerald, *British Labour Management*, pp. 7ff.

64. *Report of the Committee on Holidays with Pay*, pp. 5 and 21. The first major breakthrough was the grant of the holiday to 600,000 engineering workers: *The Times* 28 July 1937; Jones, *Workers at Play*, pp. 31–3.

65. Bevin had also served on the Amulree Committee. Angus Calder, *The People's War* (London, 1969/71), pp. 135–6, 372, 379, 405; G.C. Cameron, 'The Growth of Holidays with Pay in Britain', in G. Reid and D. Robertson (eds), *Fringe Benefits, Labour Costs and Social Security* (London, 1965), pp. 277n.1, 282, 283, 284; Russell, *Growth*, pp. 71–2; Chris Wrigley, *British Trade Unions since 1933* (Cambridge, 2002), p. 9.

66. Pimlott, *The Englishman's Holiday*, chap. 13; Walvin, *Beside the Seaside*, pp. 103–7; Walton, *Blackpool Landlady*, pp. 137–9; *The Times*, 5 Sept. 1941, 9 July, 3 Aug. 1942, 10 Apr., 13, 16 Aug. 1943; cf. Chris Sladen, 'Holidays at Home in the Second World War', *Journal of Contemporary History*, 37(1) (2002), pp. 67–89, and 'Wartime Holidays and the "Myth of the Blitz"', *Cultural and Social History*, 2(2) (2005), pp. 215–46, esp. pp. 226ff.

67. Mass-Observation [File Report 2509], *Voluntary Social Service Report no. 1:*

A Report on Holidays, August 1947, pp. 1–3; cf. Hulton Press readership survey of 1947 reporting 56 per cent spending holidays away from home, cited in A.H. Halsey (ed.), *Trends in British Society since 1900* (London, 1972), pp. 540, 548–9.

68. Paul Addison, *Now the War Is over: A Social History of Britain 1945–51* (London, 1995), pp. 115–19; Douglas A. Reid, 'Butlin, Sir William Heygate Edmund Colborne [Billy] (1899–1980)' and 'Pontin, Sir Frederick William (1906–2000)', *OxfDNB* (2004); Barton, *Working-class Organisations and Popular Tourism*, p. 190; *The Times*, 10 Jan. 1949.

69. *The Times*, 15 Sept. 1951.

70. Russell, *Growth*, pp. 117, 120; Sidney Pollard, *The Development of the British Economy, 1914–1990* (fourth edition, London, 1992), p. 229.

71. *The Times*, 25 July 1955; Walton, *British Seaside*, p. 87; cites holiday journeys by train reduced from 47 per cent in 1951 down to 37 per cent in 1955.

72. *The Times*, 26 May, 12 June 1959; *New Society*, 10 July 1980, pp. 73–4; Labour Research Department, *A Forty Hour Week and Three Weeks Holiday: How the Case Rests at Present in U.K. and Overseas* (London, [1960]), pp. 3–4; Jim [J.E.] Mortimer, *The Forty Hour Week: The Case Argued* ([London] *New Left Review*, [1960?]); Russell, *Growth*, pp. 114–20. Mortimer and LRD both imply the 42-hour stage was widespread. For an analysis which stresses the deleterious impact of overtime see John Rule, 'Time, Affluence and Private Leisure: the British Working Class in the 1950s and 1960s,' *Labour History Review*, 66(2) (summer 2001), pp. 228–32.

73. Stress on real incomes from Russell (initially in her discussion of the 1920s) and the European point from Russell, *Growth*, p. 118.

74. Labour Research Department, *A Forty Hour Week*, pp. 9–11; *idem, Shorter Hours, Longer Holidays* (London, [1965]), pp. 5–7; *Birmingham Evening Mail*, 7 Jan. 1972; *The Economist*, 4 Jan. 1975; Russell, *Growth*, pp. 119–20, 1965 = 22 per cent, 1966 = 33 per cent; Halsey and Webb, *Twentieth-century British Social Trends*, p. 632.

75. Russell, *Growth*, pp. 186–7 (three weeks+ = 15 per cent in 1969 and 52 per cent in 1970).

76. Walton, *British Seaside*, p. 66; Pollard, *British Economy*, p. 380; Barton, *Working-class Organisations*, chap. 8.

77. Gareth Shaw and Allan Williams (eds), *The Rise and Fall of British Coastal Resorts: Cultural and Economic Perspectives* (London, 1997); Walton, *British Seaside*, pp. 66–70, 156–66.

78. *Social Trends 30*, table 13.1.

79. A. Blair, L. Karsten and J. Leopold, 'The Fight over Working Hours: Trade Union Action or State Control? A British Dutch Comparative Perspective', *Journal of European Economic History*, 31(2) (2002), pp. 286–7. The engineering workers did achieve a reduction to 37 hours by 1991.

80. Halsey and Webb, *Twentieth-century British Social Trends*, p. 310; cf. M. Wareing, 'Working Arrangements and Patterns of Working Hours in Britain', *Employment Gazette*, 100 (1992), pp. 88–100.

81. Halsey and Webb, *Twentieth-century British Social Trends*, table 8.19, p. 307. I have used the 1982 figure in the chart for the entire workforce as the 1981 figure

was aberrant to the trend and would thus have been misleading. 'Yuppie' is first recorded by the *OED* from 1984. Blair *et al.*, 'The Fight over Working Hours', pp. 287–9; Pollard, *British Economy*, p. 281, re single employer bargaining in 1970s beneath the level of collective trade agreements; *Social Trends 30*, pp. 176–7.

82. Halsey and Webb, *Twentieth-century British Social Trends*, p. 631; http://www.tuc.org.uk/work_life/tuc-8507-f0.cfm: TUC press release, 'The Time is Right for a New Bank Holiday', 27 Aug. 2004.

83. Julia Lourie, *Working Time Regulations* (House of Commons Library Research Paper 98/82, 1998) http://www.parliament.uk/commons/lib/research/rp98/rp98-082.pdf; Fiona Neathey and James Arrowsmith, *Implementation of the Working Time Regulations* (London, Department of Trade and Industry, 2001), pp. i–iii, 2–6, 45–7, 71–2 – http://www.dti.gov.uk/files/file11615.pdf; TUC, *Statutory Leave and UK Bank Holidays: Closing the Bank Holiday Loophole* (London, 2002) – http://www.tuc.org.uk/em_research/tuc-5419-f0.pdf; J. Kodz, *et al.* (Institute for Employment Studies), *Working Long Hours: A Review of the Evidence*, pp. 100ff.; Amicus, *The Time of Our Lives: Facts, Figures and Arguments for Campaigning on Working Time* (n.d. [2003?]), http://www.amicustheunion.org/pdf/thetimeofourlives.pdf, esp. pp. 5–7; BMRB Social Research, *A Survey of Workers' Experiences of the Working Time Regulations* (London, Department of Trade and Industry, 2004), pp. 6–10, 52–3 – http://www.dti.gov.uk/files/file11485.pdf; National Association of Citizen's Advice Bureaux, *Wish You Were Here* (2000), pp. 17–18, http://www.citizensadvice.org.uk/macnn/wish_you_pdf.pdf.

84. Francis Green, 'It's Been a Hard Day's Night: the Concentration and Intensification of Work in Late Twentieth-century Britain', *British Journal of Industrial Relations*, 39(1) (2001), pp. 53–80; for an amusing fictional take on the problem see Allison Pearson, *I Don't Know How She Does It: A Comedy about Failure, a Tragedy about Success* (London, 2002); Keith Rankin, 'Why Do We Seek So Much Work?', *New Zealand Political Review*, 4 (1995), no. 5: http://keithrankin.co.nz/nzpr1995_5work.html; cf. Gershuny, *Changing Times*, pp. 74–5, for a different perspective.

85. Ruth Hill and Shirley Dex, *The Business and Family Consequences of Deregulating Sunday Trading in Britain* (Judge Institute of Management Working Papers 34, Cambridge, 1999); *Guardian*, 30 June 1994, 28 Aug. 1999; *Observer*, 30 Mar. 1997, 24 Jan., 24 Oct. 1999.

86. John Lowerson, 'Sport and the Victorian Sunday', *British Journal of Sports History*, 1 (1984), pp. 208–18; Sean O'Connell, *The Car in British Society: Class, Gender and Motoring 1896–1939* (Manchester, 1998), pp. 87–8, 164.

87. Jeffrey Richards, 'The Cinema and Cinema Going in Birmingham in the 1930s', in John K. Walton and James Walvin (eds), *Leisure in Britain 1780–1939* (Manchester, 1983), pp. 41–3; H.E. Browning and A.A. Sorrell, 'Cinemas and Cinema-going in Great Britain', *Journal of the Royal Statistical Society*, 117 (1954), p. 147. However, in Middlesbrough in 1913 the magistrates licensed Sunday cinema performances (possibly for charity) on the recommendation of the police to keep 'young people off the streets, and 'others out of public houses': *The Times*, 7 Mar. 1913.

88. *The Times*, 23 July 1962.

89. *The Times*, 7 May 1960. Tony Mason, 'Football', in Mason, *Sport in Britain*, p. 149.

90. *The Times*, 21 Dec. 1973.

91. *The Times*, 26 Jan. 1974, 16 Oct. 1981; Richard Cox *et al.*, *Encyclopedia of British Sport* (Oxford, 2000), pp. 88–9.

92. *HC Debs* 1969 (147), 619 ff.; Select Committee on Delegated Powers and Deregulation, *Ninth Report*, 15 Mar. 2000, paras 11–12, 37–8.

93. *The Times*, 29 Jan. 1973; Clive D. Field, '"The Secularized Sabbath" Revisited: Opinion Polls as Sources for Sunday Observance in Contemporary Britain', *Contemporary British History*, 15(1) (2001), esp. pp. 13–15; cf. *The Independent*, 19 June 2005 *re* time-budget evidence.

94. http://www.keepsundayspecial.org.uk.

95. Halsey and Webb, *Twentieth-century British Social Trends*, pp. 629–33, 646–7; Irene Harkness, 'Working 9–5?', in Paul Gregg and J. Wadsworth (eds), *The State of Working Britain* (Manchester, 1999), pp. 90–108; Gershuny, *Changing Times*, pp. 5–6.

96. Gershuny, *Changing Times*, pp. 7–9, 49–50; Chris Rojek, 'Leisure and the Rich Today: Veblen's Thesis after a Century', *Leisure Studies*, 19 (2000), pp. 1–15.

97. As is demonstrated with remarkable clarity and vivacity in the films in the Mitchell and Kenyon archive: http://www.bfi.org.uk/features/mk/. See also Vanessa Toulmin, Patrick Russell and Simon Popple (eds), *The Lost World of Mitchell and Kenyon: Edwardian Britain on Film* (London, 2004), esp. chaps 15–16.

98. McKibbin, *Classes and Cultures*, pp. 339–44, 390–410, 419–23.

99. Walton, *The British Seaside, passim*.

100. Colin Ward and Dennis Hardy, *Goodnight Campers: The History of the British Holiday Camp* (London, 1986), pp. 154–6.

101. C.B. Hawkins, *Norwich: A Social Study* (London, 1910), pp. 73, 80, 314–6; *New Survey of London Life and Labour*, IX, pp. 70–1; James Mott, 'Miners, Weavers and Pigeon Racing', in Michael Smith, Stanley Parker and Cyril Smith (eds), *Leisure and Society in Britain* (Harmondsworth, 1973), pp. 86–96.

102. John Lowerson, 'Angling', in Cox *et al.*, *Encyclopedia*, p. 8; John Lowerson, 'Angling', in Mason, *Sport in Britain*, pp. 12–43.

103. Arnold Freeman, *Boy Life and Labour: The Manufacture of Inefficiency* (London, 1914), pp. 133–52. See also John Springhall, *Coming of Age: Adolescence in Britain 1860–1960* (Dublin, 1986), pp. 128–47.

104. Dave Russell, *Football and the English* (Preston, 1997), pp. 30–4; for further discussion and sources see Reid, 'Playing and Praying', pp. 773–6, 803.

105. Michael Young and Peter Willmott, *The Symmetrical Family: A Study of Work and Leisure in the London Region* (London, 1973), pp. 13, 98–9; Richard Holt and Tony Mason, *Sport in Britain* (Oxford, 2000), pp. 3–4.

106. Holt and Mason, *Sport in Britain*, pp. 3–4, 96–100; Russell, *Football, passim*.

107. *The Times*, 21, 22 Feb. 1896; Springhall, *Coming of Age*, pp. 133–6; Nicholas Hiley, '"At the picture palace": the British Cinema Audience, 1895–1920', in John Fullerton (ed.), *Celebrating 1895: The Centenary of Cinema* (London, 1998), pp. 96–103.

108. *New Survey of London Life and Labour*, XI, p. 44; Graves and Hodge, *The*

Long Week-end, pp. 133–4; Andrew Horrall, *Popular Culture in London c. 1890–1918: The Transformation of Entertainment* (Manchester, 2001), pp. 130–1, 207–13.

109. Nicholas Hiley, '"Let's go to the pictures": the British Cinema Audience in the 1920s and 1930s', *Journal of Popular British Cinema*, 2 (1999), pp. 40–2, 45.

110. Jeffrey Richards, *The Age of the Dream Palace: Cinema and Society in Britain 1930–1939* (London, 1984); Kathleen Box, 'The Cinema and the Public', *The Social Survey*, NS 106 (1946), pp. 1–2.

111. Cited in Hiley, '"Let's go to the pictures"', p. 49.

112. *HL Debs* 1964 (258), 283–4 (Norwich).

113. Stephen Constantine, 'Amateur Gardening and Popular Recreation in the 19th and 20th Centuries', *Journal of Social History*, 14(3) (1981), pp. 387–406.

114. Hilda Jennings and Winifred Gill, *Broadcasting in Everyday Life* ([London], 1939), *passim*.

115. Halsey and Webb, *Twentieth-century British Social Trends*, p. 645; *The Times*, 13 Sept. 1985.

116. Transmitted 1998–2000 (3 series, 19 episodes): http://www.bbc.co.uk/comedy/guide/articles/r/gallery/roylefamilythe_66602940_2.shtml.

117. Mark Abrams, *The Newspaper Reading Public of Tomorrow* (London, 1964), p. 50.

118. Williams and Brake, *Drink in Great Britain*, pp. 134–5.

119. *Sunday Times*, 11 Aug. 1985. For lager louts see *OED* (1987) and *The Times*, 23 Oct. 1988. See also *The Times*, 25 Apr. 1988 and *Sunday Times*, 26 June 1988.

120. Mass-Observation, *The Pub and the People* (1938), pp. 242, 245–8; P. Marsh and K.F. Kibby, *Drinking and Public Disorder* (London, 1992), pp. 25–6 (see pp. 128–35 for comparison with the Netherlands).

121. Williams and Brake, *Drink in Great Britain*, pp. 203–4; Stanley Cohen, *Folk Devils and Moral Panics: The Creation of the Mods and Rockers* (third edn, Oxford, 1987). My thanks are due to Dr C.J. Bearman for giving me particular pause for thought on this point.

122. *HL Debs* 1999 (221), 245 (Anelay of St. Johns).

123. *Social Trends* 30, table 13.14, p. 216; cf. Mandler, 'Two Cultures – One – or Many', pp. 146–55.

124. There spring to mind Richard Desmond, owner of the *Daily Express*, *The Sun* and, of course, the proprietors of hundreds, if not thousands, of pornographic Internet sites: see *Observer*, 29 July 2003, on Richard Desmond.

Part V
Youth

–10–

The Youth Establishment in the Netherlands in the Twentieth Century

*Piet de Rooy**

Introduction

By the end of the 1960s many intellectuals had convinced themselves that Dutch culture was on the brink of an historic turning point.[1] The concept of 'youth' played a crucial role in this belief: the society of the future could be seen in the younger generation. This concept was not, however, based on detailed research. Indeed, in the Netherlands socio-historical research into young people has been neither extensive nor intellectually rigorous. It has always rested on a superficial, qualitative approach characterized by the search for a cultural label for what is considered to be characteristic 'youth behaviour'. The unspoken premise of much of this literature is that young people are attuned from birth to changes within society and that, in order to determine the future direction of society, it is first necessary to 'tune in' to young people.[2]

A distinguished exception to this tradition can be found in the work of the sociologist J.S. van Hessen, whose work *Samen jong-zijn* (Young together), was published in 1965. In this work Van Hessen rejects the idea that young people are heralds of the future. The future is just as mysterious for young people as for many adults. Van Hessen emphasizes the importance of youth as a collective experience, which, rather than simply being orientated towards the future, is equally founded in tradition. In order to research youth culture, young people should not be seen as a large group of individuals who happen to be young, but rather as a group that is 'young together'. Young people react strongly to each other and lay down the law for each other. They mimic each other's behaviour and set rules for each other, win or lose status in relation to each other, and test each other's values and norms. Whilst there are important variations within this collectivity (variations according to gender, class and urban or rural environments), these all fit within what Van Hessen terms 'the youth polity' or 'the youth establishment'. The differences are comparable with religious differences within the Christian community. The way in which these differences are dealt with is set out in codes and rituals. As a whole, the youth establishment is characterized by a limited autonomy, independent from family ties, schooling and state or market forces. It can thus be researched historically, just like any other institution. It is also obviously influenced by changes within society, although not directly: 'Youth-life has its own separate existence'.[3]

This 'separate existence' of young people has its own dynamic, a rhythm that is strongly defined by special moments when one section of youth develops a self-image (sometimes accepted by adults) which they advance as a model for all young people, for the whole youth establishment. This was the main aim of the youth movement that developed between the two world wars. It was highly successful. Indeed it was so successful that the explosion of this youth establishment on to the scene became a source of serious concern for a number of adults, particularly educators. When the long-trusted concept of youth fell by the wayside in the 1950s, educators were only able to see the youth of the period as an unstructured mass. In the 1960s a new group would come forward to help forge a new image of 'youth'. This time the reaction of adults was ambivalent. On the one hand, this new group was a nuisance, attacking all forms of power and authority. On the other hand, it contained a discernible level of utopian idealism, and it could thus count on a certain level of sympathy. This youth establishment would also disintegrate, partly because it became too difficult to contain its ideas within the parameters of a youth movement. Adults were starting to view distinctions of age as unimportant and were beginning to see themselves as 'young at heart' – and sometimes young in behaviour. People of all ages and lifestyles would meet in a remarkably large and varied marketplace of ambition and consumerism, where every taste would be catered for.

The Youth Movement

In the nineteenth century the youth establishment was highly traditional and strongly divided along class and gender lines. Children from the elite were raised strictly and were rarely allowed out of sight. According to Bourdieu, these children embodied 'family capital', which had to be preserved by upholding conventions and discouraging unwanted interaction with others (which could lead to a 'bad' marriage). The most common form of social interaction within these groups was strictly regulated parties (such as birthday parties, dance evenings and weekends spent on country estates). A son from this social milieu would later remember that, to all intents and purposes, he was not allowed to do anything on his own: 'A young boy does not always want to be supervised when he is walking, or practise his gymnastics on command, or read a useful book ... He wants freedom, he wants to stray from the path and enter into the wilderness, be amongst the trees, in the water, on the ice. But back then none of that was allowed.'[4]

At the turn of the century the social interaction of young people from lower social classes was also strongly determined by traditional customs. Generally, an evening would be set aside for the boys and girls to follow a prescribed path through the village or district and, if all went well, ultimately end up in lovers' lane. There was, of course, also the yearly fair, where all inhibitions were shed. Parental observation was suspended, and things would happen as they have always happened and not much was said about it.

For the young people of the middle classes restrictions were particularly irksome. They were excluded from the party culture of the upper classes, yet the pressure of social refinement also prevented them from taking part in the less-regulated forms of social interaction common amongst the lower classes. Autobiographical writings frequently reveal how it was precisely boys from this group who felt exceptionally lonely, and who were relieved to find a 'bosom buddy' or new worlds within easy reach in a library. It was boys from this middle stratum who would eagerly gather together fellow 'partners in adversity' and set up clubs or societies – whether these were for the common study of the Bible, for exploring nature by bike or for participating in sport. It is here that the roots of the modern youth movement can be found.

To a large extent, the Dutch youth movement took its inspiration from the German example. In 1901 a group of schoolchildren formed a society for walking in the area around Steglitz, a small town a short distance from Berlin. These *Wandervögel* (migratory birds) grew rapidly in size, organization and ideological ambition. By the eve of the First World War they had become a nationwide federation of 25,000 members. In 1913 they gathered on the *Hohe Meisner*, a mountain top near Kassel, to proclaim their almost euphoric manifesto: 'The Free-German youth will give expression to its life, according to its own goals, its own responsibility and its own truth.'[5] Such a proclamation sounds like a declaration of independence, legitimized by the idea that old age is equivalent to decline, that the future belongs to the young, and that young people have already realized true brotherhood through their mutual interaction. This interaction involved specific choices in clothing and music, and together these created a culture (both in the sense of a work of art and a form of society) which was ready to be integrated into society at large.

This style of youth movement had a huge influence on the Social Democratic youth movement the AJC (the Arbeiders Jeugd Centrale or Centre for Working Youth). In 1921 a delegation from this movement attended an 'International Day of Youth' in Bielefeld. They left in 'bourgeois' hand-me-down suits with stiff collars and came back dressed in 'Manchester' corduroy with open shirts (so-called Schiller-collars). Of even greater importance than this external transformation was the fact that these young people had picked up ideals whilst in Bielefeld. One of the most important was that being young involved seeing the world as flawed and accepting the obligation to make things better. Both characteristics – divergent clothing and social ideals – spread rapidly in the youth establishment, even if this was simply because it helped gain respect from adults. After the Great War, adults were no longer completely convinced of the stability of their own 'bourgeois' culture, and their self-confidence did not increase during the Great Depression. They increasingly placed their hopes in young people, who would create a new world. The president of the AJC, the former schoolmaster Koos Vorrink, was at the forefront of this. In his book *Om de vrije mens der nieuwe samenleving* (The free man of the new society – 1933), he condemns the bourgeois-capitalist society which makes human beings into weak-willed victims of tasteless mass consumerism. He contrasts this with the ideals which should characterize the lives of young people, and which in several respects were reminiscent of a true community (ideals he believed to have predominated in medieval guilds). It was impressed upon young people that they should renounce their immediate need for sensual pleasures and transform their sexuality into social idealism. At precisely this time, Sigmund Freud was analysing this mechanism in his classic work *Civilization and Its Discontents* (1933): essentially, without frustration there is no culture. Although the AJC did not grow very large, its format inspired admiration and imitation. Adults formed an image of young people that matched this ideal type and encouraged youth clubs and societies. One educationalist wrote quite explicitly that new forms of 'being young' were being created, ways 'which bind young people to a sense of freedom in a way that they have never felt bound before, because we place a responsibility on their shoulders that they have never known, even if in this respect the adult would never want to give up their own, higher responsibility'.[6] The question is why this appeared attractive to so many young people – for it is estimated that between the two world wars one-third of young people in the age group 12–20 were members of a club at one time or another.

This was because the youth movement offered a solution for different groups of young people. For the elite it meant more freedom, whilst for the working classes it brought contact with a richer culture. Youth clubs flourished in the youth establishment and – as demonstrated above – were fired with ambition, and thus legitimation by the educators. Above all, it was the youth movement that conceptualized 'young people' as idealistic and aesthetic: in favour of goodness, beauty and truth, and against the entertainment industry and the use of stimulants. However, as a consequence, new lines of division were drawn within the youth establishment, since many young people were quite unprepared to sacrifice the possibilities for fun offered by a greater income and more free time (possibilities such as the cinema, dancing and cigarettes). The youth movement was thus also a vanguard which came to see itself as a new elite.[7]

The Phenomenon of Mass Youth

Adults began to express serious concerns about young people during the Second World War. Young people had not only witnessed how adults had squandered all their values during the war but, perhaps more seriously, they had themselves become personally involved in dubious activities. When the schools closed, young people had nothing to do but roam around; they had to steal in order to eat and to lie in order to protect their families. People everywhere were afraid that a serious 'demoralization' might take hold. This concern grew so great because society seemed to have lost traditions and connections, and thus cut itself adrift, and to consist of 'mass-people'.[8] After the liberation, a deep-rooted concern about 'youth run wild' or 'mass youth' was repeatedly expressed – to an extent that it is possible to talk of actual 'moral panic'. In 1948 the Dutch government gave seven sociological and educational institutions the task of researching 'the origins of and the influences on the mentality of so-called mass-youth'. This was to be the largest piece of social-scientific research ever conducted in the Netherlands and would remain the largest for some time. The serious nature of the work was clearly underlined by the fact that, after five years of research, a total of 900 pages had been published. The chief editor of the key report, the renowned educator M.J. Langeveld, concluded that a loss of tradition, social convention, morality and belief lay behind the demoralization of young people, although education, youth clubs and family life provided something to hold on to. Suspicion increased that this demoralization was about to engulf all young people, including what Langeveld termed the 'bourgeois-mass youth' or the 'refined mass youth', even if this was not obvious on the surface. The crux was that young people had lost all their values and were simply driven by materialism. They lacked any self-control – which was already clear from the commotion they caused – and were victims of the hedonism introduced by market forces.[9] Educators are rarely inclined to think that young people will more or less look after themselves, but in this case the fact that many of the researchers were themselves members of a pre-war youth movement is of clear significance. Langeveld, for example, had been a member of a youth organization which had abstained from alcohol in order to better the world. What they reported was thus not so much an analysis of the situation as a misunderstanding of it: post-war youth no longer behaved according to the ideal image of youth that had been formulated a couple of decades earlier.

A considerably calmer tone is struck in a number of publications from the end of the 1950s, probably written under the influence of the German sociologist H. Schelsky's widely known work *Die skeptische Generation* (The sceptical generation – 1957). In 1959 the social psychologist Goudsblom concluded on the basis of a (non-representative) inquiry that young people actually had similar opinions to adults on a whole range of issues. What he found most striking was that young people saw no good in the 'outmoded template of rash idealism' which their parents had suffered from in the youth movement. Sociologists such as Krantz and Vercruijsse were also of the opinion that little was wrong. Their book *De jeugd in het geding* (Youth in issue – 1959) similarly suggests that adults were so troubled by their own nostalgia for the youth movement that they tended to see problems everywhere. In his 1960 dissertation *Jeugdige ongeschoolden* (Unskilled youth), Feitsma pleads that youngsters should no longer be used as scapegoats for the failings and flaws of adults.[10] In short, the problem of 'mass youth' was reformulated as a hang-up of former members of the youth movement.

Nevertheless, a fundamental change was under way in the youth establishment, as evidenced by the membership figures of youth societies. Young children were still joining clubs, but a standard complaint of the authorities had become: 'where are all the 16 to 19 year olds?' From 1952 onwards the total number of members fell so rapidly that after 1964 the Central Bureau for Statistics no longer published these figures at all. However, it was clear that youngsters still wanted to be members of sports clubs: in 1946, some 21 per cent of 8–25 year olds were members of such clubs, and by 1963 that percentage had doubled. This was unsatisfactory for concerned educators, for whilst they saw sport as a good use of time, it did not help form character or produce the idealists who would propel society on to a higher level of civilization.

In addition, it was felt young people should stay on longer in education. Participation in education began to increase after 1930, as increasing numbers of children went to school. In 1900 around 30 per cent of 12–17 year olds attended school;

by the end of the century this had risen to practically 100 per cent. The 1950s saw an important increase in this growth: in 1950 27 per cent of 12–25 year olds were in education; by 1960 that had risen to 41 per cent. These increases would continue. Not only were more children attending school, they were also remaining in education for longer. In the 1960s many children still left school at 14, but this phenomenon slowly declined. In 1950 only 2 per cent of 18–25 year olds were in full-time education; by the end of the century this had risen to just above 20 per cent.[11] This had a number of far-reaching consequences. First and foremost, there were considerably more young people who had received a better education than their parents, especially by the middle of the twentieth century. Whilst young people had enjoyed a minimum of a couple of years of secondary education, many of their parents' generation had never progressed further than primary education. In 1965 this was true for 40 per cent of fathers and 66 per cent of mothers; in 1977 these figures had shrunk to 22 per cent and 39 per cent respectively. Of even greater importance was the fact that the school environment, determined since time immemorial by the middle classes, had become of great importance in the daily lives of young people. Youngsters grew up in age-homogenized groups with their own social climate, in which the differences between young people grew smaller. Despite a general increase in education levels, and although existing mechanisms of choice and selection did not change (so that it was still impossible to talk of proportional participation by social class), the opportunities for young people from the working classes increased, the differences between boys and girls reduced considerably, and the differences between young people from the city and those from the countryside vanished almost completely.[12] The implication is clear: however important parents were, it was the influence of mutual social interaction with people of a similar age that was growing. Certainly, it should not be forgotten that in 1960 just over half of 14–19 year olds entered the working world, but it is none the less clear that the arena of youth had shifted from the open air to the school yard.

The changing financial position of young people was also of importance. Due to the gradual growth in actual income, children often had more money at their disposal. They got pocket money and, if they worked, no longer had to give all or part of their wages to their parents. Young people became key consumers: even in 1950 Dutch youth between 14 and 21 spent around 90 million euros, 12 million euros of which went on entertainment.[13] The rapidly increasing consumer power of young people was both visible and audible: the number of mopeds increased from 4,000 in 1949 to more than 1 million in 1960. On the one hand, young people were more dependent on each other and, on the other hand, they were collectively less dependent on adults. This was intensified by many parents' uncertainty about upbringing. Many felt that society was modernizing at a revolutionary pace and that their children fitted into this new world better than they did. Adults expressed this uncertainty openly. In the early 1950s there were constant discussions about the increasing divide in society between technical-material civilization and moral-ideal culture. For the time being adults held on to old values and norms, and yet they do not appear to have been sufficiently convinced of the relevance of these values to impose them on young people. There was a marked tendency to avoid conflicts with children if at all possible, even in advice on upbringing – a tendency to approach young people sympathetically and give them as much freedom as possible: 'It is a risky undertaking, without a doubt, but there is no other way to negotiate with people who are searching for their own life in a world of today and tomorrow.'[14] Increasingly, upbringing took on the characteristics of discretion and negotiation. Young people noticed this phenomenon and diagnosed it as follows: 'What strikes me is the disconcerting uncertainty amongst those who are supposed to give young people guidance. Their fear seems bigger than ours.'[15] The balance of power was shifting in favour of the young. This created the opportunity for a reconceptualization of 'youth'.

Two Youth Traditions

It was above all radio, cinema and television (in the 1960s every year 200,000 new television sets were purchased in the Netherlands) that helped promote a new youth tradition, strongly grounded in rock and roll. As early as 1956 trouble had broken out at cinemas showing the film *Rock around the Clock*, starring Bill Haley. This new youth tradition was 'discovered' by the journalist Jan Vrijman. In the magazine *Vrij Nederland* (The free Netherlands), Vrijman wrote about a group of working-class boys who dressed in leather jackets and had bryl-creamed hair, and who spent their free time seemingly aimlessly roaming through town, often on their mopeds, kicking up trouble. Vrijman called these boys *nozems*, an untranslatable term close to the concept of 'rockers'. Vrijman does not simply describe this group but transforms them – according to his own criteria – into unconscious heroes of tragic substance: '*Nozems* aren't concerned with good salaries, easy work or social security – they are about living life to the full: complete fulfilment in life, something that touches every nerve and every heartstring, an essential realization of life – or, more simply, of happiness. They consider happiness to be something other than a sense of comfort. For years on end they refused any substitute, until they couldn't take any more, and they capitulated, reaching a great compromise with society.'[16]

This modern variant of the noble savage was never appreciated by society. The police intervened heavy handedly, and from 1955 the conviction rate of young people for various offences rose quickly. It was precisely this criminalization which the criminologist Buikhuisen used as the basis for further research. In his 1965 dissertation, 'Achtergronden van nozemgedrag' (A background to *nozem* behaviour), Buikhuisen totally rejected the romantic image of Vrijman, yet agreed that the criminalization was remarkably short-sighted. In his eyes, *nozems* were young men aged between 16 and 18 from the lower socio-economic classes. For the most part they had reasonable relations with their parents, who broadly speaking left their children to their own devices. These were ordinary young men, who were simply exceptionally bored and unable to occupy themselves. Consequently they 'provoked' the police, as this provided them with excitement and entertainment. The situation would only get worse if the police allowed themselves to be provoked, and could only get better if the police handled the situation more tactfully.

Alongside this *nozem* tradition, which appealed primarily to working-class youth, a second tradition developed in the larger towns which was more suited to young people from the middle classes. At the heart of this tradition were the 'Leidseplein-youth', named after the square in Amsterdam with its many cafés and entertainment venues where they congregated. It is possible to see the Leidseplein-youth as similar to 'mods', although they are not comparable in all respects. They borrowed much from the American tradition (directly after the Second World War Amsterdam had been a centre of leave for the Allied forces). This helps explain their interest in jazz (above all for Charlie Parker) and in the somewhat melancholic French philosophy of existentialism, for which black clothes were particularly suitable. This 'youth tradition' was also actively cultivated by journalists within the trend-sensitive media. An icon of this time was the photo collection 'Wij zijn zeventien' (We are seventeen – 1956) by 17-year-old Johan van der Keuken, a student at the Montessori School in Amsterdam (who later became a renowned photographer and film-maker). The collection contained little laughter and much contemplative staring into glasses of wine. Van der Keuken would later say: 'It was a protest against the contemporary, the petty-bourgeois, the oppressive, but you only see that later – we experienced everything very romantically.' This romantic protest was not, however, directed against parents. Rather, it was primarily the expression of a strongly introspective group life. The photo collection attracted high levels of attention, although this was generally baffled rather than shocked in tone: 'It looks as if these children don't have parents.'[17]

It is interesting that both youth traditions entered into competition with each other. This had the advantage that both groups became more cohesive. However, the small scuffles between the two groups can also be seen as a battle for hegemony within the youth establishment as a whole – battles between those who were studying and those who were working, between Puch and Kreidler (two brands of moped), between jazz and rock, wine and beer. Only in the middle of the 1960s would these two different youth traditions merge into a bigger, new youth establishment. And only then would the idea grow that social differences between the young did not prevent them from having views and expectations in common – and, above all else, from having beat music in common.

Provo

At the start of the 1960s Amsterdam became the focal point for everyone who felt that something was 'happening'. They waited impatiently for what must come. The Amsterdam window-cleaner and cult figure Robert Jasper Grootveld, who had proclaimed Amsterdam to be the 'magic centre', would stride through town constantly calling: 'Something must happen, something must happen, *happening!*' At weekends this waiting was ritualized in 'happenings' on a small square in the centre of the city, around a statue of the brazen Amsterdam street lad, ironically named 'het Lieverdje' (the little rascal). Throughout 1964 these 'happenings' attracted increasing levels of attention, and when they began to obstruct traffic, the police reacted with growing force. On the basis of this, Roel van Duyn, a philosophy student, formulated a concept of a new youth establishment, which collected together all existing youth traditions and which had international presence. Van Duyn used Buikhuizen's terminology.

Young people had to 'provoke', they formed a 'provotariat', they were 'provokers' or 'provos': 'The provotariat is the latest rebellious class in affluent countries. It consists of "provos", "beatniks", "pleiners", "nozems", "Teddy boys", "rockers", "blouson noirs", "stiljagi", "mangupi", "raggare", "gammler", artists, students, anarchists, and "ban-the-bombers" – all those young people who reject a career.'[18] In Amsterdam, tensions between the police and the 'provotariat' grew rapidly, all the more so since the tensions coincided with the marriage of Princess Beatrix to Claus von Amsberg. The game of provocation was too tempting, and the inevitable reaction of the police actually helped to foster support from progressive elements of the elite and create sympathy for the Provos. There were extensive disturbances of the peace in both 1965 and 1966, which led to the dismissal of the chief of police and the mayor. It is notable that the Provo movement was discontinued in 1967, as if it had collapsed under the weight of the attention of the media. The student movement thus appointed itself as the heir of 'provocation', and confronted any authority figure they could find. However, of greater importance in this respect was the fact that Provo had promoted itself as a unifying force of the youth establishment through a new magazine: *Hitweek*. The carrier wave had become music.

The first edition of *Hitweek* came out on 17 September 1965. The motto of the magazine was: 'Years, no, centuries of total underestimation of young people have come to an absolute end with the publication of *Hitweek*.' The magazine placed the relatively new phenomenon of beat music at the heart of youth culture. In *Hitweek*'s eyes, rock was still 'nice' music (indeed, they still promoted middle-class youth's appreciation of it), but it had become dated. The readers were urgently advised to switch their allegiance to the new music. In the themed issue *Vetkuifje waarheen?* (Where now for quiffs?), of 22 April 1966, the *nozems* were told that they should not imagine themselves as symbols of revolutionary youth, for 'there is now a new youth-spirit which makes a massive game and a terrific party out of fashion, music and lifestyle'. The magazine had a circulation of 30,000 – an unheard of success for an initiative that had not been supported by a large media company. The readership itself was still many times larger, and the letters sent to the magazine reveal that it was read in the farthest reaches of the land. Radio and television programmes bred further familiarity with the magazine and powerfully supported this new party culture.

If many adults had already shown sympathy towards Provo, this even milder version of the new youth establishment was greeted with almost open arms. The historian James Kennedy has already pointed out how in the Dutch tradition change and modernization were seen as unavoidable – and thus how it was better to sympathetically accept things which could not be avoided or escaped, and to integrate them into normal life as far as possible.[19] This attitude is clearly shown in a number of quotations from a magazine for educators from 1958, which reveal the attitude of adults towards youth: 'Indeed, being open to young people is not only important for the young. Time and again life is recaptured in young people. It is not the case that the young must open up to us; rather we must open up to the young.' Two years later it would be pleaded: 'We should become partners.' By 1962 the capitulation was finally complete: 'We no longer have any idea what kind of world we should raise our children for. Let us thus give up explicit, intentional upbringing, and be satisfied with an "un-pressurized, un-emphatic, daily contact", conscious of the limited significance of our maturity and the present day'.[20]

This suggests that there was still tension between the new youth establishment and 'the authorities', but relatively little between parents and their children. Indeed, parents would partially adopt the new conventions (both in clothing and, for example, in being on first-name terms with everyone). In several respects they would start to behave as contemporaries of their children, with 'forever young' as their motto. Precisely because adults borrowed so much so quickly from the new youth establishment, it was quickly forgotten that these new conventions had to a large extent been formulated by young people for their own use. The victory could hardly have been more comprehensive.

Dancing

The new youth establishment borrowed extensively from the traditional concept of the youth movement. The idea that young people had created an ideal model for society through their mutual contact with one another (later reformulated as the Woodstock-myth) was also prevalent in the 1960s. However, these ideals were disseminated with a certain reticence in the Netherlands, mostly in the form of ironic hyperbole. Radical groups, primarily from within the student movement, seldom reached maturity, possibly because any rebellion was almost always suffocated by the sympathy it generated. Initially, asceticism was also part of the youth concept. It was above all Provo that spoke out derisively against what it saw as the thoughtless consumption of many consumer articles. The electric whisk came to be seen as the example *par excellence* of the useless product of an affluent society. People who bought these whisks were weak-willed slaves of a runaway consumer society which had lost contact with real life, and which apathetically lounged on the sofa in front of the television. Young people, so it would seem, consciously rejected the purchase of an electric whisk and thus satisfied the demands of a higher level of civilization. In this manner the idea once again returned that the new youth establishment was forming an elite.

This partially obscured what had happened in the meantime: the youth market had become ever more important. In 1975 Dutch youngsters spent over 2.5 milliard euros a year. This was the combined result of the baby boom after the war – i.e. there were more people – and the persistent increase in affluence. The baby boomers not only had much more to spend, but to a large extent they also stuck to the consumer behaviour and habits of their youth. Many of their preferences from the 1960s were also ruthlessly exploited commercially. The punk explosion of the mid-1970s can thus be seen as a stark attempt ('no future') to shake off sympathy and commercialism. From 1977 punk and new wave acts were on the bill at all the important pop venues in Amsterdam. Yet this remained a minority. Of greater importance was the reaction generated by new developments in music, which had led to increasingly large gatherings where all attention was focused on an unreachable performer. This music had to be listened to, and people could sing along and sway with raised cigarette lighters if they so wished. People were connecting more with the crowd than with the music. As a result, discos grew in importance – places where the dancing public took centre stage and not the performer. This phenomenon was manifested in disco music (Donna Summer first broke on to the Dutch scene in 1974 with her hit *The Hostage*), which would be followed a decade later by house music. By 1990 nearly one in four Dutch people between the ages of 15 and 65 went to a disco; of these, half were estimated to be under the age of 20. Between August 1989 and August 1990 there were over 64 million visits to a disco (out of a population of 12 million).[21]

Conclusion

This all leads to a mixed picture. On the one hand, 'young people' spend more time than ever in education. The differences between young people have thus become smaller, even if the remaining differences have simultaneously become more important, thanks to the mechanism Freud termed 'the narcissism of small differences'. Almost all young boys have to wear jeans, but the subtle differences in style, design and price of the jeans are critical (a similar development can be seen with trainers). Yet there has never been a solid youth establishment, and it is equally impossible to point out one group or youth tradition which has sought clear hegemony or can be suspected of such ambitions. Indeed, after the middle of the 1960s there was no longer a clear 'image' of youth. This development can to an extent be explained by the increasing fluidity of the boundaries between youth and adulthood. Certainly, young people have from time to time done their best to maintain these boundaries (think of punk), but the baby boomers have, for the most part, banished such differences. They work together in a large marketplace of moral issues, environmental concerns, anti-Americanism and the support of refugees. Adults frequently purchase the same music as young people, wear similar clothes and have the same informal approach to life. Finally, market mechanisms ensure a plentiful supply of goods for every taste and style. For however much capitalism – according to Schumpeter – is a mechanism of 'creative destruction', it would appear to have transformed the historical phenomenon of the youth establishment into an archipelago of differing tastes.

Notes

    * Translated by Benedict Schofield (University of Sheffield)

    1. This is a greatly revised version of my chapter 'Vetkuifje waarheen?', in J.C.H. Blom and G.N. van der Plaat (eds), *Wederopbouw, welvaart en onrust* (Houten, 1986), pp. 121–46.

    2. Typical is the discussion in the *Hollands Maandblad*, XXVI (1985), especially in April and May 1985.

    3. J.S. van Hessen, *Samen jong-zijn* (Assen, 1965), p. 33. This point of view shares similarities with Judith Rich Harris's excellent work *The Nurture Assumption: Why Children Turn out the Way They Do* (New York, 1998).

    4. Quoted from C. Miermans, *Voetbal in Nederland* (Assen, 1955), p. 80.

5. W. Kindt (ed.), *Grundschriften der deutschen Jugendbewegung* (Düsseldorf/ Cologne, 1963), p. 93; cf. Walter Laqueur, *Young Germany: A History of the German Youth Movement* (Somerset, NJ, 1984).

6. G. van Veen in *Volksontwikkeling*, no. 12 (1930–1), pp. 345–6.

7. The classic study is by Ger Harmsen, *Blauwe en rode jeugd* (Assen, 1961).

8. B.J. Hinnen, *Verdoolde jeugd* (Amsterdam, 1946). See also S.H. Stoffel, *De massa-mensch en zijn toekomst* (Amsterdam, 1946), with an interesting preface by the prime minister of the day.

9. *Maatschappelijke verwildering der jeugd* (The Hague, 1952), pp. 17–18, 21, 32, 59; *Bronnenboek* (The Hague 1953).

10. J. Goudsblom, *De nieuwe volwassene* (Amsterdam, 1959); D.E. Krantz and E.V.W. Verkruijsse, *De jeugd in het geding* (Amsterdam, 1959); H. Feitsma, *Jeugdige ongeschoolden* (Assen, 1960).

11. Source: Central Bureau of Statistics; cf. Geert de Vries, *Het pedagogisch regiem* (Amsterdam, 1993); Peter Selten, 'Vroeg rijp, later volwassen', in Corrie van Eijl, Lex Heerma van Voss and Piet de Rooy (eds), *Sociaal Nederland. Contouren van de twintigste eeuw* (Amsterdam, 2001), pp. 69–85.

12. *Achtergrondstudies ten behoeve van de planning van het voortgezet onderwijs*, VI, *Schoolloopbanen in het voortgezet onderwijs* (The Hague, 1983).

13. J. Diederich, *Werkende jeugd en zakgeldbesteding* (Leiden, 1951).

14. *Dux*, XXIII (1956), p. 159; cf. C. Brinkgreve and M. Korzec, *Margriet weet raad* (Utrecht/Antwerp, 1978).

15. J. Goudsblom, *De nieuwe volwassenen* (Amsterdam, 1959), pp. 53–4.

16. Quotation from 1955 in *Vijfentwintig jaar Vrij Nederland* (Amsterdam, 1965), p. 139.

17. J. van der Keuken in *De Groene Amsterdammer*, 21 December 1983; *Dux*, XXIII (1956), pp. 157ff.; there was also a counter-publication, *Wij zijn ook zeventien* (We are also seventeen) (Nijmegen, n.d.).

18. Roel van Duyn, *Het witte gevaar* (Amsterdam, 1967), p. 64; cf. Niek Pas, *Imaazje! De verbeelding van Provo 1965–1967* (Amsterdam, 2003).

19. James C. Kennedy, *Nieuw Babylon in aanbouw* (Amsterdam, 1995).

20. H.J.H. Brentjens in *Dux*, XXV (1958), p. 129; J.J. Dijkhuis in *Dux*, XXVII (1960), p. 237; H. Ruygers in *Dux*, XXIX (1962), p. 249.

21. Lutgard D.M. Mutsaers, *Beat crazy. Een pophistorisch onderzoek naar de impact van de transnationale dansrages twist, disco en house in Nederland* (Utrecht, 1998).

–11–

'Seized by Change, Liberated by Affluence'

Youth, Consumption and Cultural Change in Post-war Britain

Bill Osgerby

The 'Youth Question' and Post-war Britain

The early 1960s saw Britain beset by 'Beatlemania'. Liverpool pop group the Beatles first leapt to fame in 1963, as seven of their records soared up the Top Twenty and their every public appearance was besieged by hordes of screaming young fans. In November they even got a regal seal of approval, the 'Fab Four' headlining a Royal Variety Show at the Prince of Wales Theatre to perform before the Queen Mother. 'On this next number I want you all to join in', quipped Beatles guitarist John Lennon. 'Would those in the cheap seats clap their hands. The rest of you can rattle your jewellery.' Further esteem came in 1965, as Harold Wilson, then prime minister of Britain's Labour government, forwarded the Beatles for investiture as Members of the Order of the British Empire – the Queen awarding the band their prestigious MBE medals, while outside Buckingham Palace a crowd of 4,000 youngsters chanted 'Long live the Queen, long live the Beatles'.[1] But not everyone was caught up in the fervour. Complaining that the Beatles' awards had sullied the noble traditions of the British honours system, several MBE recipients returned their medals in disgust. 'The British House of Royalty had put me on the same level as a bunch of vulgar numbskulls,' protested Hector Dupuis, a former Canadian MP, while irate author Richard Pape remonstrated: 'If the Beatles and the like continue to debase the Royal honours list, then Britain must fall deeper into international ridicule and contempt.'[2]

To some, 'Beatlemania' and the passions it provoked might seem a relatively trivial episode in the development of modern Britain. But, rather than being an inconsequential historical footnote, the colossal fame of the Beatles, and their resonance in British social life, were profoundly significant, the band's huge success underlining the growing economic and aesthetic impact of youth culture in post-war Britain.

During the 1950s and 1960s the youth market emerged as a key sector of the British economy. Indeed, in February 1964 Sir Alec Douglas Home, then Britain's Conservative prime minister, had his tongue only slightly in his cheek when he

175

acclaimed the Beatles as 'our best exports' and 'a useful contribution to the balance of payments'.[3] Earlier that year the Beatles had played their first concerts in America and, in 1964 alone, US stores sold an estimated $50 million worth of Beatles merchandise.[4] At home, meanwhile, high streets brimmed with all manner of Beatle-booty (from collarless 'Beatle jackets', to plastic figurines and bubblegum cards), and in London's Bethnal Green a factory toiled round the clock to meet the voracious demand for 'Beatle Wigs'. Youth culture had become big business, the Beatles boom representing just the tip of a mammoth iceberg of commercial interest targeting the spending power of the young.

But 'youth' also acquired powerful symbolic significance. The American authors Joe Austin and Michael Willard have highlighted the important emblematic connotations that invariably surround popular debates about young people. 'The youth question', they argue, acts as 'an important forum where new understandings about the past, present, and future of public life are encoded, articulated and contested'.[5] This was especially true of Britain during the 1950s and 1960s. Commentators made recurring use of the themes and images of 'youth' as a vehicle for comment on broader patterns of social change – young people were both celebrated as the exciting precursor to a prosperous future and (sometimes simultaneously) vilified as the most deplorable evidence of woeful cultural decline. When premier Harold Wilson furnished the Beatles with august awards, therefore, it was more than a good-natured gesture by an affable man of the people. It was a calculated political manoeuvre. Wilson was coopting a 'language' of dynamic youth and 'swinging' modernity that had come to the fore in 1960s Britain. 'Let's Go with Labour!', Wilson's decisive 1964 election slogan, borrowed from the exhilarating idioms of 1960s pop culture, while courting the Beatles allowed the Labour leader to tap into a positive, pulsating iconography in which youth culture was configured as the vanguard of Britain's march into a new era of progress and optimism.

Visions of youthful hedonism, however, were not universally applauded. The establishment figures who derided the Beatles as 'vulgar numbskulls' were indicative of a broader antipathy often elicited by modern youth culture. From this perspective, the commercial youth market and its growing impact on contemporary cultural life were viewed with disdain. Here, trends in youth style and music were regarded as the baleful nadir of a broader cultural decay in which the rise of consumerism and commercial entertainment were seen as ushering in an age of banal and homogenized 'mass culture'.

This chapter, then, charts the major social and economic changes that combined to highlight the 'visibility' of British youth as a distinct cultural group during the 1950s and 1960s. But it also emphasizes the way the 'youth question' operated as an 'ideological vehicle', debate about young people and youth culture serving as a symbolic medium through which fundamental shifts in Britain's social boundaries and cultural relationships were explored, made sense of and interpreted.

'A Distinctive Teenage World': The Growth of the Youth Market

Contrary to popular assumptions, distinct forms of youth style did not suddenly materialize amid a 1950s explosion of rock 'n' roll records and Bryl-creamed quiffs. Working youngsters first emerged as a distinct consumer group during the Victorian era, with a commercial youth market becoming better defined during the 1920s and 1930s. The inter-war depression meant levels of youth unemployment were a problem in some regions, but demand for young workers remained generally high since their labour was relatively inexpensive (compared to that of adults) at a time when employers were cutting costs. According to David Fowler, working youngsters' earnings rose by between 300 and 500 per cent between the wars and a 'hard-sell youth market' began to blossom as cinemas, dance halls and magazine publishers all chased the spending power of young workers.[6] Nevertheless, while a long history exists to British youth culture, there remain grounds for seeing the mid-twentieth century as a distinct phase in its development.

After 1945 a number of factors combined to accentuate young people's social and cultural profile. Demographic shifts were crucial. A 'baby boom' in the wake of the Second World War meant the number of people aged under 20 years grew from around 3 million in 1951 to just over 4 million by 1966.[7] Changes in the organization of education also helped 'formalize' notions of young people as an identifiable social group. The 1944 Education Act brought a major expansion of secondary education, while the school-leaving age was raised to 15 years in 1947 and there was a significant expansion of the youth service (which administered youth clubs and other organizations intended to marshal young people's leisure). Taken together, these moves worked to institutionalize 'youth' as a discrete social group associated with specific needs and problems. Youth was further bracketed as a distinct social category by the introduction of National Service in 1948. On average 160,000 young men were annually conscripted for two years' training in the Forces, and the looming 'call up' encouraged many youngsters to make the most of their freedom while they could. As one lad explained to *Picture Post* in 1957: ' "Between now and the time I'm eighteen I've got to 'do the lot'. 'Ave a good time, I say, before I get called up, blown up or married".'[8]

Above all, however, economic trends were the decisive factor working to enhance youth's social visibility. After 1945 the workforce as a whole felt the impact of economic realignment – with a decline in heavy industry, movement of capital into lighter forms of production (especially consumer goods), the expansion of production-line technologies and trends towards 'de-skilling'. But these changes had particular consequences for the young. The labour market shifts created a demand for flexible, though not especially skilled, labour, and young people (because they were cheaper to employ than adults) were ideally suited to the role. As a consequence, the 1950s and early 1960s saw buoyant levels of youth employment. Indeed, rather than undertaking a period of relatively poorly paid training or apprenticeship, many youngsters much preferred the comparatively high immediate rewards offered by unskilled and semi-skilled work.

As a consequence, the equation of 'youth' with 'affluence' became a prevalent post-war theme. During the late 1950s research conducted for the London Press

Exchange by Mark Abrams played a key role in popularizing the notion that youth, more than any other social group, had prospered since 1945. Widely cited in an array of official reports (and a welter of books, magazines and newspaper articles), Abrams' data suggested that since the war young people's real earnings had risen by 50 per cent (roughly double that of adults), while youth's 'discretionary' spending had risen by as much as 100 per cent – representing an annual expenditure of around £830 million.[9] Abrams also maintained that this spending was concentrated in particular consumer markets (representing, for example, 44 per cent of total spending on records and 39 per cent of spending on motorcycles), which, he concluded, represented the rise of 'distinctive teenage spending for distinctive teenage ends in a distinctive teenage world'.[10]

Abrams' figures probably exaggerated the scale of young people's economic muscle, but notions of 'affluent youth' had a degree of foundation. The wage packets of British youngsters were certainly not bulging but, compared to earlier generations, their levels of disposable income were tangibly enhanced – a spending power that underpinned a huge expansion of the commercial youth market. As Derek Hawes observed in a report published in consultation with the Standing Conference of National Youth Organizations during the mid-1960s:

> The quality of life lived by the average young person in Britain today is much affected by the realization by commercial interests that the age group fourteen to twenty-five represents, in economic terms, a vast multi-million pound market; a well-defined consumer group, affluent and innocent, to be attracted and exploited and pandered to; second only to the housewife in potential spending power.[11]

Indeed, by the late 1950s the range of products geared to the young was already boundless. Popular music, in particular, became closely tied to the youth market. Teen spending, for example, underpinned the meteoric rise of the seven-inch, vinyl single. Launched in 1952, vinyl singles accounted for 80 per cent of British record sales by 1963, with the success of new releases gauged in new, sales-based charts (the first appearing in *New Musical Express* in 1952, followed by *Record Mirror*'s 'Top Fifty' in 1954). Rock 'n' roll also emerged as a pop genre closely related to the youth market. The initial wave of American rock 'n' rollers (Bill Haley, Chuck Berry and Elvis Presley) was soon joined by home-grown talent such as Cliff Richard, Tommy Steele and Marty Wilde. And, with the British beat boom of the early 1960s, bands such as the Beatles and the Rolling Stones soon presided over the world of pop.

The British film industry, too, made overtures to youth. Britain had nothing to match the huge American 'teenpic' industry of the 1950s, but British film-makers made a pitch to young cinema-goers with films featuring pop stars such as Tommy Steele, Cliff Richard and the Beatles. In contrast, British radio reacted slowly. During the 1950s rock 'n' roll could be heard only by tuning in to the American Forces Network or Radio Luxembourg. At the BBC it was largely ignored as a consequence of 'needle time' restrictions on the broadcast of recorded music and officialdom's disdain for a music it deemed crassly commercial. Radio stations specifically geared to a youth audience appeared in Britain only during the early 1960s, with the rise of unlicensed, 'pirate' stations such as Radio Caroline and Radio London – the BBC finally responding in 1967 with the launch of its own pop music station, Radio One. The younger medium of television responded more swiftly. Initially, pop programmes such as *Hit Parade* (BBC, 1952) and *Off the Record* (BBC, 1956) were low key in their youth appeal. By the later 1950s, however, competition between the BBC and ITV (the new commercial rival, launched in 1955) helped generate a TV genre targeted more specifically at youth. Pop programmes such as *Six-Five Special* (BBC, 1957) and *Juke Box Jury* (BBC, 1959) still made concessions to an adult audience through the inclusion of variety entertainers and dinner-jacketed compères, but the launch of *Oh Boy!* (ITV, 1958) – a pop show broadcast live from the Hackney Empire – heralded the rise of a quick-fire format aimed squarely at youth.

Consumption, Meaning and the Symbolic Connotations of Youth Culture

The eruption of 'Beatlemania' in 1963, then, was one constituent in a broader proliferation of the commercial youth market. Increases in the disposable income of many young workers during the 1950s and early 1960s laid the basis for a burgeoning commercial sector whose scope and scale helped popularize notions of the post-war youth experience as qualitatively different from that of earlier generations. Beyond this, however, the period also saw the youth market take on symbolic significance, with perceived changes in the lifestyles of young people increasingly treated as a benchmark of wider shifts in British cultural life.

In the media, youth culture could often be presented in glowing terms – as an energetic and uplifting force displacing the dead hand of tradition. The *Daily Mirror* led the field, attempting to boost its circulation with enthusiastic coverage of pop music, the newspaper even sponsoring a train (the 'Rock 'n' Roll Express') to take Bill Haley to London after the American rocker arrived in Southampton for his first British tour in 1957.

More widely, an increasing association between youth and notions of social dynamism found its purest manifestation in the concept of the 'teenager'. First coined by American market researchers during the 1940s, the term 'teenager' was imported into Britain during the early 1950s. Presented by the media and cultural commentators as the quintessence of contemporary social trends, 'teenagers' were configured as the standard-bearers of a new consumer culture. As Peter Laurie contended in his taxonomy of *The Teenage Revolution*, published in 1965: 'The distinctive fact about teenagers' behaviour is economic: they spend a lot of money on clothes, records, concerts, make-up, magazines: all things that give immediate pleasure and little lasting use'.[12] During the 1950s and early 1960s, then, the term 'teenager' did not simply describe a generational category. Rather, the 'teenager' was an ideological terrain upon which a particular definition of post-war social change was constructed. Central to notions of the 'teenager' was the idea that traditional class boundaries were being eroded by the fashions and lifestyles of a newly affluent 'gilded youth'.[13] 'Teenagers' were presented as a class in themselves, what Laurie termed a 'solidly integrated social bloc',[14] whose vibrant, fun-loving culture seemed to be a symbolic foretaste of good times waiting around the corner for everyone. It was hardly surprising, then, that astute politicians like Harold Wilson sought to capitalize on the dynamic aura of youth, enlisting grandees of youth culture like the Beatles in his crusade for a rejuvenated and vigorously modern 'New Britain'.

Social responses to youth culture, however, were never unanimously positive. As Dick Hebdige has argued, a recurring duality has characterized popular debate about youth, with breathless celebrations of teenage consumption coexisting alongside fearful accounts casting juvenile delinquency and commercial youth culture as depressing indices of social decline.[15] During the 1950s, within both popular opinion and academic enquiry, there arose the widely held belief that the destruction of the war, the absence of fathers and the long working hours of mothers had contributed to a breakdown in processes of socialization and a consequent rise in levels of delinquency. A leading exponent of the view was the journalist T.R. Fyvel, who, through a number of articles and his 1961 study *The Insecure Offenders*, popularized the idea that post-war increases in juvenile crime were 'the expression of a particularly disturbed generation, a delayed effect of the war'.[16]

Fyvel's opinions found empirical support from research conducted for the Home Office by Leslie Wilkins and published as *Delinquent Generations* in 1960. Juggling with reams of statistics, Wilkins claimed that children born between 1935 and 1942 were more prone to delinquency than those born in any other seven-year period and, he argued, the highest delinquency rates were to be found among those who had been aged between four and five years old during the war.[17] Nevertheless, Wilkins judged that wartime conditions alone did not account for subsequent rises in levels of juvenile crime. In addition to the destabilizing effects of the war, Wilkins also cited the recent styles adopted by the young as an important contributory factor, arguing that: 'One of the most disturbing features of the pattern of post-war criminal statistics is the recent crime-wave among young adult males between seventeen and twenty-one years of age. The crime wave among young males has been associated with certain forms of dress and other social phenomena'.[18]

During the 1950s specific anxiety cohered around the Teddy boy. The characteristically 'Edwardian' style of the Teddy boy's long, draped jacket was actually a variation of the zoot suit, imported with American GIs during the war. First identified in the working-class neighbourhoods of south London in 1954, the Ted was soon presented as a shockingly new apparition haunting street corners and dance halls throughout the country. And the Ted's negative image was further compounded in wildly exaggerated press reports of cinema 'riots' by Teddy boys following screenings of American 'youth' films such as *Blackboard Jungle* (1955) and *Rock around the Clock* (1956). Press claims that the Ted was a perpetrator of a 'new' wave of uniquely violent street crime, however, were well wide of the mark. According to Geoffrey Pearson, the concerns of the 1950s were just the latest episode in a long and connected history of fearful complaint stretching back to the Victorian era in which 'each succeeding generation has understood itself to be standing on the brink of some radical discontinuity with the past, and in which the rising generation has been repeatedly seen as the harbinger of a dreadful future'.[19]

But delinquency and violence were not the only issues that worried 1950s commentators. Often, the very styles adopted by the young were viewed as symptomatic of a wider cultural decline. Richard Hoggart, for example, argued that a post-war proliferation of commercial entertainment had spawned a shallow and insipid 'candy-floss world'. Looking back to his working-class boyhood, Hoggart happily validated popular culture as a meaningful field of collective experience, but in contemporary cultural life he found little reason for optimism. Hoggart derided trends towards 'canned entertainment and packeted provision' that seemed, for him, to offer an 'unvaried diet of sensation without commitment' that induced 'an underlying sense of purposelessness in existence outside the limited range of a few appetites'.[20] And, significantly, Hoggart singled out contemporary youth as a benchmark of this general cultural paucity. Denouncing modern youth as a 'hedonistic but passive barbarian', Hoggart poured scorn on 'the juke box boys' with their 'drape suits, picture ties and American slouch', who spent their evenings in 'harshly lighted milk bars' putting 'copper after copper into the mechanical record player' – a realm of cultural experience that, Hoggart argued, represented 'a peculiarly thin and pallid form of dissipation'.[21]

Nor was Hoggart alone. During the late 1950s and early 1960s numerous commentators decried the rise of a debased 'mass culture' they perceived as the corollary of modern consumerism – and young people were invariably cited as the worst offenders. As Bryan Wilson contended in 1959:

Today's high income receivers are without background, education and information necessary to the cultivation of stable tastes ... They are exposed in innumerable ways to commercial exploitation, and induced to pay high prices for the merely novel and ephemeral ... Consequently people, and especially young people, become confused about their norms, values, tastes and standards.[22]

Such antipathy towards commercial leisure and entertainment was nothing new. Similar sentiments had existed during the late nineteenth century, while the 1930s had seen notions of cultural decline increasingly cohere around the concept of 'Americanization'. America, the home of monopoly capitalism and commercial culture, came to epitomize the processes of debasement and deterioration that, many commentators argued, were coming to characterize British popular culture.[23] As Dick Hebdige shows, this use of America as a paradigm 'for the future threatening every advanced industrial democracy in the western world' intensified after 1945, the growth of working-class affluence prompting heightened anxieties that British culture was set to become a degraded mass.[24] And it was trends in youth culture that were invariably cited as the worst example of this drift towards tawdry 'Americanization'. Richard Hoggart's views were exemplary. Hoggart's critique of the 'spiritual dry rot' in post-war cultural life zeroed in on the 'juke-box boys' who, Hoggart argued, were 'living to a large extent in a myth-world compounded of a few simple elements which they take to be those of American life'.[25]

Crucially, however, what Hoggart's kind of cultural pessimism missed were the meanings that young people invested in their style. Rather than seeing youth as the passive victim of exploitative cultural industries, since the 1960s researchers have given more attention to the meanings young people construct around the products of the commercial market. An early move in this direction was Stuart Hall and Paddy Whannel's argument that teenage culture was 'a contradictory mixture of the authentic and the manufactured'.[26] Surveying the 'popular arts' in Britain during the early 1960s, Hall and Whannel acknowledged that the youth market represented 'a lush grazing ground for the commercial providers', but they resisted sliding into pessimistic notions of 'mass culture'. Instead, they highlighted the potential of consumers to engage actively with the products of the market, insisting that 'the use intended by the provider and the use actually made by the audience never wholly coincide, and frequently conflict'.[27]

During the 1970s and 1980s there was a tendency for some theorists to interpret young people's use of fashion, music and style as a strategy of class-based rebellion. In what became known as 'subcultural theory', theorists such as Stuart Hall and Dick Hebdige argued that young people's subcultural styles (like those of the 1950s Teddy boys) were acts of symbolic resistance to ruling class power structures.[28] This neo-Marxist perspective interpreted youth subcultures as forms of cultural insubordination – sartorial expressions of defiance in which working-class youths appropriated the articles, artefacts and icons generated by the commercial market, and symbolically reworked them to take on new, threatening and subversive meanings. During the 1990s, however, this emphasis on 'resistance' gave way to more nuanced approaches, with authors such as Paul Willis[29] and Steven Miles[30] seeing the commercial market as offering 'symbolic resources' that young people drew upon as they made sense of their social experiences and carved out their social identities.

From this perspective, therefore, Britain's 'juke-box boys' of the 1950s were not the passive victims of an exploitative commercial machine but discriminating consumers whose fascination with American style was full of cultural meaning. Indeed, as Steve Chibnall argues, American popular culture bore powerful symbolic associations for many youngsters in post-war Britain. Against the drab conventions of 1950s Britain, American style 'offered a sense of worth, individuality and empowerment'.[31] In these terms, then, the Teddy boy's drape jacket represented a 'blasphemous mixture of orthodox British dandyism and Yank style' and was recognized by both brash young tearaways and upstanding authority figures as an emblem of 'fundamental disrespect for the old class modes and manners – a disrespect born of a romance with an alien culture'.[32]

'Everything New, Uninhibited and Kinky': The 1960s

By the 1960s the Teddy boy's drape jacket had been displaced by the chic, Italian-inspired styles associated with mod style. The smoothly tailored lines of Italian fashion were first sported in Britain during the late 1950s by the 'modernists' – the hip, West London cliques immortalized in Colin MacInnes' 1959 novel *Absolute Beginners*.[33] As the 'modern' look caught on, young mods' quest for exquisitely cut suits took them to Soho tailors such as John Stephen in Carnaby Street, which was transformed into the throbbing heart of the mod universe. Other mod haunts included London nightclubs such as the Scene and the Flamingo, where white, British mods encountered black, American soul music and rhythm and blues (the latter emulated by 'mod' groups The Who and The Small Faces). West Indian ska and bluebeat were also popular, and the intersection of black and white style became a recurring trait in post-war British youth culture.

Responses to the mods reproduced the recurring duality that had come to characterize post-war debates surrounding youth culture. Stylish and clean-cut, the mods were often fêted by the media as pace-setters of 1960s social dynamism. At the same time, however, they could also be reviled as the *bête noire* of the affluent society – a negative stereotyping that climaxed in reactions to the 1964 mod seaside 'invasions'. During the 1964 Easter Bank Holiday, Clacton (a sleepy seaside resort) had seen scuffles between local youths and visiting Londoners. The violence was minor, but headline stories in national newspapers suggested there were full-scale battles between gangs of mods and rockers, the latter presented as the mods' leather-clad, motorcycle-riding rivals. In his landmark study of the episode (first published in 1972), sociologist Stanley Cohen argued that the sensationalized media alarm was a 'moral panic' – a moment of heightened social anxiety in which the media escalated events by exaggerating the activities of real or imagined deviant groups.[34] In the case of the 1964 'invasions', Cohen argued, the mods and rockers were initially ill-defined youth styles. The polarization of the two camps developed only as a consequence of the sensational news stories, Cohen contending that youngsters came to identify with the 'folk devil' images conjured up by the press. The melodramatic reporting also influenced agencies of social control. Arrest rates soared as the police felt obliged to react strongly to the slightest hint of trouble, while the government even considered special legislation to deal with the mods and rockers 'problem'.[35]

Similar processes took place in relation to the procession of youth subcultures that followed the mods and rockers. From the skinheads of the late 1960s, through the punks of the 1970s, to the gangsta rappers of the 1990s, British youth subcultures have been subject to processes of media stigmatization that (paradoxically) have worked to popularize and lend substance to styles that were initially small scale and vaguely defined.

Even amid moments of fraught moral panic, however, popular fascination with youth culture was never far away. In 1964, for example, at the height of concerns about 'marauding' mods and rockers, the *Sunday Times Magazine* featured a nine-page photospread spotlighting the mods' sartorial flair.[36] The fashionable nightclubs and boutiques of 'Swinging London' also fed into notions of Britain entering an age of bold, liberated modernity. It was an image that caught on abroad. In America, especially, British cultural exports such as 'Beatlemania', mod style and Mary Quant's chic fashion designs accrued connotations of exciting vitality. *Time* magazine's 1966 cover story on 'London: The Swinging City' captured this sense of Britain as the font of youthful dynamism: 'Youth is the word and the deed in London,' *Time* enthused, 'seized by change, liberated by affluence . . . . everything new, uninhibited and kinky is blooming at the top of London life'.[37]

The transatlantic trade in youth culture continued during the late 1960s. In Britain the American counterculture exerted particular influence. Always a loose coalition of bohemian groups and political factions, the counterculture's various strands developed from earlier artistic and political movements. On both sides of the Atlantic the 1950s 'Beat Generation' had fused existentialist philosophy with jazz, poetry, literature, eastern mysticism and drugs – themes that were all sustained in the 1960s counterculture. In Britain the Campaign for Nuclear Disarmament (CND, formed in 1958) had also won many young supporters and its direct action campaigning helped pioneer the forms of protest that became a feature of later radical movements.

In the 1960s the spiritual home of the counterculture was Haight-Ashbury, a once-genteel neighbourhood of San Francisco that was colonized by a motley assortment of hippies, rock bands and student militants. But Britain also hit a psychedelic groove. By 1966 venues such as the Roundhouse and UFO (Unlimited Freak Out) were focal points of a burgeoning London underground. New rock bands such as Pink Floyd (regulars at UFO) sought to push back the frontiers of musical creativity, while festivals, concerts and assorted 'happenings' helped generate a sense of collective identity and 'alternative' lifestyle. The underground press was also important. Publications such as *International Times* (or simply *It*, launched in 1966) and *Oz* (launched in 1967) took the lead, exploring the aesthetics of dissent through their surreal cartoons and fantastic visuals. The same creative strategies featured in the counterculture's posters, films and the various experimental projects of the Arts Lab movement. Nonconformity and exoticism also became bywords in the world of style, hip boutiques abounding with bell-bottomed trousers, kaftans and a pot-pourri of faded denim and tie-dye. Self-exploration was also a countercultural preoccupation, inspiring 'journeys' through both space and consciousness. Trips (to India and elsewhere) in search of spiritual karma were not uncommon, while trips of another kind were undertaken through the use of hallucinogenic drugs – in particular, Lysergic Acid Diethylamide (generally known as LSD or 'Acid').

Sociological accounts have often presented the 1960s counterculture as a middle-class phenomenon. Stuart Hall and his colleagues, for example, argued that the counterculture was a revolt by middle-class youth against the machinery of social power. The Teddy boys and mods, they suggested, had been working-class subcultures that challenged the status quo from 'below', but the counterculture represented an attack from 'within' – middle-class youth turning against the ideas and institutions maintained by their parents' culture.[38] Elements of truth exist to this perspective, though it is overly simplistic. In Britain (and elsewhere) the 1960s counterculture was never a homogeneous movement; it was a network of loosely affiliated causes with a disparate membership drawn from a variety of class backgrounds.

Also diverse were the responses to the counterculture elicited from the state and the media. The more explicitly radical strands of the counterculture often faced firm repression. Activism in Britain did not match the scale of '*les evenements*' that rocked Paris in May 1968, nor the intensity of opposition to the Vietnam War in America, but there were still significant moments of dissent. Fierce confrontations occurred between student groups and administrators at many academic institutions, especially the London School of Economics and Hornsey College of Art. Opposition to the Vietnam War, meanwhile, superseded CND as a cause for protest, and in 1967 and 1968 massive demonstrations were held outside the US Embassy, where aggressive policing saw violence flare between protestors and police 'snatch squads'. Further clashes came in 1974, with a demonstrator killed as the police broke up a rally against the extreme right-wing National Front in Red Lion Square. Other elements of the counterculture also faced resolute police action. The late 1960s saw drug laws enforced more vigorously, while police raids on clubs such as UFO led to their closure. The offices of underground publications such as *It* were also raided and in 1970 *Oz* editors Richard Neville, Jim Anderson and Felix Dennis were prosecuted – and subsequently imprisoned – for obscenity.

In contrast, the counterculture's aesthetics and lifestyles often elicited sympathy and even a degree of admiration. This was especially apparent in reactions to the Rolling Stones' drugs trial of 1967. Amid a blaze of publicity, rock stars Keith Richards and Mick Jagger were convicted and sentenced to three months' imprisonment for the possession of illegal drugs (though both walked free after an appeal). Rather than denouncing the Stones, however, significant sections of the media rallied to their defence. Famously, *The Times* published an editorial asking 'Who Breaks a Butterfly on a Wheel?' – the newspaper defending Jagger and Richards and attacking their sentences as unacceptably draconian.[39] The media were also spellbound by the counterculture's hedonistic lifestyles. In 1968, for instance, in a feature series spotlighting 'The Restless Generation', *The Times* praised hippy communes such as the Tribe of the Sacred Mushroom for generating 'a fresh approach to living' that provided its members with 'livelihood and fulfilment'.[40]

Rather than being universally reviled, then, the 1960s counterculture was often a source of fascination. Indeed, Ron Eyerman and Andrew Jamison argue that during the 1960s youth 'became the model and set standards for the rest of society in many spheres of culture, from the most superficial like clothing and hair-styles, to the most deeply rooted like the basic social interactions of men and women and blacks and whites'.[41] The lifestyles of the counterculture won particular appeal. The libertine ethos of self-expression and 'doing your own thing' proved widely attractive at a time when cultural values were rapidly changing. And, as traditional ideals of restraint and respectability gave way to an emphasis on hedonism and personal consumption, the fashions, hair-styles, music and attitudes of the counterculture all percolated into mainstream social life.

'Whatever Happened to the Teenage Dream?': Shifting Perceptions of British Youth Culture

The media's representations of youth in Britain during the 1950s and 1960s were stereotypes that often bore a tenuous relation to social reality. Yet their symbolic power was potent, images of youth serving as a key motif around which dominant interpretations of social change were constructed. For a number of critics, post-war youth culture was emblematic of Britain's broader slide into cultural torpor. More generally, however, the late 1950s and early 1960s saw a more positive set of images of British youth come to the fore – personified in the irrepressible *joie de vivre* of the Beatles. Here, teenage lifestyles were taken as the epitome of a Britain in which the sheer pace of economic growth seemed set to engender a newly prosperous age of fun, freedom and social harmony.

The 'teenage myth', however, depended on an unsteady economic and political base. In retrospect, the prosperity of the post-war decades can be seen as a transient 'age of illusion'.[42] Much of the consumer 'boom' of the late 1950s and early 1960s, for example, was based on the shaky foundation of short-term credit, with Britain's hire purchase debt rising faster between 1956 and 1959 than at any other time either before or since. Moreover, post-war 'affluence' depended on a level of growth that the British economy, drained by the strains of wartime and increasingly struggling in ruthlessly competitive world markets, was simply unable to maintain. As a consequence, economic decline and an atmosphere of crisis and conflict was beginning to characterize British society by the end of the 1960s. In this context the ideologies of consensus and dynamism that had taken shape during the late 1950s became untenable and steadily gave way to a more confrontational social and political climate.

Against this background, representations of youth culture also changed. Though responses to youth were never exclusively negative, the late 1960s and early 1970s saw a greater degree of hostility within political comment and media coverage. For example, the skinhead style, which first began to make its presence felt in British youth culture during the late 1960s,[43] was unequivocally presented as a violent and menacing presence stalking British streets. Whereas the mods' clean-cut *élan* allowed them to be easily incorporated within a discourse of dawning classless affluence, no such co-option was possible with the skinheads, whose self-conscious invocation of a 'traditional' working-class heritage (through their distinctive 'uniform' of steel toe-capped work boots, rolled-up jeans, braces and convict-style cropped hair) was irreconcilable with notions of disappearing social divisions in a prosperous 'New Britain'.

Notions and representations of 'youth', therefore, have the capacity to play a metaphorical role in the ways sense is made of more general social developments, especially at times of dramatic social change. This was especially true of Britain in the two decades that followed the Second World War, young people becoming an important (possibly the *most* important) ideological vehicle for the discussion of wider shifts in social relations and cultural life. During the late 1950s and early 1960s 'the affluent teenager' was promoted as the figurehead of Britain's march into a new era of prosperous consumerism. By end of the 1960s, however, the confident rhetoric of growth and social cohesion had begun to crumble in the face of economic crisis and industrial decline – a shift that found its corollary in the rise of an increasingly negative set of responses to British youth culture.

Notes

1. Cited in Philip Norman, *Shout!: The True Story of the Beatles* (London, 2004), p. 251.
2. Ibid.

3. Cited in Hunter Davies, *The Beatles: The Authorized Biography* (London, 1978), p. 219.

4. Ibid.

5. Joe Austin and Michael Willard, 'Angels of History, Demons of Culture', in Joe Austin and Michael Willard (eds), *Generations of Youth: Youth Cultures and History in Twentieth-century America* (New York, 1998), p. 1.

6. David Fowler, *The First Teenagers: The Lifestyle of Young Wage-earners in Interwar Britain* (London, 1995), pp. 93, 170.

7. Department of Employment, *British Labour Statistics Historical Abstract 1886–1968* (London, 1971), pp. 206–7.

8. *Picture Post*, 8 April 1957.

9. Mark Abrams, *The Teenage Consumer* (London, 1959), p. 9.

10. Abrams, *Teenage Consumer*, p. 10.

11. Derek Hawes, *Young People Today: An Account of Young People in Voluntary Youth Organisations* (London, 1966), p. 25.

12. Peter Laurie, *The Teenage Revolution* (London, 1965), p. 9.

13. *The Economist*, 11 January 1958.

14. Laurie, *Teenage Revolution*, p. 11.

15. Dick Hebdige, 'Hiding in the Light: Youth Surveillance and Display', in Dick Hebdige (ed.), *Hiding in the Light: On Images and Things* (London, 1988), p. 19.

16. T.R. Fyvel, *The Insecure Offenders: Rebellious Youth in the Welfare State* (London, 1961), p. 51.

17. Wilkins' calculations and conclusions were, in fact, seriously flawed. Not only were his statistical inferences invalid, but he failed to consider variations of delinquency rate between different types of offence and ignored non-indictable offences altogether.

18. Leslie Wilkins, *Delinquent Generations* (London, 1960), p. 9.

19. Geoffrey Pearson, 'Falling Standards: a Short, Sharp History of Moral Decline', in Martin Barker (ed.), *The Video Nasties: Freedom and Censorship in the Media* (London, 1984), p. 102. See also Geoffrey Pearson, *Hooligan: A History of Respectable Fears* (London, 1983).

20. Richard Hoggart, *The Uses of Literacy* (London, 1957), p. 246.

21. Ibid., pp. 248–50.

22. Bryan Wilson, 'The Trouble with Teenagers' (originally published in 1959), in Bryan Wilson (ed.), *The Youth Culture and the Universities* (London, 1970), p. 23. Wilson advanced similar sentiments in 'Victims of the Youth Culture', *Spectator*, No. 7210, 2 September 1966.

23. Dominic Strinati provides a thorough survey of British perceptions of, and responses to, processes of 'Americanization'. See Dominic Strinati, 'The Taste of America: Americanization and Popular Culture in Britain', in Dominic Strinati and Stephen Wagg (eds), *Come on Down? Popular Media Culture in Post-war Britain* (London, 1992), pp. 46–81.

24. Dick Hebdige, 'Towards a Cartography of Taste, 1935–1962', in Dick Hebdige (ed.), *Hiding in the Light: On Images and Things* (London, 1988), pp. 52–3.

25. Hoggart, *Uses of Literacy*, p. 248.

26. Stuart Hall and Paddy Whannel, *The Popular Arts* (London, 1964), p. 276.

27. Ibid., pp. 269–70.

28. The 'founding texts' of British subcultural theory were Stuart Hall and Tony Jefferson (eds), *Resistance through Rituals: Youth Subcultures in Post-war Britain* (London, 1976); Dick Hebdige, *Subculture: The Meaning of Style*, (London, 1979); and Paul Willis, *Profane Culture* (London, 1978).

29. Paul Willis, *Common Culture: Symbolic Work at Play in the Everyday Cultures of the Young* (Milton Keynes, 1990).

30. Steven Miles, *Youth Lifestyles in a Changing World* (Buckingham, 2000).

31. Steve Chibnall, 'Counterfeit Yanks: War, Austerity and Britain's American Dream', in Philip Davies (ed.), *Representing and Imagining America* (Keele, 1996), p. 155.

32. Steve Chibnall, 'Whistle and Zoot: the Changing Meaning of a Suit of Clothes', *History Workshop*, 20 (1985), pp. 74, 69.

33. Colin MacInnes, *Absolute Beginners* (London, 1959).

34. Stanley Cohen, *Folk Devils and Moral Panics: The Creation of the Mods and Rockers*, third edition (London, 2002).

35. See Richard S. Grayson, 'Mods, Rockers and Juvenile Delinquency in 1964: the Government Response', *Contemporary British History*, 12(1) (1998), pp. 19–47.

36. *Sunday Times Magazine*, 2 August 1964.

37. *Time*, 15 April 1966.

38. John Clarke, Stuart Hall, Tony Jefferson and Brian Roberts, 'Subcultures, Cultures and Class: a Theoretical Overview', in Hall and Jefferson (eds), *Resistance through Rituals*, pp. 57–71.

39. *The Times*, 1 July 1967.

40. *The Times*, 18 December 1968.

41. Ron Eyerman and Andrew Jamison, *Music and Social Movements: Mobilizing Traditions in the Twentieth Century* (Cambridge, 1998), p. 113.

42. Vernon Bogdanor and Robert Skidelsky (eds), *The Age of Affluence, 1951–64*, (London, 1970), p. 7.

43. Informed histories of the development of British skinhead style can be found in Nick Knight, *Skinhead* (London, 1982) and George Marshall, *Spirit of '69: A Skinhead Bible* (Dunoon, 1991).